Focus:
Writing Sentences
and Paragraphs

Focus:
Writing Sentences
and Paragraphs

MARTHA E. CAMPBELL
St. Petersburg Junior College

PRENTICE HALL, UPPER SADDLE RIVER, NEW JERSEY 07458

Library of Congress Cataloging-in-Publication Data

Campbell, Martha E.
   Focus—writing sentences and paragraphs / Martha E. Campbell.
      p.   cm.
   Includes index.
   ISBN 0-13-901141-2
   1. English language—Sentences—Problems, exercises, etc.
2. English language—Paragraphs—Problems, exercises, etc.   3. English
language—Grammar—Problems, exercises, etc.   4. Report
writing—Problems, exercises, etc.   I. Title.
   PE1441.C29   1999
   808'.042—dc21   99-11753
                                    CIP

Editor-in-Chief: Charlyce Jones Owen
Senior Acquisitions Editor: Maggie Barbieri
Director of Production and Manufacturing: Barbara Kittle
Senior Managing Editor: Bonnie Biller
Senior Project Manager: Shelly Kupperman
Manufacturing Manager: Nick Sklitsis
Prepress and Manufacturing Buyer: Mary Ann Gloriande
Director of Marketing: Gina Sluss
Marketing Manager: Sue Brekka
Creative Design Director: Leslie Osher
Interior and Cover Designer: Carmela Pereira
Editorial Assistant: Joan Polk

This book was set in 11/14 Janson by Progressive Information Technologies and printed
by Press of Ohio. The cover was printed by Press of Ohio.

Acknowledgments
Grateful acknowledgment is made to the following copyright holders: Dave Barry, "Motivate Then
Fail," Miami Herald; John J. Macionis, *Sociology*, 6th ed., Prentice Hall; Gary Shelton, "Boggs Delivers
Hit for the Ages," 7/26/98, St. Petersburg Times: St. Petersburg, FL. Grateful acknowledgment is
made to the following student writers for their contributions: Jennifer Sanders; Michelle Pinciotti;
Patricia Montgomery Smith; Jane Dietz; Ken Sparks.

Printed in the United States of America
10 9 8 7 6 5 4 3 2 1

ISBN 0-13-901141-2

Prentice-Hall International (UK) Limited, *London*
Prentice-Hall of Australia Pty. Limited, *Sydney*
Prentice-Hall Canada, Inc., *Toronto*
Prentice-Hall Hispanoamericana, S.A., *Mexico*
Prentice-Hall of India Private Limited, *New Delhi*
Prentice-Hall of Japan, Inc., *Tokyo*
Pearson Asia Pte. Ltd., *Singapore*
Editora Prentice-Hall do Brasil, Ltda., *Rio de Janeiro*

*To my loving family
and in memory of two special teachers,
Kathy and Len*

Contents

Preface   xv

CHAPTER 1: FOCUS ON WRITING   1

Writer's Inventory   1
Understanding the Writing Process   2
Why Writers Write   3
  Writing to Express   4
  Writing to Entertain   5
  Writing to Inform   5
  Writing to Persuade   6

The Writer's Audience   7

  Speaking versus Writing   7
  General Readers versus Specialized Readers   8

The Writer's Rewards   10
Writing Assignment   11
Writers as Spiders   11

CHAPTER 2: FOCUS ON THE WRITING PROCESS   14

Stage 1: Planning   14
  Freewriting   15
❖ *Student Sample — Freewriting*   15
  Brainstorming   16
❖ *Student Sample — Brainstorming*   16
  Clustering   17
  Journal Writing   19

viii *Contents*

❖ *Student Sample—Journal Writing*   19

Stage 2: Organizing   20

❖ *Student Sample—Experimental Draft*   20

Stage 3: Revising   21

❖ *Student Sample—Revised Draft*   22

Stage 4: Editing   23

❖ *Student Sample—Edited Draft*   23

Stage 5: Finishing   24

❖ *Student Sample—Final Draft*   25

Writing Assignment   26

Writers as Spiders   26

CHAPTER 3: FOCUS ON THE TOPIC SENTENCE   28

Limiting a Topic   30

Writing a Topic Sentence   31

Locating the Topic Sentence   34

Discovering Topic Sentences in Textbooks   40

Writing Assignment   40

Writers as Spiders   41

CHAPTER 4: FOCUS ON THE SUPPORTING DETAILS   42

Creating Supporting Details   42

The Reporter's Questions   43

How Many Details?   45

The Underdeveloped Paragraph   45

Organizing Details   48

Order of Importance   48

Time Order   51

Spatial Order   52

Writing a Concluding Sentence   54

Sticking to the Topic   56

Using Transitions   59

Writing Assignment   62

Writers as Spiders   63

CHAPTER 5: FOCUS ON THE SENTENCE: PART I — 64

Focus on Subjects: The Actors of the Sentence — 65

Identifying Subjects — 66
Complete Subjects — 69
Simple Subjects — 70
The Three-Step Method of Finding Subjects — 71
Subjects in Inverted Sentences — 72
Subjects in Questions — 73
Subjects in Commands — 75
Compound Subjects — 76

Focus on Verbs: The Heartbeat of the Sentence — 77

Action Verbs — 78
Helping Verbs — 81
Verbs in Questions — 84
Verbs in Commands — 85
Linking Verbs — 86
Compound Verbs — 88

Focus on Editing: Avoiding Fragments — 90

Fragments with Missing Subjects — 90
Fragments with -ing Words — 91
Fragments with Missing Helping Verbs — 92
Example Fragments — 93

Writing Assignment — 95
Writers as Spiders — 95

CHAPTER 6: FOCUS ON THE SENTENCE: PART II — 96

Focus on Phrases: The Music of the Sentence — 97

Prepositional Phrases — 97
Infinitive Phrases — 101
-ing Phrases — 102
Present Participle Phrases — 103

Focus on Clauses: The Backbone of the Sentence — 104

Independent Clauses — 105
Dependent Clauses — 108

Focus on Editing: Dependent Clause Fragments — 114
Focus on Punctuation: The Breath of the Sentence — 117

x *Contents*

Commas   117
Apostrophes   121

Writing Assignment   124
Writers as Spiders   125

CHAPTER 7: FOCUS ON NARRATION   126

What Is Narration?   126
Choosing a Topic   128
Organizing a Personal Narrative   129

The Topic Sentence   129
Supporting Details   132
The Concluding Sentence   135

Transitions in Narrative Paragraphs   136
Focus on Diction   137

Using Lively Verbs   137

Focus on Revising: Unrelated Details   139
Revising Tip: Writing with a Computer   140

Cut and Paste   140

Focus on Editing   140

Avoiding Run-ons   141
Avoiding Comma Splices   148

Focus on Peer Review   153

❖ *Student Sample—Final Draft*   155

Writing Assignment   155
Writers as Spiders   156

CHAPTER 8: FOCUS ON DESCRIPTION: PART I   158

What Is Description?   158
Choosing a Topic   159
Organizing a Descriptive Paragraph   160

The Topic Sentence   160
Supporting Details   162
The Concluding Sentence   167

Transitions in Descriptive Paragraphs   168

Focus on Diction   169

 Adjectives: The Color of the Sentence   *169*
 Adverbs: The Energy of the Sentence   *171*

Focus on Revising: Using a Thesaurus   173
Focus on Editing   175
 Subject-Verb Agreement   175
 Two Problem Verbs: Be and Do   183
 Using Past Tense   184
Focus on Peer Review   190

❖ *Student Sample*   191

Writing Assignment   192
Writers as Spiders   192

CHAPTER 9: FOCUS ON DESCRIPTION: PART II   194

Describing People   195
Describing Places   195
Choosing a Topic   196
Organizing a Description of a Person or Place   197

 The Topic Sentence   *197*
 Supporting Details   *199*
 The Concluding Sentence   *202*

Transitions in Descriptive Paragraphs   204
Focus on Diction   205

 Using Lively Adjectives and Adverbs   *206*
 Using Similes   *208*

Focus on Editing   208

 Capitalizing Proper Nouns   *209*
 Using Commas with Appositives   *210*

Pronoun Agreement   211

 Pronoun Choice   *216*
 Troubleshooting Problems with Antecedents   *222*

Focus on Peer Review   225

❖ *Professional Writing Sample*   226

Writing Assignment   226
Writers as Spiders   227

CHAPTER 10: FOCUS ON DEVELOPMENT BY EXAMPLE 228

Choosing a Topic 229
Organizing a Development-by-Example Paragraph 231

The Topic Sentence 231
Supporting Details 233
The Concluding Sentence 237

Transitions in Development-by-Example Paragraphs 238
Focus on Revising: Sentence Combining 240
Focus on Editing 249

Parallelism 249

Focus on Peer Review 253

❖ *Student Sample* 254

Writing Assignment 254
Writers as Spiders 255

CHAPTER 11: FOCUS ON PROCESS 256

Choosing a Topic 257
Organizing a Process Paragraph 258

The Topic Sentence 258
Supporting Details 260
The Concluding Sentence 265

Transitions in Process Paragraphs 266
Focus on Revising 268

Shifts in Person 268
Gender Bias 270

Focus on Editing 272

Dangling Modifiers 273
Misplaced Modifiers 274

Focus on Peer Review 277

❖ *Student Sample* 278

Writing Assignment 278
Writers as Spiders 279

Appendix A   Spelling   280

   Spelling Rules   280
   Commonly Confused Words   282
   Using a Spell Checker   285

Appendix B   Manuscript Form   286

   Preparation of a Title Page   286
   Page Numbering   286
   Spacing   289
   Margins   289
   Titles   289

Appendix C   Glossary of Key Grammatical Terms   290

Answers to Selected Odd-Numbered Exercises   293

Index   321

Preface

PURPOSE/OVERVIEW

Students often enter basic writing courses unprepared for the challenges that await them in college. Some have been out of school for many years and need a review of grammatical and rhetorical principles. Others lacked proper instruction in elementary and secondary school or may not have been ready to receive the instruction that was offered. Because writing well is often a matter of confidence, it is important that students experience writing success in their developmental writing courses early and often. The goal of this textbook is to provide instruction for student writers as well as support for their teachers.

This book features an integrated approach. Because students are more likely to remember grammatical principles taught within context, most of the book's plentiful, high-interest exercises are continuous discourse with the sentences working together to form a paragraph. The purpose of this integrated approach is to help students improve their writing and prepare themselves for the challenges of writing in their college courses and in their careers.

This textbook features

- Clear, readable, and practical instruction
- An overview of the writing process with a student's paragraph in progress
- A review of paragraph and sentence basics
- Topic suggestions, organizational techniques, revising and editing strategies, and peer review questions for each rhetorical purpose
- Emphasis on writing with a computer
- Abundant exercises to reinforce grammar and rhetorical concepts
- Extensive use of writing samples (written by students as well as professional writers)

In addition, there are several features not commonly found in developmental writing textbooks:

- A "Writers as Spiders" section in each chapter with links to Internet sites that reinforce grammatical/rhetorical principles
- Writing assignments based on web sites
- Attention to English as a second language instruction (see ESL Tip boxes)

- Graphical icons to help students locate information and remember key concepts
- Answers to selected odd-numbered exercises
- An appendix on manuscript form

ORGANIZATION OF CHAPTERS

Chapter 1 begins with an inventory of writing habits, introduces students to audience and purpose, discusses the rewards of writing well, and briefly outlines the stages of the writing process. Chapter 2 discusses the stages of the writing process and includes a student's paragraph in progress. Chapter 3 focuses on the topic sentence. Chapter 4 emphasizes supporting details and transition. Chapter 5 examines sentence structure, specifically identifying subjects and verbs. Chapter 6 teaches students to identify phrases and clauses and to edit their compositions for fragments. Chapter 7 through 11 each focus on a particular purpose for writing paragraphs. Narration, description, development by example, and process are introduced along with related grammatical, punctuation, and diction skills.

ANCILLARY PACKAGE

- *Instructor's Manual*
- *Prentice Hall Test Manual* (includes diagnostic/mastery tests); also available in WIN, MAC, or DOS format
- *ESL Workbook* with exercises and tips for ESL writers
- *Writer's Solution: Writing Lab*, a dual-platform (MAC/WIN) interactive CD-ROM introducing students to the writing process and rhetorical modes and using professional writing as examples (ISBN 0-13-639000-3)
- *Writer's Solution: Language Lab*, a dual-platform interactive CD-ROM helping students improve their writing with grammar, usage, and diction activities (ISBN 0-13-616418-8)
- *Writer's Toolkit*, a disk-based (WIN or MAC) program featuring activities from *Writer's Solution;* networking capability for lab use
- Supporting web site at http://www.prenhall.com/campbell that features

  - Syllabus creator
  - Objectives/summaries of each chapter
  - Online quizzes and student exercises available in various formats, including multiple choice, true-false, and essay questions
  - Teacher management features including quiz scoring and e-mail capabilities
  - Links to helpful web sites
  - Site search feature

ACKNOWLEDGMENTS

I thank the reviewers for their helpful comments: Patrick Haas, Glendale Community College; Kate Gleason, Berkeley College; and Ted Walkup, Clayton College and State University.

I am especially indebted to Jan Ballantine, my great friend and fellow traveler, for authoring the ESL Tip boxes in this edition as well as the *ESL Workbook*.

I am also grateful for my students over the last twenty-five years. They have been a constant source of inspiration and surprise.

I thank my colleagues at the Tarpon Springs Center of St. Petersburg Junior College, who have supported me through the valleys and the heights of my life as a teacher and as a writer.

A special word of thanks to the fine Prentice Hall staff: sales representative Beth Rechsteiner for convincing me that I could write a textbook; Phil Miller, president of the humanities and social sciences division, for offering me a contract; and English editorial assistant Joan Polk for answering every question I asked her. This book, however, would not exist without senior acquisitions editor Maggie Barbieri, who has unswervingly supported my efforts over the last five years, and freelance editor Harriett Prentiss, whose prompting, cajoling, and upholding pushed me to do my best.

Finally, I thank my mother and father, Evelyn and George Etheredge, for giving me a love for language; my husband, Dan, for loving me; and my daughters, Jenny and Leah, for teaching me.

Martha E. Campbell

How to Use the Icons in This Book

In this textbook you will often find icons (visual images) in the margins. Each icon represents a grammatical concept or punctuation rule. Use these icons as your guide when you are searching for information. To improve your understanding, try to associate the icon with the related grammatical concept or punctuation rule.

Following is a list of the icons used in this text:

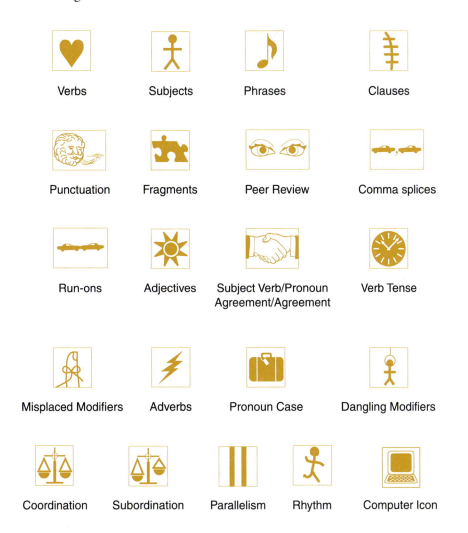

Focus:
Writing Sentences
and Paragraphs

CHAPTER 1

Focus on Writing

Do you want to improve your writing skills? Do you believe that writing well is necessary for your future success in the classroom and in your career? If so, this textbook is for you.

You probably need to review some basics. Maybe you have difficulty organizing your ideas. Perhaps you are not confident about your ability to express your thoughts, or you worry about whether your writing is "correct." This book will help build your confidence as a writer.

Writing is not just about rules. Writing is a creative exchange between you and your reader. You want your reader to receive the messages you send and respond to them.

Think about yourself as a writer. If you are like many other college students, you think of yourself as a student, an adult, a friend, a son or daughter, a worker—but as *a writer?* What are your writing habits?

WRITER'S INVENTORY

The following inventory will help you examine your habits as a writer.

EXERCISE 1.1

Writer's Inventory—Part 1

Write **Y** for **yes** or **N** for **no** in each blank. There are no right or wrong answers, so be honest in your responses.

_____ **1.** I can always find a good topic to write about.

_____ **2.** I spend time planning what I am going to say before I begin writing.

_____ **3.** I use some type of outline to help me organize my ideas.

_____ **4.** I read through my papers to decide what ideas should be omitted.

_____ **5.** I read through my papers to decide what ideas should be added.

_____ **6.** I check my spelling with a dictionary or spell checker.

_____ **7.** I use a textbook or a handbook to look up punctuation rules.

_____ **8.** I read my papers aloud so I can check the flow of my sentences.

_____ **9.** I ask someone else to read my papers aloud to me so I can check the flow of my sentences.

_____ **10.** I read over my writing assignments many times looking for mistakes.

If you answered no to any of the above questions, congratulations! You admit that some of your writing habits need improvement. The first step toward writing improvement is recognizing the need for change.

This textbook will help you change your writing habits in several ways. It will teach you about

- The writing process
- Paragraph organization
- Sentence structure
- Grammar
- Punctuation

Writing, however, is not just about habits. The _attitude_ of the writer is important.

Writer's Inventory—Part 2

These statements will help you examine your attitudes as a writer. Write **Y** for **yes** or **N** for **no** in each blank.

_____ **1.** I should be able to write for a long time without being distracted.

_____ **2.** I always allow enough time to complete my writing assignments.

_____ **3.** I feel confident when I submit my writing assignments to my teacher.

_____ **4.** I reward myself when I complete a writing assignment to my satisfaction.

_____ **5.** I dread getting my papers back from the teacher.

Look again at each of these statements:

1. I should be able to write for a long time without being distracted.

Most people do not lead uninterrupted lives. The demands of family and work occupy much of our time. Writers learn to work around interruptions by using small "chunks" of time and taking a step-by-step approach.

2. **I always allow enough time to complete my writing assignments.**

   No one has a foolproof system for meeting deadlines. Most writers struggle to finish their writing in a timely manner so they don't end up rushing at the last minute. If you get an early start on an assignment and allow time to get help when you need it, you will likely be successful in handing in your papers on time.

3. **I feel confident when I give my writing assignments to my instructor.**

   You want to do the best you can with every assignment. However, it is natural to feel unsure about your ability as a writer. The important thing is to believe that you will improve your writing with practice and guidance.

4. **I reward myself when I complete a writing assignment to my satisfaction.**

   When you know you have done a good job, don't forget to reward yourself! You know when you have put forth your best effort.

5. **I dread getting my papers back from the instructor.**

   Keep your focus on improving your writing skills. Read your teacher's remarks carefully, and decide how you will use them to become a better writer. The more you practice, the more you will learn.

With the help of this textbook, you can become a confident writer. You can begin developing this confidence by looking at the process writers use to develop their compositions.

UNDERSTANDING THE WRITING PROCESS

There is no mystery to good writing. Effective writers move through various stages when they write. The stages that writers move through are called the *writing process*.

Stage 1: Planning
In this stage, writers consider possible topics and collect ideas about these topics.

Stage 2: Organizing
During stage 2, writers focus the topic, determine the main idea, and arrange the supporting ideas in order. Then they write a first draft.

Stage 3: Revising

When writers revise, they add, omit, or rearrange sentences to improve the organization of their ideas. They also check to see if each sentence flows smoothly into the next. Afterward, they write a revised draft.

Stage 4: Editing

In the editing stage, writers correct spelling, punctuation, and grammatical errors and check their word choice.

Stage 5: Finishing

During this last stage of the writing process, writers make last-minute corrections and prepare the final draft according to the reader's (or instructor's) instructions.

If you follow these stages, you can change your writing habits and improve your attitudes about writing. You will also be more satisfied with your writing and ready to share your writing with others.

EXERCISE 1.3

The five stages of the writing process are planning, organizing, revising, editing, and finishing. Read the following. Write in the blank the correct stage of the writing process.

_____ Checking for spelling errors

_____ Making last-minute corrections

_____ Gathering your ideas about the topic

_____ Arranging your supporting points

_____ Adding ideas where necessary

Each chapter of this textbook provides more information about the writing process. Chapters 2 through 4 introduce strategies for organizing paragraphs. Strong paragraphs depend on effective sentences, so Chapters 5 and 6 review the basic elements of sentences. Chapters 7 through 11 offer you a chance to practice writing several types of paragraphs while continuing to learn grammar and punctuation skills.

WHY WRITERS WRITE

As a writer, you want to share your ideas with a reader. Generally, writers write for four reasons or *purposes:*

- To express their personal feelings
- To entertain their readers
- To inform their readers
- To persuade their readers

Writing to Express

One of the most common purposes for writing is to express personal feelings. When you write for this purpose, the results are often surprising. You may uncover thoughts and responses that you did not even know you had.

Some examples of writing for self-expression include personal letters, diaries, electronic mail, and chat rooms.

In 1887, Elizabeth Etheredge wrote this letter to her sons, who were freshmen at a nearby university:

> My Dear Sons,
>
> I received your letter last Friday. It gave me so much pleasure to receive it from you. I am so glad that you are having a good time. I suppose today is the first day of classes. You need not fear at all. Always try to do what is right. Write to me what books you are studying. You do not know how much I miss you. I must close now. Write me often, for you do not know how much I love to receive your letters.
>
> Your beloved Mother,
>
> Elizabeth Etheredge

Because this mother's feelings were written rather than spoken, her voice can still be heard over a hundred years later.

Today, a mother might send this e-mail message to her daughter who is away at college:

> Hey! What's up? I was glad to get your e-mail message this morning. How are your classes going? Are you getting along with your new roommate? I'm glad you're making lots of new friends. I hope you're studying hard. (I know; don't lecture, Mom!) Not much new here. I mailed your care package yesterday. We miss you.
>
> Write back soon,
>
> Mom

Like the letter from 1887, this e-mail message expresses a mother's concern for her child. However, will this message still be around in a hundred years?

One popular form of self-expression is musical lyrics. Copy the lyrics from one of your favorite songs. What emotions do you think the songwriter is trying to express? What do these lyrics mean to you?

EXERCISE 1.4

Writing to Entertain

Some writers are entertainers. They enjoy relating an amusing story or just poking fun at the little things in everyday life. When you read your daily newspaper, you will find columnists relating funny stories to communicate with their readers. Other writers compose screenplays for television sitcoms and movies or manuscripts for short stories or novels—all *to entertain* their readers.

Here is a paragraph by Dave Barry, one of America's most popular humorists:

> Let's say that, like millions of weight-conscious Americans, you think you eat sensibly: Your diet consists . . . of mineral water and low-calorie, low-fat foods. And yet you're still gaining weight. Why? I'll tell you why. You're drinking water with minerals in it. Minerals are among the heaviest substances in the universe. . . . Think about it. The Appalachian Mountains and most major appliances are essentially big wads of minerals, and you're putting those things into your body. No wonder you're gaining weight!
>
> —Dave Barry, "Motivate! Then Fail!"

Writing to Inform

Most of the reading you do every day is written *to inform*. When you read a newspaper, you can check the articles on the front page so you can learn about the events of the previous day. Journalists compose newspaper articles to tell you the *who, what, when,* and *where* of each event. For example, maybe you want to know the score from last night's basketball game or the damage from yesterday's storms. Informational writing is based on fact. Other examples of informational writing are encyclopedias, technical manuals, autobiographies, and textbooks.

Here is an example of informative writing taken from a sociology textbook:

> Factories sprouting across much of Europe became magnets attracting people in need of work. This "pull" of work in the new industrialized labor force was accentuated by an additional "push" as landowners fenced off more and more ground, turning farms into grazing land for sheep—the source of wool for the thriving textile mills. This "enclosure movement" forced countless tenant farmers from the countryside toward cities in search of work in the new factories.
>
> —John J. Macionis, *Sociology*

EXERCISE 1.5 Write a few sentences informing someone about an activity (for example, a sport or a hobby) that you enjoy. What is the activity? How long have you been doing this activity? Why do you enjoy this activity?

Writing to Persuade

Some writers not only want to inform you of the facts but also try *to persuade* you to accept a particular viewpoint on the issue. If you leave the front page of the newspaper and turn to the editorial page, you will find editorials and columns that set forth an opinion and try to convince you to accept it. For example, an editorial might support a particular political candidate or argue for a waiting period before handguns can be purchased. Other examples of persuasive writing include letters to the editor, sermons, and advertisements.

A student wrote the following persuasive paragraph on the topic "Should Congress pass a law making flag burning a federal crime?"

> Burning the flag should not be a federal crime. First of all, the American red, white, and blue symbol is private property. Since the government does not own the flag, as it does public property, it should not interfere with the method in which citizens use it. Next, the foundation of American government is based on the right of citizens to dissent. The First Amendment guarantees that U.S. citizens have the right to speak and act against the government's decisions in a legal manner. Therefore, citizens who express their dissent by burning the flag are exercising their rights as provided by the founders of this country. Even though some Americans may see burning the flag as disagreeable, it is not a criminal act.
>
> —Mike Conroy

Read each of the following topics. Decide on the topic's purpose. Then place the appropriate letter in the blank: **X** (express personal feelings), **I** (inform), **P** (persuade), or **E** (entertain).

_____ 1. A letter to the editor against new property taxes

_____ 2. A catalog of computer software

_____ 3. A letter of recommendation for a scholarship

_____ 4. A technical manual for installing a dishwasher

_____ 5. A medical article about new treatments for breast cancer

_____ 6. A novel about two long-separated lovers who are reunited

_____ 7. A column about the top ten reasons not to vacation in Siberia

_____ 8. A job application letter

_____ 9. A mathematics textbook

_____ 10. A political candidate's television advertisement

THE WRITER'S AUDIENCE

As a writer, you have a voice to give expression to your ideas. You rely on your speaking voice every day; however, your writing voice may not get as much practice.

Speaking versus Writing

Speaking is an important skill for the classroom and workplace, but writing is more than just "speaking on paper." Understanding how speaking and writing are alike and how they differ will help you become a better writer.

First, both speaking and writing have three key elements:

- Someone sending the message
- Someone receiving the message
- The message itself

However, these elements interact with each other in different ways when you speak and when you write.

When you are speaking, your audience (one or more people) is usually present. You can tell if your audience is listening carefully. Attentive listeners will often make eye contact, nod their heads when they agree with you, and respond to your ideas. For example, your classroom teacher knows that if students are reading a textbook for another class or looking around the room, they are probably not listening carefully to the lecture.

If members of your audience are listening actively, they can ask questions if they do not understand part of your message. You see this give-and-take exchange in talk shows, political debates, and active classrooms.

However, when you are writing, your reader is absent. You cannot see your reader in front of you reading your message. What is happening when the reader is receiving your message? Are there any distractions? Is the reader able to focus on what you have to say? If not, you probably will never know. What if the reader has questions? Perhaps a sentence is unclear, or the reader just wants more information about the topic. Generally, you will not be there to answer your reader's questions.

There is another important difference between speaking and writing. Everyday conversation moves back and forth between the speaker and the audience. Speakers often interrupt each other and jump from topic to topic. The conversation continues freely until it is time to move on to something else.

Most writing, on the other hand, is organized for the reader. Because you want to communicate your ideas clearly to your reader, you plan what you want to write before you write it. Also, you work to arrange your ideas so that the reader receives your ideas and does not misunderstand your message. Suppose you write a paragraph for your English class, and one of your sentences is unclear. It is unlikely that your instructor is going to call you on the telephone and ask you what you meant in the second sentence on page 2. Because you are not available to answer your reader's questions, your writing must be clear and organized. This textbook will help you send clear, organized messages to your reader.

Finally, speakers do not have to worry about spelling and punctuation. Even when you are making a formal speech, your audience cannot tell if you have misspelled words or punctuation errors in your notes. Also, your audience will not know whether you use periods, commas, apostrophes, and other punctuation marks correctly. When you speak, you rely on pauses or changes in your tone of voice—not punctuation—to signal the end of a sentence or to create dramatic effect.

However, when you write, correct spelling and punctuation are important. Errors can keep your reader from understanding your message. For most readers, *how* you say something is closely connected to *what* you say.

Table 1.1 on the next page summarizes the differences between speaking and writing:

General Readers versus Specialized Readers

All serious writers work hard to communicate with their readers. However, it is sometimes difficult to picture the reader. Who is he or she? What does he or she expect?

Your reader can be an individual person or a group of people. Readers can be divided into two types.

TABLE 1.1	Speaking versus Writing
Speaker	*Writer*
Can see audience.	Audience is absent.
Can tell if audience is listening.	Cannot tell if reader understands message.
Can view audience's response.	
Can communicate back and forth with audience.	Ideas must be organized to help reader understand the message.
Doesn't have to worry about spelling.	Spelling is important.
Doesn't have to worry about punctuation.	Punctuation is important.

The first type of reader is a general reader. When you write for a general reader, you do not assume that the reader has any specific knowledge about your topic. Therefore, your writing must be clear since you cannot expect the reader to read between the lines. Also, you should avoid using any special terms that your reader may not know. Here is a paragraph written for a general reader:

> The Internet is a global network of computers connected by phone lines, satellites, and cable wires. To use the Internet on a home computer, you will need to contact a company that provides the software necessary to access the Internet. This company will also provide the software you need to use the World Wide Web, part of the vast network known as the Internet.

The second type of reader is a specialized reader. Specialized readers already have knowledge of your topic. You can assume they will be interested in what you are writing. You can also use special terms you would expect specialized readers to understand. Here is the same paragraph written for a specialized reader.

> The Internet is a global network of computers connected by modems, satellites, fiber optic cable, and leased data lines. To use the Internet on a home computer, you will need an Internet service provider that provides TCP/IP software to access the information superhighway. This company will also provide the graphical user interface you need to use the World Wide Web, a hypermedia subset of the Internet.

Good writers are reader-friendly. They keep in mind whether their readers are general or specialized and try to meet the reader's expectations. Here is a table comparing general and specialized readers:

TABLE 1.2	General Readers versus Specialized Readers
General Reader	*Specialized Reader*
Writer must attract the interest of a general reader.	Specialized reader is already interested in the subject.
General reader may not have any knowledge of the subject.	Specialized reader knows the subject.
General reader probably will not recognize use of specialized vocabulary.	Specialized reader understands specialized vocabulary.

EXERCISE 1.7

Consider each of the following types of writing. Write **G** in the blank if the writing is intended for general readers. Write **S** if the writing is intended for specialized readers.

_____   **1.**   A restaurant review in a big-city newspaper

_____   **2.**   A review of a ballet in a dance magazine

_____   **3.**   A technical manual for installing a hard drive on a computer

_____   **4.**   A cookbook of easy recipes

_____   **5.**   A repair manual for videocassette recorders

_____   **6.**   A book of quilt patterns for experienced quilt makers

_____   **7.**   A review of a movie for a general newspaper

_____   **8.**   A travel guide for visitors to Chicago

_____   **9.**   An investment guide for stockbrokers

_____   **10.**   A guide to children's health for all parents

THE WRITER'S REWARDS

Writing means taking risks. Will the reader enjoy what you have to say? Will your reader be bored? Will the reader understand your message? Will the reader agree with what you have to say?

What are your rewards for taking these risks? Why make a commitment to learning to write well? There are three major reasons to work hard in this class and learn to write well:

- **Your grades will improve.**

  Success in the classroom demands good writing. If you can express your understanding of a subject in a clear, organized composition, you will get a higher grade.

- **Your chances of finding a better job will increase.**

  If your application letter for a job is well written, you will be more likely to get your foot in the door. After you get a job, your chances for promotion will increase if you can write good reports and memos.

- **You will be proud of your efforts.**

  Seeing your finished paper, you can be satisfied with your accomplishments.

WRITING ASSIGNMENT

Write a few sentences answering one (or more) of the following questions:

1. How do you think writing well will help you in your future career?

2. Write about a time when you were proud of something you had written.

Writers as Spiders

At the end of every chapter in this textbook is a section called "Writers as Spiders." This section encourages you to "crawl" through the World Wide Web, using it as another resource to help you become a better writer.

The World Wide Web is part of the Internet. The Internet was first developed as a research tool for the military, the government, and educational institutions. At first, all users could see on the Internet was text. Now, thanks to the World Wide Web, users can see graphics as well as text and can move easily from one site to the next.

To access the World Wide Web, you will need an Internet service provider or ISP (either at home or through your school) and a connection (often a modem). Once you reach the World Wide Web, you can explore various sites. Each site on the World Wide Web has a location (or address).

The Writers as Spiders sections will give you World Wide Web addresses for accessing information about the writing topics you are studying. You will recognize these addresses because they all begin with *http://.* To access a web site on most browsers (provided for you by your ISP), you go to *File. . . Open Location* (or *File. . . Open Page*) and type in the address. Once you are within a web site, you can move to related sites by clicking on *hyperlinks,* which are underlined words in blue. Then you can use the back key to return to your original location or type in another address to move to a new site. If this process sounds complicated, ask a friend or a teacher for help.

Keep in mind that the number of World Wide Web sites is growing rapidly, and sites frequently change addresses or are deleted or modified. Also, the address must be typed in exactly, or the site will not open. So if you have trouble opening one of the sites listed in this textbook, first check to be sure you have entered the address correctly. If you still cannot open the site, it may have moved, so try another address.

For an overview of the writing process, try

http://www.tri-c.cc.oh.us/west/faculty/write/docs/
process.htm#Overview

For a humorous way to remember the stages of the writing process, see

http://www.davison.k12.mi.us/elementary/rap.htm

ESL TIP 1

This textbook offers resources for students whose native language is not English. The web sites below are especially helpful for ESL (English as a second language) students; they are also excellent resources for native speakers who want to improve their communication skills. You will find additional ESL resources in later chapters.

Purdue University: ESL Resources for Students

http://owl.english.purdue.edu/ESL-student.html

Planet English

http://www.tesol.com/planet/

On-Line English Grammar

http://www.edunet.com/english/grammar/toc.html

Grammar Quizzes

http://www.aitech.ac.jp/~iteslj/quizzes/grammar.html

Portland Community College Links for Students

> http://thor.pcc.edu/~ap-sec/links.htm

English Pages

> http://www.pratique.fr/~green/english.html

English Grammar for ESL Students

> http://www.gl.umbc.edu/~kpokoy1/grammar1.htm

Selected Links for ESL Students

> http://www.aitech.ac.jp/~iteslj/ESL.html

ESL Grammar Notes: Count and Non-Count Nouns

> http://www.fairnet.org/agencies/1ca/grammar1.html

ESL Grammar Notes: Articles

> http://www.fairnet.org/agencies/1ca/grammar2.html

ESL Grammar Notes: Verb Tenses

> http://www.fairnet.org/agencies/1ca/grammar3.html

CHAPTER 2

Focus on the Writing Process

In Chapter 1, you learned that writing is a process. The five stages of the writing process are

- Planning
- Organizing
- Revising
- Editing
- Finishing

This chapter will explore each stage of the writing process. You will also see how one student—Jennifer Sanders—uses the stages of the writing process to complete a writing assignment in her English class.

STAGE 1: PLANNING

You should begin this stage as soon as you can after you receive a writing assignment. In stage 1, you

- Consider possible topics
- Discover what you already know about various possible topics
- Gather ideas about each possible topic

Sometimes instructors assign writing topics, but often they do not. If your topic was not assigned, you must come up with your own topic. The possibilities are endless. Fortunately, this stage is "thinking about" rather than "committing to." Your responsibility is to explore different writing topics.

Be sure to allow enough time in stage 1. If you rush through this stage to begin actually drafting your paper, you will likely have to go back to the drawing board because you are unhappy with your topic. Take the time to explore your ideas fully. Remember, too, that you are writing for yourself—not your reader—so relax and let the ideas flow.

Writers use several strategies to help them gather ideas about their topics:

- **Freewriting**

  When you freewrite, you write nonstop about a topic and see what ideas come to mind.

- **Brainstorming**

  Brainstorming is thinking about as many ideas as you can related to a topic.

- **Clustering**

  A cluster is a visual diagram of words and phrases related to your topic.

- **Journal Writing**

  A journal is a collection of your written observations about the world around you.

Freewriting

Suppose your instructor gives you a general writing topic, such as "friend-ship." Where do you begin? Many writers start with freewriting.

Freewriting is a way to "free up" your ideas. When you freewrite, the goal is to write continuously for a set length of time, usually three to five minutes. If you cannot think of something to say, just write "I can't think of anything to write" until your ideas start to flow.

Do not worry about grammar or sentence structure. Keep writing.

Following is Jennifer Sanders's freewriting on the topic of friendship:

Student Sample—Freewriting

Friendship. What do I think about friendship? I know it's not easy to find a good friend. Trusting this person to keep promises. Suppose I lend a friend money to pay a late bill or to make repairs on her car. A true friend will keep the promise to repay me. What if I ask a friend to attend a birthday party or a cookout. A true friend will go knowing it means something to me. I can't think of anything to write. I can't think of anything to write. I can't think of anything to write. I need a friend who will keep my secrets and listen to me. No matter what the personal trauma may be. My friend will be their and help keep me encouraged. To help me when I fall down, to say it's a tough time right now, but here is a shoulder to cry on. To explain to me even though I'm having family difficulties, to say my family only wants the best for me and I am special the way I am. No matter what choices or mistakes I make. These are the qualities of a true friend.

Jennifer has written freely, not worrying about grammar, spelling, or punctuation. Jennifer realizes that freewriting is an exploratory activity. It is like stirring a stew to see what floats to the top.

EXERCISE 2.1

Try freewriting on one of the following topics or a topic of your own choice. Write for three to five minutes nonstop.

1. Television
2. Growing up
3. Cars
4. Where you live
5. Today's popular music

Brainstorming

When you *brainstorm*, you try to think of as many ideas about your topic as possible.

The goal of brainstorming is to let your ideas flow freely. Do not take the time to organize your thoughts or judge your ideas as "good" or "bad." Instead, just write down your ideas in the order that they come to you. Later you can go through your list and pick out the good ones.

You can also brainstorm as part of a group. If you are working in a small group, you should listen to each person's ideas and give everyone a chance to speak without interruption. Everyone should have a chance to participate in the discussion. Do not criticize anyone's ideas even if you do not agree with them. Be sure someone in the group records everyone's ideas for later use.

Some writers prefer brainstorming to freewriting. Others find it useful to freewrite and then brainstorm an idea that comes out of freewriting.

After reading over her freewriting, Jennifer decides to focus on the idea of trust between friends.
Here is Jennifer's brainstorming:

Student Sample—Brainstorming

Trust Between Friends
Very important
Keeping promises
Showing up for special times
Not telling secrets
Loaning money for car repair
Paying back money
Keeping secrets

➡

Hugging me when I'm sad
Picking me up when I'm down
Listening to me
Giving advise
Being their for me

Jennifer has made spelling errors in her brainstorming list, but she can correct those later. She has written her brainstorming list quickly so she can get down all her ideas.

Form a group with two or three other students in your class. Then brainstorm the topic "What are the qualities of a good parent?" Someone in your group should record the ideas mentioned by each group member. Someone should also be prepared to report your group's responses to the class. After you listen to the reports from all the groups, consider these questions:

EXERCISE 2.2

- What qualities of good parents were mentioned by more than one group?
- Why do you think so many students considered these qualities important?
- Which qualities did only one group address?
- Of the qualities mentioned by all the groups, which two or three do you think are most important?

Try brainstorming on one of the following topics or on a topic from your freewriting. Remember not to judge your ideas. Just write them down.

EXERCISE 2.3

1. A sport you enjoy
2. A favorite restaurant
3. A special relative
4. A dream vacation
5. An ideal job

Clustering

When you brainstorm, you list your ideas in no particular order. Clustering goes a step further by also grouping your ideas. *Clustering* is a visual diagram of your ideas about a topic and the relationship of those ideas to each other. To create a cluster diagram, write your general topic in the center of a piece of paper. Circle your topic. Then draw lines out from the topic to create narrowed subtopics, each represented by one or two words. Circle the subtopics. Then draw lines again as you generate words associated with each subtopic.

Clustering reveals relationships between ideas. Clustering also provides the opportunity for you to be sure you have not repeated any key ideas.

Some writers prefer clustering to brainstorming, and some writers use both techniques along with freewriting to gather ideas. There is no right or wrong way to get ideas. Use whichever techniques work best for you. Figure 2.1 shows Jennifer's clustering diagram on trust and friendship.

Figure 2.1   Student Sample—Clustering Diagram

Jennifer's clustering diagram has some of the same ideas as her brainstorming list, but she also added some new thoughts. The more you explore, the more ideas you will get, and the more interesting your writing will be. Once again, Jennifer ignored grammar and spelling and concentrated on getting her ideas down on paper.

EXERCISE 2.4   Create your own clustering diagram on one of the following topics or a topic of your choice.

1. Movies

2. Hobbies

3. Your college

4. Your family

5. The planets

Journal Writing

You can also collect ideas for writing by keeping a journal. A *journal* is a record of your observations about daily life—observations that would easily slip into the past unless they were recorded.

You can use a regular 8½-by-11-inch spiral notebook for your journal, or you can keep your journal on a computer. Most students date their entries. It's a good idea to get in the habit of writing daily. Some days you may feel like writing more, and other days you may write only a few sentences.

A journal is more than a diary. A journal gives you a chance to write about *what* has happened to you and *why* things have happened to you. When you keep a journal, not only will your own observations sometimes surprise you, but your journal entries will also be available to you later as a resource for writing topics.

Jennifer keeps a journal and tries to write something daily. Here are some entries from her journal:

Student Sample—Journal Writing

Journal Entry 1

When it's football season and I have those good old football parties, I want to have friends over who are going to enjoy watching the games. Let's face it. Nobody likes party poopers, and if I'm up for a rough and tumble football game, I want everyone to join in.

Journal Entry 2

There's nothing better than sitting with friends and talking about the juicy romance novel we're reading. That adds to the excitement of the novel. If we get tired of reading, we can always pull out the old sewing machine and make seat covers for the furniture, or even work on next year's Halloween costumes.

We all need to take the time and realize that friends aren't something we can just throw away and pick new ones later. It's about hanging in no matter what the situation may be.

Jennifer may find that one of these journal entries gives her an idea to write about later. Even if she never gets an idea from her journal, writing regularly will help her become a better writer. Writing is a skill, and practice helps.

EXERCISE 2.5

Begin a journal of your own. Buy a notebook, or set up a file on a computer. Date your entry. Write about something that happened to you or something you thought about during the day. Don't worry about how many words you write. If you write every day, you'll find yourself loosening up and writing more.

STAGE 2: ORGANIZING

Now that Jennifer has collected her ideas on her topic, she is ready to organize those ideas. During stage 2, you

- Focus your topic
- Determine your main idea
- Consider which ideas you will use to support your main idea (and which ideas you will omit)
- Determine the order in which your ideas will appear
- Write an experimental draft(s)

In the organizing stage, an important change takes place. You are now writing for a reader. You make the decisions in this stage that will allow you to communicate your ideas clearly to the reader.

Your readers are busy people. When they read your writing, they want to know what your point is. They expect you to stick to your main idea and use good supporting details. They also expect you to organize your thoughts. If your writing is confusing, they will likely stop reading. Your readers will appreciate your efforts to organize your ideas, and you will build your confidence as a writer.

When Jennifer reviews her brainstorming and clustering diagram, she decides she has more ideas than she can use in a single paragraph. She decides to focus on one quality of a true friend—trustworthiness. She supports her main idea with three supporting details—keeping promises, not telling secrets, and being supportive.

Here is Jennifer's experimental draft:

Student Sample—Experimental Draft

Everyone has opinions about the qualities of a true friend. The most important quality of a true friend is being trustworthy. Trusting my friend to keep promises. Suppose I lend a friend money to pay a late bill or to make repairs on her car. A true friend will keep the promise to repay me. What if I ask a friend to attend a birthday party or a cookout. A true friend will go knowing it means something to me. Trusting in the person to keep my innermost secrets, the skeletons in my closet. Helping me calm my fears and enjoy happy moments. To explain to me that even though I'm having family difficulties, my family wants the best for me. I want this person to hug me when I cry, to listen, to give me advise even if it's wrong. A friend should not judge me

➡

for my mistakes or for the things they would do different or not do at all. A true friend will be their to believe in me and support my goals and dreams. Whatever path I take, to give me the confidence to take risks and chances, to say it's okay when I fail. To let me know I am accepted for me, not what society says I should be. These are the things that I find to be the true genuine qualities in a friend.

Notice how Jennifer's ideas have begun to take shape. Her paper still has some grammatical errors and spelling mistakes, but she has not yet made her corrections. She is still concentrating on ordering her ideas and supporting them with details.

STAGE 3: REVISING

Revising is challenging work. When you revise your compositions, you need to take off your writer's glasses and put on your reader's glasses. In other words, you need to see your paper from your reader's point of view.

In the revising stage, you

- Rearrange sentences to improve the organization
- Reword unclear or vague sentences
- Omit sentences that are unrelated to the topic
- Add ideas where your support may be insufficient
- Check the flow of ideas
- Revise your draft(s)

You need time, energy, and patience when you revise (meaning "to see again") because this stage requires discipline and concentration. You may find it difficult to revise your writing after you have finished your experimental draft. Sometimes you become so familiar with what you are trying to say that it is challenging to read your paragraph from someone else's point of view.

ESL TIP 2   **Writing in English**

Writing in a language other than our own involves more than knowing grammar and vocabulary. We must also have a sense of the culture because people from different cultures have different communication styles. Here are some tips to help you write for English-speaking readers:

1. **Be direct from the beginning.** State clearly the main point of your paragraph in a topic sentence. Usually, this will be your first sentence.

2. **Go directly to your supporting points.** Present your supporting ideas in a direct, logical fashion.

3. **Stick to your topic.** Make sure every detail and example supports your topic sentence.

4. **Remember that written and oral language differ.** Speakers often talk in fragments and use incorrect grammar. However, in the United States, we use Standard English in written communication. Also, sometimes a non-native English speaker will hear a word but not be able to produce it in writing because the English language has so many irregular pronunciations and spellings.

5. **Be original within the instructor's guidelines.** Your instructor wants you to master various types of writing and to share your ideas. So feel free to state your opinions and to challenge or question existing ideas. In our democracy, every individual has the right to express well-supported claims. One of your goals in writing will be to get your audience to think about your topic. The audience may not necessarily agree with your ideas, but that is certainly acceptable (just as you may disagree with someone else's ideas). Your audience will take your well-supported ideas seriously.

6. **Immerse yourself in the language.** To see significant improvement in your ability to read, write, and speak English, do more than the assigned work in your classes. Reading, writing, and speaking will help you master English because repetition plays a key role in learning. Remember, too, that it is natural to make mistakes. When you use your mistakes to improve, you will learn and grow more rapidly.

Following is Jennifer's revised draft:

Student Sample—Revised Draft

Trustworthiness is the most important quality of a true friend. Trusting my friend to keep promises. For instance, if I lend a friend money to pay a late bill or make repairs on her car. A true friend will keep her promise to repay me. Also, if I'm asked to attend a special occasion such as a birthday party or a cookout. A true friend will go knowing it means something to me. Above all, I expect secrets we share together to remain secrets. For example, listening to my fears about my boyfriend and not telling anyone else. Surely when family difficulties arise, I would hope my friend would be their to give me that shoulder to cry on and to give me advise even if it's wrong. A ➤

friend should not judge me for my mistakes. Whatever path I take, to give me the confidence to take risks and chances. To let me know I am accepted for me, not what society says I should be. Overall, these are the genuine qualities I find in a true friend.

In her revised draft Jennifer has made some important changes. She has placed the main idea of her paragraph in the first sentence. She has provided additional examples to support her points. For example, she mentions fears about her boyfriend to support her point about friends keeping secrets. She has also added words like *for instance, also, above all,* and *overall* to improve the flow of her sentences. Jennifer is satisfied with what she has written and is ready for the next stage in the writing process—editing.

STAGE 4: EDITING

Many students confuse the revising stage with the editing stage. However, editing is a distinct stage in the writing process. The editing stage includes

- Correcting spelling errors
- Correcting capitalization errors
- Correcting punctuation errors
- Correcting grammatical errors
- Checking for effective word choice
- Preparing your edited draft(s)

Most readers are used to reading work that has been carefully edited. It is difficult for many readers—particularly educated readers—to concentrate if a paper is filled with errors in spelling, capitalization, punctuation, and grammar. Remember that for most readers, *what you say is directly related to how you say it.*

Editing can be time-consuming. You must read your paper several times. Read once looking just for grammatical errors. Read again to look for misspelled words. Then read for errors in capitalization and again for punctuation mistakes. Of course, every time you read, you must be alert. In other words, don't try editing at three o'clock in the morning!

Here is Jennifer's edited draft:

Student Sample—Edited Draft

Trustworthiness is the most important quality of a true friend. I must be able to trust my friend to keep promises. For instance, if I lend a friend money to pay a late bill or make repairs on her car, a true friend will keep her promise to repay me. Also, if I'm asked to attend a special occassion such as a birthday party or a cookout, a true friend will go. Above all, I expect the secrets we share to remain secrets. For example, she will listen to my fears about my boyfriend and not tell anyone else. Most importantly, family problems should be kept a secret. Surely when family difficulties arise, I would hope my friend would be there to help calm my fears, to give me that shoulder to cry on, and to give me advice even if it's wrong. A friend should not judge me for my mistakes. Whatever path I take, a true friend will give me the confidence to take risks and chances. A friend will let me know I am accepted for who I am, not what society says I should be. Overall, trustworthiness is a genuine quality of a true friend.

When Jennifer edited, she found several sentence fragments as well as misspelled words (*their/there* and *advise/advice*). She also omitted some unnecessary words, for example, changing *share together* to *share*. She is now ready to finish her paper.

STAGE 5: FINISHING

Before she turns in her paper, Jennifer completes the finishing stage. This stage consists of

- Proofreading the final draft for last-minute corrections
- Choosing a title
- Preparing the final draft according to the teacher's instructions

Should your paper be typed or word-processed, or will your teacher accept it handwritten?

When you proofread your paper, look for any corrections you may have overlooked. Don't be afraid to make last-minute corrections to your draft. Every writer has had the experience of finding an error just before the assignment is due. If you make your corrections neatly, most readers will not object.

You will also need a title for your paper. Your title should be short (usually three to five words) and should appear at the beginning of your composition. Think of your title the same way you think of the title of a book on a library shelf. Will the title of your paper attract your reader's interest? Does the title let your reader know the topic of your paper? If you have difficulty writing a title, write down the key words from your topic. Then write a title that includes those words.

Follow these guidelines when writing your title:

- Do not underline your title or place it in quotation marks (unless your title is quoting someone else's words).
- Do not follow your title with a period.
- Capitalize the first and last words.
- Capitalize all other words except *a, an, the, and, nor, but, or, yet, so,* and short prepositions such as *in, of, at, into, by, to, for, from,* and *on.*

To prepare your paper to hand in to your instructor, be sure to include your name, the course title, your instructor's name, and the date (see Appendix B). Use the same format as Jennifer does below (unless your instructor gives you different instructions). Also, double-space your paper and use a minimum margin of 1 inch at the left, right, top, and bottom of each page.

When you complete your paper, reward yourself for a job well done!

Here is Jennifer's final draft. Notice her last-minute spelling correction (*occassion* to *occasion*). She has also added a title.

Jennifer Sanders
Basic Writing
Ms. Campbell
18 January 1999

Student Sample—Final Draft

A True Friend

Trustworthiness is the most important quality of a true friend. I must be able to trust my friend to keep promises. For instance, if I lend a friend money to pay a late bill or make repairs on her car, a true friend will keep her promise to repay me. Also, if I'm asked to attend a special occasion such as a birthday party or a cookout, a true friend will go. Above all, I expect the secrets we share to remain secrets. For example, she will listen to my fears about my boyfriend and not tell anyone else. Most importantly, family problems should be kept a secret. Surely when family difficulties arise, I would hope my friend would be there to help calm my fears, to give me that shoulder to cry on, and to give me advice even if it's wrong. A friend should not judge me for my mistakes. Whatever path I take, a true friend will give me the confidence to take risks and chances. A friend will let me know I am accepted for who I am, not what society says I should be. Overall, trustworthiness is a genuine quality of a true friend.

Although these stages of the writing process have been presented here in a step-by-step arrangement, the writing process does not usually work in a lockstep fashion. Instead, writers often find themselves circling back to stages they thought they had finished. This recycling is natural, so do not worry if you have to repeat some steps. Just be sure to allow enough time for the writing process to work.

WRITING ASSIGNMENT

Use the stages of the writing process to write a paragraph. Look over your responses to the freewriting, brainstorming, clustering, and journal exercises in this chapter. Choose a topic that appeals to you, and write an experimental draft. Then revise, edit, and prepare a finished copy.

Writers as Spiders

How do you locate information on the World Wide Web? One way is to use search engines. Search engines "crawl" through web sites looking for a keyword or phrase that you have provided. The search engine then creates a list of web sites for you to explore.

There are more than 250 search engines. Some popular search engines are AltaVista, InfoSeek, Excite, WebCrawler, and Yahoo. Each search engine has advantages and disadvantages for the user.

Search engines use keywords that you must provide in a particular format. You can use a single keyword or combine keywords to form a phrase. For example, if you were searching for articles on the issue of censorship and television, you could search for "censorship and television." Some search engines use a + sign to replace the word *and*. On these search engines, you would enter "censorship + television." Each search engine provides the user with information regarding search techniques.

For more information about the advantages and disadvantages of various search engines as well as information about using search engines effectively, see

http://www.spjc.cc.fl.us/0/research/home.html

Web Exercise 1

Conduct a World Wide Web search for one of the topics in Exercise 2.2 or Exercise 2.3. Then explore one or more web sites suggested by the search engine.

Web Exercise 2

The following sites offer a number of journal topics for writers:

http://www.boker.org.il/eng/etni/teacjour.htm
http://www.dsusd.k12.ca.us/schools/amistad/
Informal_Journal_Writing_Topics.htm

Write about one of these topics in your journal.

CHAPTER 3

Focus on the Topic Sentence

A paragraph is a group of sentences that presents a main idea and related details to a reader. You can write compositions that consist of one paragraph, or you can combine paragraphs to create longer papers. In this textbook, you will concentrate on writing good paragraphs.

You can easily recognize paragraphs because the first line of a paragraph is indented. Without paragraphs, each page in this textbook would be a solid block of type, and you would have to decide where one major idea ends and another begins. Writers indent the first lines of their paragraphs so readers will know that a new idea is being introduced.

A good paragraph has the following key elements:

- A focused topic
- A main idea expressed in a topic sentence
- Details supporting the main idea
- A concluding sentence

In this chapter, you will learn

- How to narrow a topic
- How to write a topic sentence

In Chapter 4, you will learn about supporting details.

Paragraphs vary in length. Some paragraphs are only a few sentences long while others can be as lengthy as a page. In general, the paragraphs that you write in the classroom will be between six and twelve sentences long—approximately the length of the sample paragraph below.

Here is a typical six-to-twelve-sentence paragraph:

> ## Walking to Physical Fitness
>
> <u>Walking is my favorite way to exercise.</u> Walking thirty to forty minutes every morning is a great way to relax. When I walk with a friend, I can talk about the day ahead or share some challenges I am facing. When I walk by myself, I can meditate and get rid of my stress. Walking regularly also improves my general health. Fitness experts recommend an exercise routine to keep the heart strong. Furthermore, walking every day lessens my risk of disease. I know the positive effects walking has made in my life, and I will continue my walk to physical fitness.

"Walking to Physical Fitness" has all the elements of a good paragraph:

- A focused topic (walking as a form of exercise)
- A main idea expressed in a topic sentence (Walking is my favorite way to exercise.)
- Details supporting the main idea (a great way to relax, walk with a friend, walk by myself, improves my general health, keeps the heart strong, lessens my risk of disease)
- A concluding sentence (I know the positive effects walking has made in my life, and I will continue my walk to physical fitness.)

Read the following paragraph, and then answer the questions that follow.

EXERCISE 3.1

Using a spell checker on a computer can be a great advantage for a writer. First, the writer can check the spelling of many of the words in the paper. The spell checker tries to match the spelling of the word with a word in its dictionary. Many spell checkers have at least 100,000 words in their dictionaries. Second, the writer can ask the spell checker to suggest a spelling. If the word is already spelled correctly, the writer can ask the program to ignore the suggested spelling. If the word is misspelled, the writer can request that the program correct the error. Many writers rely on spell checkers to improve the accuracy of their writing.

1. What is the topic of the paragraph?

_____

2. What is the main idea of the paragraph? Underline the topic sentence.

3.   What points does the author use to support the main idea?

_____

4.   Circle the concluding sentence.

LIMITING A TOPIC

The first step in writing a strong paragraph is limiting the topic. Suppose you were asked to write a paragraph about your childhood. It would be impossible to write all the details of your childhood in just six to twelve sentences! You must, therefore, narrow the topic. Your topic must be limited enough that you can write about it *completely* within a single paragraph.

Here are three possible ways to narrow the topic "childhood":

1.   <u>Childhood</u>
    Birthday parties
        The best birthday party I ever had

2.   <u>Childhood</u>
    My friends
        My friends in the seventh grade
            My best friend in seventh grade

3.   <u>Childhood</u>
    Summer vacations
        Family trips
            The time my family went camping
                The night it rained and our tent collapsed

EXERCISE 3.2

Narrow each of the following topics so that you could write about it completely in a single paragraph. Be sure that each time you fill in a blank, you are limiting the topic further. Fill in as many levels as necessary to narrow your topic.

1.   Sports

_____

    _____

      _____

        _____

2.   High school

_____

    _____

      _____

        _____

3. Music

_____

_____

_____

_____

4. Books

_____

_____

_____

_____

5. Exercise

_____

_____

_____

_____

You can also use the strategies you learned in Chapter 2—freewriting, brainstorming, and clustering—to help you focus your topic. Even after you think you have limited the topic sufficiently, you may discover that you have too much information for a single paragraph. If that is the case, you must narrow your topic further.

Choose one of the general topics below, and narrow it using one of these methods—freewriting, brainstorming, or clustering.

EXERCISE 3.3

1. Topic: Animals
Limited topic: _____

2. Topic: Political leaders
Limited topic: _____

3. Topic: Holidays
Limited topic: _____

4. Topic: Travel
Limited topic: _____

5. Topic: Pollution
Limited topic: _____

Writing a Topic Sentence

After you have narrowed your topic, you are ready to begin organizing your paragraph. Start by writing a topic sentence.

The topic sentence of a paragraph expresses the single main idea the writer wants to communicate to the reader. All the other sentences in a paragraph explain the topic sentence.

The topic sentence is important to you, the writer, because it helps keep you on track as you write your paper. Readers also rely on topic sentences to help them understand the message of the paragraph.

A topic sentence has two parts. It names the topic, and it expresses an idea about it. Here are some examples:

Topic sentence: Successful students know how to manage study time.

Topic: Successful students

What about the topic? Know how to manage study time

Topic sentence: Knowing how to study for tests is important in college.

Topic: Knowing how to study for tests

What about the topic? Is important in college

Topic sentence: Taking notes in class is another essential study skill.

Topic: Taking notes in class

What about the topic? Is another essential study skill

EXERCISE 3.4

Underline the key words from the topic, and draw a circle around the idea to be discussed. Use the first example as a model.

1. One <u>characteristic of a good teacher</u> is (treating students with respect.)
2. An important benefit of regular exercise is weight control.
3. One essential quality of a good movie is an unpredictable plot.
4. My favorite type of music is jazz.
5. An effective way for college students to manage time is to prepare a daily "to do" list.
6. Reducing cholesterol levels is another benefit of regular exercise.
7. Assigning grades fairly is also a trait of a good instructor.
8. Scheduling regular conferences with instructors can help college students manage their time.
9. A lively sound track is a characteristic of a good movie.
10. Another type of music I enjoy is the blues.

EXERCISE 3.5

Copy your limited topics from Exercise 3.3. Then write a topic sentence for each limited topic. Use the first example as a model.

1. Topic: Animals

   Limited topic: <u>Tropical birds</u>

   Topic sentence: <u>My favorite tropical bird is the macaw.</u>

2. Topic: Political leaders

   Limited topic: _____

   Topic sentence: _____

3. Topic: Holidays

   Limited topic: _____

   Topic sentence: _____

4. Topic: Travel

   Limited topic: _____

   Topic sentence: _____

5. Topic: Pollution

   Limited topic: _____

   Topic sentence: _____

A good topic sentence is neither too broad nor too narrow. If your topic sentence is too broad, you will not be able to discuss the topic sufficiently in a single paragraph. If your topic sentence is too narrow, you will probably have difficulty writing six to twelve sentences on the topic.

Too broad: Many students have difficulty solving word problems in math.

Too narrow: Janine missed word problem 4 on her homework last night.

Good topic sentence: Students can use a step-by-step approach to solve word problems in mathematics.

Too broad: Eating correctly is important.

Too narrow: Spinach is an excellent source of iron.

Good topic sentence: An important step in preventing heart disease is eating fruits and vegetables daily.

Too broad: Mystery novels are fun to read.

Too narrow: The last mystery novel I read was 300 pages long.

Good topic sentence: The plot of the novel *May Tomorrow Never Come* is suspenseful.

EXERCISE 3.6

Read each sentence below. Place a check mark in the blank next to the sentences that you think are focused topic sentences. If the sentence is unfocused, place an **X** in the blank.

_____ **1.** Good teachers can be found in any school.

_____ **2.** Everyone can benefit from regular exercise.

_____ **3.** Good movies are hard to find.

_____ **4.** A good teacher listens patiently to her students.

_____ **5.** One excellent benefit of regular exercise is muscular fitness.

_____ **6.** A good dramatic movie has realistic characters.

_____ **7.** Every college student needs time management skills.

_____ **8.** There are many forms of music in the world today.

_____ **9.** One of my favorite types of music is rap.

_____ **10.** College students who want to manage their time well must avoid procrastination.

Readers expect the topic sentence to help them understand the writer's ideas. If the topic sentence is too broad or too narrow, the reader will be confused. A good topic sentence makes the writer's job easier.

LOCATING THE TOPIC SENTENCE

A topic sentence can appear anywhere in a paragraph, but it is usually the first sentence. When you place your topic sentence first, you provide a road map of your paragraph for your reader. The reader's attention is focused on your main idea from the beginning. Your reader then expects the rest of your paragraph to support the main idea.

In the following paragraph, the topic sentence appears in the first sentence:

> One important study skill critical for college success is doing homework completely. Students who are working for academic success know that it is important to follow the directions for each exercise. For example, if the math instructor has asked students to show all their work on a homework assignment, then the students should complete all steps of each problem. Furthermore, serious students review their homework to see ➡

> if they have followed all the directions. Successful students also attempt to answer all the questions in every homework assignment. If a problem is easy, the student can place a check mark next to it in the margin. If one of the problems is especially difficult, the student can place a question mark next to it as a reminder to ask the instructor for assistance. All in all, students who work hard to complete their homework to the best of their ability are well on their way to success in the classroom.

Because the topic sentence appears at the beginning, the reader's attention is immediately drawn to the importance of *doing homework completely*. The writer does not have to worry whether the reader will figure out the main idea of the paragraph—the main idea is in the first sentence! For this reason, beginning writers usually place their topic sentences at the beginning of their paragraphs.

Sometimes, however, a topic sentence will be the last sentence in the paragraph. Writers place their topic sentences last when they want to present the supporting details first and then lead their readers to the topic sentence. This technique can attract the reader's interest or add suspense to the paragraph.

In the paragraph below, the topic sentence appears at the end.

> Anthony sighs as he thinks about his humanities test on Friday. How should he prepare for the test? He has never taken a test in college, and now he faces studying three chapters on the history of Rome. Fortunately, his instructor provided a review sheet with key terms and concepts from each chapter. Anthony finds each term and concept in his textbook and highlights the related information. Then he reads through his class notes. Finally, he makes an index card for each item on the review sheet and records the information he wants to recall on the test. Afterward, he spends several hours reciting and reviewing the details on his note cards. <u>Even though Anthony has never taken a college test, he has already discovered the importance of reviewing his textbook and his class notes and preparing study cards before each test.</u>

In this paragraph, the writer wants the reader to "sweat it out" with Anthony. Therefore, the topic sentence appears last in the paragraph.

In other paragraphs, the topic sentence is not stated directly.

> Brianna had been worrying all night. All kinds of questions popped into her mind. What if she were to fail the math test tomorrow? She had never had success taking tests. Why should she think that this test should be any different? Her hands were already beginning to shake, just from thinking about sitting at that desk in the front row of her math class. Then ideas of escape entered her mind. She thought to herself, "Maybe I can sleep late tomorrow and take the test some other time. Or maybe I should just quit school altogether. What is the point in staying in school if I can't make good scores on tests?"

Professional writers often write paragraphs with implied (understood) topic sentences. The reader, then, must discover the paragraph's main idea. One possibility for a topic sentence for this paragraph might be "Brianna, like many college students, suffers from test anxiety."

EXERCISE 3.7   Read each of the following paragraphs. Then underline the sentence that best represents the topic sentence of the paragraph.

1. Many college students find study groups an effective way to review for tests. Members of the study group can ask each other questions. For example, each student can make up several possible test questions. Then all the questions can be added together to form a sample test. Study group members can also review each other's notes. For instance, one group member may have missed an important class lecture. The others can share their notes with the student who needs to make up work before the test. Finally, study groups can divide up the review work. If the instructor has distributed a test review sheet covering several chapters, each group member can be responsible for a specific chapter. Students who join study groups will be more likely to enjoy studying for tests.

   A. Finally, study groups can divide up the review work.
   B. Many college students find study groups an effective way to review for tests.
   C. Study group members can also review each other's notes.
   D. If the instructor has distributed a test review sheet covering several chapters, each group member can be responsible for a specific chapter.

2. Juan is worried about his history test next week. He remembers that he has promised to take his son to the baseball game and his wife to the movies. When will he find time to study? Then Juan remembers a study technique his history instructor suggested. He stops by the store and buys 4-by-6-inch index cards. When he gets home, he pulls out the review sheet his instructor distributed. He starts with the terms he has to define. He writes each term on a separate index card. Then he turns the card over and writes the definition. Now he has a set of flash cards he can carry with him through the next week. Juan has discovered a way to study for tests whenever he has a few moments of quiet.

A. Juan is worried about his history test next week.
B. When will he find time to study?
C. He stops by the store and buys 4-by-6-inch index cards.
D. Juan has discovered a way to study for tests whenever he has a few moments of quiet.

3. Frances is tapping her feet on the floor as she tries to stay awake in English class. Then she yawns just as the instructor looks her way. She got only a few hours sleep last night because she was out with her friends until two o'clock in the morning. What was she thinking about? Now she cannot concentrate on what the instructor is saying. Maybe if she picks up a pencil and takes notes, she can keep herself from falling asleep on the desk.

A. Frances is tapping her feet on the floor as she tries to stay awake in English class.
B. Frances, like many other college students, needs a good night's sleep.
C. Now she cannot concentrate on what the instructor is saying.
D. Maybe if she picks up a pencil and takes notes, she can keep herself from falling asleep on the desk.

4. The first step in critical reading is to survey the assigned pages. Read through the table of contents to check the chapter's contents. Then preview any subheadings in the chapters. The second step is to ask questions. What do you want to learn from the reading? Why is the reading important? The third step is to read carefully. Underline the main ideas in each paragraph. Place a check mark in the margins beside any important points. The fourth step is to review what you have read. Write an outline of what you have learned. Look for any points you may have omitted. These four steps can help you become an effective reader and improve your confidence as a student.

A. The first step in critical reading is to survey the assigned pages.
B. The second step is to ask questions.
C. The fourth step is to review what you have read.
D. These four steps can help you become an effective reader and improve your confidence as a student.

5. A key to comprehending textbooks is making notes in the margins. Students should be careful to mark important ideas. For example, students can write check marks in the margins to indicate major points. A check mark followed by a + sign can also highlight a significant passage. Furthermore, students should ask themselves questions when they read. If a passage is unclear, the student can write a question mark in the margin. A student can also use two question marks for a particularly puzzling section. These marginal notes help students build confidence in their ability to read their textbooks.

A Furthermore, students should ask themselves questions when they read.
B. A check mark followed by a + sign can also highlight a significant passage.
C. A key to comprehending textbooks is making notes in the margins.
D. If a passage is unclear, the student can write a question mark in the margin.

EXERCISE 3.8   Write a topic sentence for each paragraph below. Check your topic sentence to be sure that it relates to all of the paragraph's supporting details.

1. Many students use word processing programs to check their spelling. Some programs automatically underline words that may be misspelled. The student can then either ignore the computer's spelling suggestion or replace the misspelled word with another spelling. Furthermore, many word processing programs feature style checkers. Most style checkers include a grammar checker to check for incomplete sentences and weak wording. Students can also use style checkers to check the reading level of their compositions.

_____

_____

2. One student in my writing class uses a small cassette recorder to tape the instructor's lectures. Taping the lectures allows the student to listen to what the instructor has to say without worrying about writing down all the information. After class, the student listens to the recording and takes notes. This recorder has a special feature that allows the student to slow down the voice playback. The feature is important because this instructor can talk very quickly! When

the student plays the tape after class, he can slow down the lecture so that he can take accurate notes.

_____

_____

3. Daily reviews of material learned in class are important. Psychologists report that most of the information that people learn is forgotten during the first twenty-four hours. A daily review will help move learned information from short-term to long-term memory. Furthermore, weekly reviews are necessary for many students. A weekly review of notes will reinforce learned material. Weekly reviews also help students discover any information that remains unclear.

_____

_____

4. Some students are early risers. They like to use the early morning hours to finish homework or study for tests. Their creative juices kick in before the sun rises. Other students are night owls. They may not get started studying until after midnight. They can study for several hours before exhaustion overcomes them. Many students, though, find that the best study time is in the afternoon or evening when they return home from classes.

_____

_____

5. One memory technique, known as a mnemonic device, is to use an acronym to remember something. An acronym is a word made up of the initial letters of a series of words. UFO, for instance, is an acronym for an **u**nidentified **f**lying **o**bject. Another memory technique is to use a song or a rhyme to help remember information. For example, the ie/ei rule of spelling is "I before E except after C or when sounding like A as in *neighbor* and *weigh*." Some students even create their own songs or poems to help them recall specific facts.

_____

_____

DISCOVERING TOPIC SENTENCES IN TEXTBOOKS

Learning to recognize the main idea of a paragraph is an important reading comprehension skill. When you read your college textbooks, for instance, you should work to discover the main idea of each paragraph. You might want to mark it with a highlighter for future reference—for example, when you are studying for a test.

EXERCISE 3.9

1. Using one of your textbooks, locate a paragraph in which the topic sentence appears first. Copy the paragraph, and underline the topic sentence.

2. Using one of your textbooks, locate a paragraph in which the topic sentence is not the first sentence. Copy the paragraph, and underline the topic sentence. If the topic sentence is not stated, write a topic sentence for the paragraph.

WRITING ASSIGNMENT

Using one of your topic sentences from Exercise 3.5, write a paragraph. Follow the stages of the writing process. First, write an experimental draft. Then revise, edit, and prepare a finished copy.

Writers as Spiders

The World Wide Web offers many sites related to paragraph development. For more background information about topic sentences, try

http://www.as.ttu.edu/uwc/topicsen.html

You can find another explanation of topic sentences at

http://aix1.uottawa.ca/academic/arts/writcent/hypergrammar/partopic.html

If you need help identifying topic sentences, see

http://myst.hunter.cuny.edu/~rwcenter/writing/on-line/topicsup.html

http://www.bell.k12.ca.us/BellHS/Departments/English/idtopicsentence.html

For more study skills suggestions, see

http://www.loyalistc.on.ca/calendar/counsel/learn1.htm

CHAPTER **4**

Focus on the Supporting Details

Much of the success of a paragraph depends on its supporting details. Supporting details develop the topic sentence and communicate the paper's major points to the reader.

Where do writers find supporting details? They draw on their personal experiences, their imagination, their reading, and their observations.

Your paragraph's supporting details should be interesting because you do not want to bore your reader. Furthermore, you want your readers to learn something about your topic while they are reading your paragraph.

This chapter is designed to help you

- Generate supporting details for your paragraphs
- Arrange these supporting details in order
- Connect these details so that your paragraphs will flow smoothly

CREATING SUPPORTING DETAILS

How many details do you need to support your topic sentence? How do you know what kind of supporting details to add to your paragraph? The answers to these questions depend on your purpose and your audience.

Remember that there are four main purposes for writing. People write to express themselves, to entertain, to inform, and to persuade. If you are writing to entertain, you may use a funny story to support your main point. If you are writing to inform or to persuade, you are more likely to use facts, statistics, and reasons as supporting details.

You must also consider your audience. Are you writing to someone who knows a great deal about your topic? Or are you writing to a general audience? (To review purpose and audience, see Chapter 1.)

The supporting details you include in a paragraph also depend on your topic sentence. Your topic sentence is a promise to the reader of what is to come. Consider how these topic sentences tell you the kind of details you must supply your reader:

Topic Sentence	Supporting Details That Are Promised
On a hot April afternoon ten years ago, I was in a bad car accident.	The writer will provide details about the accident, including what happened and why it happened.
The four-year-old girl sits by the window watching the gentle rain.	The writer will describe the child, and the reader will learn why she is watching the rain.
You can prepare an excellent résumé using six steps.	The writer will list the six steps.
One quality of an effective leader is honesty.	The writer will give examples of effective leaders who are honest.

For each of the following topic sentences, tell what kinds of details the writer is promising.

EXERCISE 4.1

Topic Sentence	Supporting Details That Are Promised
1. You can prepare for a job interview if you follow these four steps.	_____ _____ _____
2. Michael Jordan is a great basketball player.	_____ _____
3. Last fall, I made a decision that changed my life.	_____ _____
4. An effective parent is a good listener.	_____ _____
5. The small jewelry box glistens in the morning sun.	_____ _____

The Reporter's Questions

One excellent method for creating supporting details is to ask the same questions a reader will ask about your main idea: "Who?" "What?" "When?" "Where?" "Why?" and "How?" These questions are the *reporter's questions*. Not every question will fit every topic, but asking these questions will help you come up with the support you need for your topic sentence.

43

Look again at this topic sentence:

On a hot April afternoon ten years ago, I was in a bad car accident.

Here is how you can apply the reporter's questions to this topic sentence:

Who?	I (the writer)
What?	Broke my arm and leg in a car accident
When?	Ten years ago this April
Where?	At the corner of Dover Street and Lakeside Drive
Why?	The driver swerved to avoid a child on a bicycle.
How?	I was a passenger in a car driven by my best friend. My friend swerved to avoid the child, and our car hit a tree.

EXERCISE 4.2

Apply the reporter's questions to the following topic sentences. Remember that not all the questions fit every topic.

1. You can prepare for a job interview if you follow these four steps.
   Who? _____
   What? _____
   When? _____
   Where? _____
   Why? _____
   How? _____

2. Michael Jordan is a great basketball player.
   Who? _____
   What? _____
   When? _____
   Where? _____
   Why? _____
   How? _____

3. Last fall, I made a decision that changed my life.
   Who? _____
   What? _____
   When? _____
   Where? _____
   Why? _____
   How? _____

4. An effective parent is a good listener.
   Who? _____
   What? _____
   When? _____

Where? _____
Why? _____
How? _____

5. The small jewelry box glistens in the morning sun.
Who? _____
What? _____
When? _____
Where? _____
Why? _____
How? _____

How Many Details?

How many details do you need to support a topic sentence? There is no single answer to this question. In general, though, writers usually need two to three supporting details in each paragraph.

Look at these topic sentences from Exercise 4.2.

Topic sentence: You can prepare for a job interview if you follow these four steps.

The writer will need four supporting details in this paragraph because that is the promise made in the topic sentence. The reader will be cheated if the writer skips necessary steps.

Topic sentence: Last fall, I made a decision that changed my life.

This topic sentence does not indicate how many details the writer will need. The writer must make this decision. This paragraph will need enough supporting details to answer the reader's questions: What was the decision? How did it change the writer's life? When the paragraph is finished, the writer should ask, "Does my reader know enough to understand why this decision was so important in my life?" Or does the paragraph lack important details?

Topic sentence: An effective parent is a good listener.

Again, the topic sentence does not promise how many details the writer will provide. Will one supporting detail be enough? Probably not. Will two satisfy the reader? If the details were strong, perhaps so. However, three supporting examples will probably be the most convincing.

There is no magic number for how many supporting details are needed to develop a topic sentence. You must use your best judgment and give your reader enough details to be complete and convincing.

The Underdeveloped Paragraph

If you do not supply your reader with enough details, your paragraph will be underdeveloped. Compare the following two paragraphs.

Paragraph A

The four-year-old girl sits by the window watching the gentle rain. She is not stirring as the rain falls softly. The girl has long, soft, wavy, strawberry blonde hair, big blue eyes, and a petite nose. Her hair is softly curled around her petite face. Her small nose is pressed against the glass. Her small nose must be cold, but she does not seem to mind. What is she thinking? Maybe she is thinking about the sound the rain makes as it hits the glass. It sounds like her feet when she tiptoes through the kitchen. Her small body is amazingly still for such a small child.

Paragraph B

The four-year-old girl, Shannon, sits quietly by the window watching the gentle afternoon rain. Shannon's long, wavy, strawberry blonde hair is softly curled around her petite face. Her small nose pressed against the glass must be cold, but she does not seem to mind. What is she thinking? Maybe she is thinking that the rain hitting the glass sounds like her feet tapping the floor when she tiptoes through the kitchen. Perhaps she is wondering where the rain comes from. She is probably making a sad face because she cannot play with her friends outside in the park. Her small body is amazingly still for such a young child.

Paragraphs A and B both contain approximately 110 words, but paragraph B is much more interesting to read because it has more details. Paragraph A could be developed using more of the reporter's questions. Also, paragraph A repeats some of the same details in slightly different words instead of adding details. For example, the first two sentences in paragraph A make the same statement. Also, some words, such as *small nose*, are repeated.

In your own writing, be sure not to repeat details or repeat the topic sentence using different words. Every detail should be different and should add to the topic.

EXERCISE 4.3

Read the following paragraphs. If a paragraph is well developed, write **Developed** in the blank following it. If a paragraph is underdeveloped, write **Underdeveloped.**

1. Jennifer St. Johns is the best softball player I have ever seen. She is just wonderful in every game. She hits the ball very hard. When she is in the outfield, she almost always catches the ball. The other

players know they can count on her to catch the ball. She is the greatest softball player.

_____

2. The attractive red convertible sits in the new car lot. Its sleek exterior design draws attention. The glistening paint, aerodynamic style, and shiny wheel covers add to the sporty look. The car's interior promises comfort. The black leather seats are inviting. A six-footer or a petite teenager would have no trouble driving this car. The precision instruments demonstrate its potential power on the road. Safety features are also prominent. Front-passenger air bags and antilock brakes are standard. This beautiful car is a treat for the eye but not for the wallet.

_____

3. Caladesi Island on the west coast of Florida is a tropical paradise. This island is protected from the traffic of nearby Clearwater Beach because it can be reached only by boat or ferry. The island's beach seems to stretch endlessly. Its fine white sand is perfect for walking or sunbathing. Seashell lovers will have no problem finding plenty of specimens for their collections. The water is also a delight. The Gulf of Mexico is comfortable for swimming most of the year. Many days the water is clear enough for swimmers to see the sandy bottom. No wonder this island is consistently ranked among the best beaches in the United States.

_____

4. Many college students are undecided about their future career. They do not know which career they should pursue. They are uncertain about their career goals. Some have had a number of jobs but have not pursued a "career." Therefore, they come to college not knowing what kind of employment they will pursue. These students should speak with a counselor about their job goals. Many colleges also have career centers where students can seek job counseling and explore new job opportunities.

_____

5. An ideal job offers excellent medical benefits. These medical benefits are part of the job package. The employer should pay for all these benefits. Medical coverage is important on a job. Medical coverage should include fees for doctors' visits and hospitalizations. Employers should make sure all their employees have medical benefits.

_____

EXERCISE 4.4 Choose one of the underdeveloped paragraphs from Exercise 4.3. Rewrite it, leaving out repeated details. Use the reporter's questions to think of new, interesting details to add.

ORGANIZING DETAILS

There are three common ways of organizing supporting details:

- **Order of importance**

  This method arranges examples, reasons, or facts supporting your topic according to their importance.

- **Time order**

  This method organizes your supporting details in chronological order.

- **Spatial order**

  This method organizes your supporting details in a pattern according to space or direction.

Order of Importance

This method arranges supporting details from most important to least important or from least important to most important. These details can be facts, reasons, or examples. Most often, writers choose to end with their most important point. Your reader is more likely to remember what you state last in your paragraph rather than what you state first. Also, your last point appears just before you make your final statement to your reader—your concluding sentence. Therefore, you will probably want your last major point to be your strongest.

Here is a paragraph developed according to order of importance. The most important example is given last.

Successful college students carefully manage their study time. First, they set aside time each day to complete their homework. Many teachers assign approximately two hours of homework for every hour of class time. Successful students block out that much homework time in their daily schedules. Second, successful students schedule time for long-term projects. Often students need several weeks to complete a project. Motivated students will break the project into small steps and work an hour or two each day until the project is complete. Most importantly, successful students schedule adequate study time for tests. This time may involve working in a small group to review for the test. Most students will also need several hours for individual review the day before the test. Successful college students know the value of time management.

Develop a topic sentence based on each of the following topics. Add two or three major points to support each topic sentence. You can use phrases rather than complete sentences for these supporting details. Use the first example as a model.

1.   Topic: Time management for college students

     Topic sentence: College students should carefully schedule their

     study time.

     Least important detail: Scheduling time for homework

     Next detail: Scheduling time for long-term projects

     Most important detail: Scheduling study time for tests

2.   Topic: A favorite musical performer or group

     Topic sentence: _____

     Least important detail: _____

     Next detail: _____

     Most important detail: _____

3.   Topic: A favorite movie

     Topic sentence: _____

     Least important detail: _____

     Next detail: _____

     Most important detail: _____

4.   Topic: A characteristic of an effective teacher

     Topic sentence: _____

     Least important detail: _____

     Next detail: _____

     Most important detail: _____

5.   Topic: A dream vacation spot

     Topic sentence: _____

     Least important detail: _____

     Next detail: _____

     Most important detail: _____

6.   Topic: A quality of a true friend

Topic sentence: _____

Least important detail: _____

Next detail: _____

Most important detail: _____

Some writers use an outline to help them arrange their ideas in order of importance. In a formal outline, a Roman numeral identifies the focused topic of the paragraph. Capital letters beginning with the letter A identify major points.

The most common type of formal outline is the topic outline (also called a key word outline). In a topic outline, each part of the outline is a phrase composed of key words from the paragraph. All the major points appear in the outline. The concluding sentence is usually omitted from an outline.

Table 4.1 illustrates a topic outline format for a paragraph. Table 4.2 outlines the focused topic and major points listed in Exercise 4.5.

TABLE 4.1	Outline Format for Paragraph

I. Focused topic
   A. Least important detail
   B. Next detail
   C. Most important detail

TABLE 4.2	Sample Topic Outline

I. Managing study time
   A. Scheduling time for homework
   B. Scheduling time for long-term projects
   C. Scheduling study time for tests

EXERCISE 4.6

You can outline *before* you write so that you can check the order of your ideas. You can also outline *after* you finish your paragraph to check whether all your major points are related to your focused topic.

Use any two of your answers to Exercise 4.5 to complete the following outlines. Be sure every part of your outline is a phrase (not a complete sentence).

1.   I. _____
     A. _____
     B. _____
     C. _____

2.   I.   _____

      A.   _____

      B.   _____

      C.   _____

Time Order

Writers use time order when they tell a story, remember an event, or relate a step-by-step process. When writers use time order, they arrange the paragraph's supporting details in the order in which they occur. For example, a paragraph about a car accident would tell about this event from beginning to end following a specific time sequence. A writer of a technical manual for a videocassette recorder would also use time order to describe the steps needed to record a television program.

Here is a paragraph remembering an event:

> One hot April afternoon ten years ago, I was in a bad car accident. My best friend was driving me home from school. The radio was blaring, and we were laughing about a joke we had heard at school. When we reached the corner of Dover Street and Lakeside Drive, a girl on a bicycle suddenly appeared in front of us. My friend swerved to avoid the child, and our car hit a tree. The next thing I remember is being in the back of an ambulance. My head was bleeding all over my new dress, and my head and neck were throbbing. After a few hours in the emergency room and several stitches in my head, I finally got home. The doctor told me I was lucky I was wearing a seat belt. Otherwise, my injuries would have been much worse. I learned a valuable lesson that day—always buckle up!

Here is a paragraph telling how to do something step by step:

> You can prepare an excellent résumé using six steps. First, center your name, address, and phone number at the top of the résumé. Second, state your job objective. Third, list your educational experience, including dates, names of schools, and honors or awards. Fourth, provide all related job experience, with dates, names and addresses of employers, and job duties. Fifth, proofread carefully for spelling and punctuation errors. Finally, give a list of references. A well-prepared résumé can help you get the job you desire.

EXERCISE 4.7

For each of the following topics, write a topic sentence. Then write some supporting details using time order. Consider whether you are being asked to tell a story or describe a step-by-step process. (Add more lines if necessary.)

1. Topic: Registering for classes

   Topic sentence: _____

   Details in time order:

   A. _____

   B. _____

   C _____

   D. _____

2. Topic: A valuable lesson you learned

   Topic sentence: _____

   Details in time order:

   A. _____

   B. _____

   C _____

   D. _____

3. Topic: Studying for a test

   Topic sentence: _____

   Details in time order:

   A. _____

   B. _____

   C _____

   D. _____

Spatial Order

Some paragraphs are arranged according to spatial order—that is, in a particular direction. You might describe a photograph from left to right, a person from head to toe, or a painting from top to bottom. When writers describe an object, a person, or a place, they generally organize the supporting details in a spatial pattern.

As long as the writer moves in a clear direction, the reader should be able to follow. Skipping around from left to top, then from bottom to right will confuse your reader.

Here is a paragraph organized spatially. What direction is the writer following?

> The beautiful oil painting features a peaceful landscape. The painting is approximately 8 inches by 15 inches. To the right is a high, majestic sand dune covered with sea oats. Below the sand dune is a view of the curving sandy shoreline. To the left is a bright blue, calm sea. The upper half of the painting is a morning sky with high clouds. There are no human beings in the painting—just earth, water, and sky.

For each of the following topics, write a topic sentence. Then tell what direction you would use to develop your topic sentences. Also list—in order—some of the supporting details you might include. (Add more lines if necessary.) **Hint:** There is no single way to organize a paragraph spatially. Choose the way you think would be easiest for your reader to follow.

EXERCISE 4.8

1. Topic: A favorite photograph

Topic sentence: _____

Direction: _____

Details in spatial order: _____

A. _____

B. _____

C. _____

D. _____

2. Topic: A special relative

Topic sentence: _____

Direction: _____

Details in spatial order: _____

A. _____

B. _____

C. _____

D. _____

3. Topic: A special place

Topic sentence: _____

Direction: _____

Details in spatial order: _____

A. _____

B. _____

C. _____

D. _____

EXERCISE 4.9

Read the following topic sentences. Write **OI** in the blank next to each topic sentence for which supporting details would be arranged in order of importance. Write **TO** next to the topic sentences that would be developed using time order. Write **SO** next to the topic sentences that would be developed using spatial order.

_____ **1.** I remember the last time I crammed for an English test.

_____ **2.** The poster on the wall of my classroom has an unusual design.

_____ **3.** A student can take several steps to organize paperwork.

_____ **4.** Many college students find study groups helpful.

_____ **5.** The instructor's notes are neatly arranged on the bulletin board.

_____ **6.** I will never forget my first day of college.

_____ **7.** Students should follow several steps to find the main idea of a reading passage.

_____ **8.** One important study skill is taking notes in class.

_____ **9.** Students can improve their short-term memory by following several steps.

_____ **10.** College students who work part-time often have a problem finding time for a social life.

WRITING A CONCLUDING SENTENCE

Your paragraph should have a concluding sentence. It should not stop suddenly. A good concluding sentence

- Reminds the reader of the main idea
- Creates a strong impression in the reader's mind

Look again at the concluding sentence of this paragraph:

> One hot April afternoon ten years ago, I was in a bad car accident. My best friend was driving me home from school. The radio was blaring, and we were laughing about a joke we had heard at school. When we reached the ➡

corner of Dover Street and Lakeside Drive, a girl on a bicycle suddenly appeared in front of us. My friend swerved to avoid the child, and our car hit a tree. The next thing I remember is being in the back of an ambulance. My head was bleeding all over my new dress, and my head and neck were throbbing. After a few hours in the emergency room and several stitches in my head, I finally got home. The doctor told me I was lucky I was wearing a seat belt. Otherwise, my injuries would have been much worse. <u>I learned a valuable lesson that day—always buckle up!</u>

This concluding sentence is good because the reader knows not only what happened on that day ten years ago but also what the writer learned from the experience.

Concluding sentences are not hard to write. There are some common mistakes students make, however, and you should avoid them.

- **Do not repeat your topic sentence.**

  Before you write a concluding sentence, reread your topic sentence to remind yourself that you should refer to the key words. However, do not say the same thing again. Instead, your concluding sentence should give the reader a signal that your paper has come to an end.

- **Do not begin your concluding sentence with *In conclusion* or *As you can see*.**

  These expressions do not add to the concluding sentence's effectiveness. They are empty expressions.

- **Do not introduce a new idea.**

  Though you want to leave your reader with something to think about, it should not be an idea that you have not discussed in your paper. Instead, use your concluding sentence as the finishing touch on your paragraph.

For each topic in Exercise 4.5, recopy your topic sentence in the spaces provided. Then write a concluding sentence for each one. Use the first example as a model.

EXERCISE 4.10

1. Topic: Time management for college students

   Topic sentence: <u>College students should carefully schedule their</u>

   <u>study time.</u>

Concluding sentence: <u>Students who manage their study time will</u>

<u>likely experience less stress and more academic success.</u>

2.   Topic: A favorite musical performer or group

Topic sentence: _____

_____

Concluding sentence: _____

_____

3.   General topic: A favorite movie

Topic sentence: _____

_____

Concluding sentence: _____

_____

4.   Topic: A characteristic of an effective teacher

Topic sentence: _____

_____

Concluding sentence: _____

_____

5.   Topic: A dream vacation spot

Topic sentence: _____

_____

Concluding sentence: _____

_____

6.   Topic: A quality of a true friend

Topic sentence: _____

_____

Concluding sentence: _____

_____

STICKING TO THE TOPIC

All the supporting details of your paragraph must be clearly related to your topic sentence. Your topic sentence is a road map for your reader. Your supporting details must follow this road map. If you take off in some other direction in your paragraph, your reader will be lost. Therefore, it is important to check each sentence to make sure it is related to your topic sentence.

Read the following paragraph, and cross out the sentences that are off track.

> One of my favorite vacation spots is Durango, Colorado. Durango is located in the southwestern corner of Colorado. One of Durango's landmarks is the Strater Hotel. This hotel offers a taste of the Old West. When was the last time you took a vacation? It is so easy to work too hard and forget to take time to relax. The Strater Hotel has rooms that are decorated to look like the hotel rooms of a hundred years ago. Another tourist attraction in Durango is the Silverton Railroad. Tourists can take an old-fashioned railroad ride to the mining town of Silverton. The train clings to cliffs, and the scenery is breathtaking. I am so afraid of heights. I highly recommend Durango, Colorado, to anyone looking for a trip to the Old West.

Did you cross out the following sentences?

When was the last time you took a vacation?

It is so easy to work too hard and forget to take time to relax.

I am so afraid of heights.

When you revise, you need to put on your reader's glasses. In other words, you should read your paper as if you were the reader. When you see a sentence that is unrelated to the topic, ask yourself, "If I were the reader, would this sentence leave me confused?" If the answer is yes, then eliminate this sentence.

Read each paragraph below. Then read the selections that follow, and underline the sentence that is unrelated to the topic of the paragraph.

EXERCISE 4.11

1. Many college students find that using a daily planner helps them manage their time effectively. First, students should schedule their sleep time, mealtimes, and recreation time. Eight to nine hours of sleep is generally recommended. I cannot remember the last time I had eight hours of sleep! Mealtimes are important because they keep energy levels high for studying. Recreation, especially exercise, is also critical for avoiding stress. Students need to use their planners to make sure they do not omit these essential activities.

   A. Students need to use their planners to make sure they do not omit these essential activities.

   B. First, students should schedule their sleep time, mealtimes, and recreation time.

   C. I cannot remember the last time I had eight hours of sleep!

   D. Recreation, especially exercise, is also critical for avoiding stress.

2.   Second, college students should make sure their planners include their class time. Students should not only write in their exact class times; they should also schedule time before and after class. Some students may need to allow extra time before class so that they will not be tardy. Jonathan was tardy to his English class six times last semester. The time scheduled after class can be used to ask the instructor questions or to review class notes.

   A. Jonathan was tardy to his English class six times last semester.

   B. The time scheduled after class can be used to ask the instructor questions or to review class notes.

   C. Students should not only write in their exact class times; they should also schedule time before and after class.

   D. Second, college students should make sure their planners include their class time.

3.   Third, students should schedule at least two hours of study time for every hour of class time. Some of that study time should be spent reviewing notes from the previous class. Students can highlight important ideas and place question marks beside information that is still unclear. Most of the study time, however, will be spent doing homework. One of the math teachers, Ms. Schmitt, forgot to assign homework yesterday. Students must also reserve study time for test preparation.

   A. Students can highlight important ideas and place question marks beside information that is still unclear.

   B. Students must also reserve study time for test preparation.

   C. Some of that study time should be spent reviewing notes from the previous class.

   D. One of the math teachers, Ms. Schmitt, forgot to assign homework yesterday.

4.   Many students benefit from studying routinely in a specific place. One such place is the college library. Many libraries offer individual desks for studying as well as rooms designated for small groups. Our study group was so noisy last week we were nearly kicked out of the library. Other students prefer to study at home or in their dorm rooms. Some students even put a "Do Not Disturb—I'm Studying" sign on their doors so that friends and family members will not distract them. Studying in the same place helps to establish

a study routine that leads to academic success.

   A. One such place is the college library.

   B. Some students even put a "Do Not Disturb—I'm Studying" sign on their doors so that friends and family members will not distract them.

   C. Other students prefer to study at home or in their dorm rooms.

   D. Our study group was so noisy last week we were nearly kicked out of the library.

5.   Students should ask their friends and family members to support them when they need study time. Sometimes friends will beg to go out for a few hours. Students who have tests the next day should say, "Ask me again another time. I have to study for a test this week." Some friends have a hard time hearing the answer "No." However, serious students realize that studying has to come first, and they ask their friends to accept their priorities. Family members can be persistent interrupters, too. Some students ask their families to leave them alone when they are studying in a certain chair or in some other place in the house. I can never find a comfortable place in my house to study. Most friends and family members will accept the fact that getting an education must be first priority.

   A. I can never find a comfortable place in my house to study.

   B. Most friends and family members will accept the fact that getting an education must be first priority.

   C. However, serious students realize that studying has to come first, and they ask their friends to accept their priorities.

   D. Family members can be persistent interrupters, too.

USING TRANSITIONS

As a writer, you know in what order you are presenting your ideas, but how does the reader know? *Transitions* are words and phrases that help the reader follow the order of your ideas. Transitional words and phrases connect your sentences to one another and show the reader the relationship between your ideas. Transitions help make your writing smooth, not choppy. Here is a paragraph without transitions:

> Good parents are respectful to their children. They are patient listeners. When a child talks to them about a personal problem, they let the child speak without interruption. They encourage their child and offer their support during difficult times. If the child is having trouble in school, they may
>
>

> encourage the child to speak with the teacher. They may offer to speak to the teacher on their child's behalf. Good parents are not judgmental. If the child is having trouble with a friend, good parents will try not to criticize the child but will help the child understand how to be a friend to others. Good parents who are respectful to their children earn their children's respect.

Now try reading this paragraph with added transitions:

> Good parents are respectful to their children. *First,* they are patient listeners. *For example,* when a child talks to them about a personal problem, they let the child speak without interruption. *Second,* they encourage their child and offer their support during difficult times. If, *for instance,* the child is having trouble in school, they may encourage the child to speak with the teacher. They may *also* offer to speak to the teacher on their child's behalf. *Third,* good parents are not judgmental. If the child is having trouble with a friend, good parents will try not to criticize the child but will help the child understand how to be a friend to others. *Overall,* good parents who are respectful to their children earn their children's respect.

Writers use transitional words and phrases as signals to their readers. As the preceding paragraph shows, transitions can appear at the beginning of a sentence or in the middle. Notice, too, that not every sentence needs a transitional word or phrase.

Some transitional expressions tell the reader that the writer is adding an idea. In paragraphs, these transitions commonly appear when the writer is introducing a major point. Here are some common transitional expressions:

first	second	third	also	then
next	in addition	additionally	moreover	furthermore

EXERCISE 4.12

This exercise features pairs of sentences. In the blank that starts the second sentence, write an appropriate word or words from the list of common transitional expressions. Do not use any transitional expression more than once. Use the first example as a model.

1. First, when I see my test on the desk, I breathe slowly and deeply for two or three minutes. <u>Second</u>, I focus my attention on my feet and make my foot muscles relax.

2. I close my eyes and picture myself walking along a peaceful mountain trail. _____, I check for any tense places left on my body and try to release the tension.

3. When I open my eyes, I scan the entire test. _____, I look for problems that I think will be easy for me as well as problems that might be difficult.

4. I work on the easiest problems first so that I can build my confidence. _____, I tackle the harder problems.

5. When I finish the test, I go over the test beginning with the last problem and working backward to the first problem. _____, I check to make sure I have marked the correct answer on the answer sheet.

Other transitional expressions signal the reader that the writer is adding an example or an illustration. Some of these transitional expressions are

for example	for instance	as an illustration	to illustrate
as a case in point	in particular	in general	

This exercise features pairs of sentences. In the blank that starts the second sentence, write an appropriate transitional expression from the above list. Do not use the same transitional expression more than once. Use the first example as a model.

1. Many students have discovered successful strategies for taking multiple-choice tests. <u>In general</u>, a student's first instinct when answering a multiple-choice question is correct.

2. Furthermore, students can learn to make intelligent guesses on multiple-choice tests. _____, if a student does not know the answer to a question, it is better to guess C or D as the answer instead of A or B.

3. True-false questions often contain clues that help give students the answers. _____, true-false questions with words such as *never* or *always* are generally false.

4. Students should have a test-taking strategy. _____, many students prefer to answer easy questions first and then approach the hard questions.

5. Successful test takers proofread their tests before they return them to the instructor. _____, these students make sure they have not accidentally misread or omitted questions.

Transitional expressions can also signal the reader that the paragraph is coming to a close. The following transitional words and phrases can be used to begin the concluding sentence of a paragraph:

overall	all in all	finally	in brief	in other words
lastly	on the whole	to sum up	in sum	

EXERCISE 4.14

Add a transitional expression from the above list to the beginning of each of your concluding sentences in Exercise 4.10. Do not use any expression more than once. Be sure to follow each transitional expression with a comma.

EXERCISE 4.15

Underline the transitional words and phrases in the following paragraph.

One important study skill critical for college success is doing homework completely. Students who are working for academic success know that it is important to follow the directions for each exercise. For example, if the math instructor has asked students to show all their work on a homework assignment, then the students should complete all steps of each problem. Furthermore, serious students review their homework to see if they have followed all the directions. Successful students also attempt to answer all the questions in every homework assignment. If a problem is easy, the student can place a check mark next to it in the margin. If one of the problems is especially difficult, the student can place a question mark next to it as a reminder to ask the instructor for assistance. All in all, students who work hard to complete their homework are well on their way to success in the classroom.

WRITING ASSIGNMENT

Using one of your topic sentences from Exercise 4.5, write a paragraph following the stages of the writing process. First, write an experimental draft. Then revise, edit, and prepare a finished copy.

Writers as Spiders

Many online writing centers feature information about paragraph development. For more information about supporting details in a paragraph, see

http://k12s.phast.umass.edu/~hharg/FRESCA.htm

If you would like more suggestions for coping with test anxiety, try

http://www.ufsa.ufl.edu/counsel/Ta.htm
http://ub-counseling.buffalo.edu/stress/study.htm

CHAPTER 5

Focus on the Sentence: Part I

The sentence is the heart of written communication. Just as the human heart pumps blood through the body, a sentence delivers the meaning of the message from the writer to the reader.

A sentence must be complete in order for its meaning to be clear. A complete sentence has three parts: subject, verb, and message.

1. **Subject**

    A subject tells who or what is performing the action of the sentence or who or what is being discussed in the sentence.

    subject
    The doctor examines the patient.

    subject
    Maria is class president.

2. **Verb**

    A verb expresses action or links the subject to the words following the verb.

    verb
    The doctor examines the patient.

    verb
    Maria is class president.

3. **Message understood by the audience or reader**

In casual conversation, people do not always speak in complete sentences. Consider this conversation:

What time is the game?

Two o'clock.

You going?

Yeah.

With Matt?

Yeah. And Karen.

Pick up Mike, too.

I'll see you there.

If you had this conversation with a friend, the meaning would be clear even though not all the sentences are not complete. Even if your message is misunderstood, your friend can ask you what you meant to say.

However, when you send a written message, you need complete sentences so that the reader will be able to receive your message. If your written message is not clear, your reader will be confused, and you will not be there to answer questions about what you meant.

Sentences deliver three kinds of messages. They can

1. **Make statements**
    I'll see you there.

2. **Ask questions**
    What time is the game?

3. **Issue commands**
    Pick up Mike, too.

The goal of this chapter is to help you write complete sentences that will communicate with your reader. In this chapter you will learn to

- Identify subjects
- Identify verbs
- Improve the effectiveness of your sentences

FOCUS ON SUBJECTS: THE ACTORS OF THE SENTENCE

All complete sentences require subjects. Subjects "act out" the action expressed in the sentence or name the person, place, or thing that is the focus of the sentence.

Consider these word groups:

have been exercising thirty minutes each day

is the new English instructor

have leading roles in the play

The meaning of each of these word groups is incomplete without a subject. Fill in the blanks:

_____   have been exercising thirty minutes each day.

_____   is the new English instructor.

_____   have leading roles in the play.

The words you have written in the blanks are subjects. Here are some possible answers (your responses will vary):

Molly and Steve have been exercising thirty minutes each day.

Mr. Fernandez is the new English instructor.

Leah and Ruth have leading roles in the play.

Identifying Subjects

The subject of a sentence answers these questions:

- Who or what is performing the action of the sentence?
- Who or what is being discussed in the sentence?

A subject is often a noun. A *noun* is a word that identifies a person, place, or thing. A *proper noun* names a specific person, place, or thing. Proper nouns are easy to recognize because they begin with capital letters. Here are some examples of proper nouns used as subjects:

subject
Jonathan is my favorite neighbor.

subject
Kate has been my friend since sixth grade.

subject
The Blue Spruce Restaurant serves great ribs.

subject
South Carolina is my home state.

subject
Furman University won the football championship.

EXERCISE 5.1   Use proper nouns as subjects in the following sentences.

1. _____   will be coming for a visit next week.

2. _____   lives down the street from me.

3. _____   sits next to me in biology.

4. _____ will be going with us to the movies.

5. _____ is my favorite city.

Sometimes subjects are common nouns. A *common noun* does not identify a specific person, place, or thing. Common nouns are not capitalized. The following sentences have common nouns as subjects:

subject
The mountains are beautiful in the distance.

subject
The lake looks calm even on a winter day.

subject
Several friends are coming home with me on Friday.

subject
Loyalty is important in a friendship.

ESL TIP 3   **Nouns**

Nouns (words used to name a group or class of people, places, or things) come in many forms. Use the guidelines below to help you choose the correct form of count and noncount nouns.

- **Count nouns** can be counted. They can be used in singular or plural form (note the plural endings).

Singular:	one student	one glass	one story	one child
Plural:	two student**s**	three glass**es**	four stor**ies**	five child**ren**

- **Count nouns** that follow *one of* should be written in the plural form.

  One of the chair**s** fell over.

- **Noncount nouns** cannot be counted and are written in one form. Here are some examples:

Abstract ideas: beauty, love, hate
Activities: tennis, homework, writing
Liquids: water, coffee, blood
Gases: air, steam, oxygen
Diseases: flu, measles, cancer

School subjects: economics, history, biology
Food: bread, rice, lettuce
Natural elements: rain, weather
Other: clothing, furniture, machinery, money, news

- Some nouns are countable or noncountable depending on their use.

Time is on our side.	At **times,** Alexander knew all the answers.
Death is unpredictable.	The police expect 100 **deaths** this holiday weekend.

ESL TIP 4 | **Articles and Determiners**

- Use *a*, *an*, or *the* before **singular count nouns** to qualify the noun. Usually, *a* and *an* indicate a nonspecific noun while *the* indicates a specific noun.

    Henry wants **a** <u>pizza</u>. He likes **the** <u>pizza</u> I make.

- Use *the* before **plural count nouns.**

    The <u>restaurants</u> close early in this town.

- **Noncount nouns** frequently do not require determiners.

    I drink **coffee** for breakfast. My brother drinks **milk.**

When you need to qualify **noncount nouns,** use one of the following:

much	any	some	a little	lots of	a lot of	this	that

Usually, *any* indicates a negative element, and *some* means certainty:

I <u>don't want</u> **any** lunch, but I <u>will take</u> **some** cake.

For an uncertain idea, either *any* or *some* may be used:

Do you suppose they <u>want</u> **some** ice cream?

EXERCISE 5.2

Underline the common nouns used as subjects in the sentences below.

1. The girls quickly left the building.
2. My supervisor completed the report.
3. The officers made the arrest.
4. The class finished the test.
5. The team scored a touchdown.

EXERCISE 5.3

Use common nouns to complete the subjects in the following sentences.

1. The _____ took our orders.
2. Several _____ are moving down the highway.

3. The _____ made the announcement.

4. _____ is my favorite sport.

5. The _____ will lead the team to victory.

Subjects can also be pronouns. A *pronoun* is a word that takes the place of a noun. Pronouns that can be used as subjects are *I, you, he, she, it, we,* and *they.*

subject
They   will not be coming with us.

subject
You   must turn off your computer at the end of the day.

Use a pronoun subject in each blank. Use a different pronoun for each sentence.

EXERCISE 5.4

1. _____ was the best player on the team.

2. _____ share many interests.

3. _____ could not go with us to the park.

4. _____ will finish the project on Friday.

5. _____ have applied for a scholarship.

Complete Subjects

One type of subject is a *complete subject.* A complete subject consists of the noun or pronoun and all the descriptive words that surround it. Like all subjects, a complete subject answers these questions:

- Who or what is performing the action of the sentence?
- Who or what is being discussed in the sentence?

For example, suppose you write

A day on the beach is my idea of relaxation.

To find the complete subject, ask yourself, "What is my idea of relaxation?" The answer is the complete subject, *A day on the beach.*

One of the keys to writing effective sentences is a lively, descriptive complete subject. You can use adjectives (descriptive words) to add interest to your subjects. Adjectives are words that describe nouns by answering the questions "What kind of?" "Which one?" or "How many?"

Consider this sentence:

The most difficult problem on the test appears at the end.

To find the complete subject, ask yourself, "What appears at the end?" In this sentence the complete subject is *The most difficult question on the test*. The words *most difficult* are adjectives answering the question "What kind of problem?"

Here is another example:

The sleek 24-foot sailboat sits in the last slip in the marina.

The complete subject is *The sleek 24-foot sailboat*. Think, "What sits in the last slip in the marina?" The adjectives *sleek* and *24-foot* describe the subject, *sailboat*.

Sometimes adjectives answer the question "How many?"

Three hundred passengers were waiting for the train.

The complete subject is *Three hundred passengers*. The words *three* and *hundred* are adjectives that answer the question "How many?"

EXERCISE 5.5

Fill in the blanks below with complete subjects. Be sure to include adjectives to make your subjects more specific and interesting.

1. _____ is increasing each year.
2. _____ will meet us this weekend.
3. _____ is the assignment for next week.
4. _____ will appear on the next test.
5. _____ is the car of my dreams.
6. _____ will be coming soon.
7. _____ is a challenge.
8. _____ is my dream vacation.
9. _____ would be my ideal house.
10. _____ is my favorite meal.

Simple Subjects

A *simple subject* is the main noun or pronoun in the complete subject. For example, in the sentence

A day on the beach is my idea of relaxation.

the simple subject is *day*. *Day* is the most important word in the complete subject because it answers the question "What is my idea of relaxation?"

In the following sentence ask, "What sits in the last slip in the marina?"

The sleek 24-foot sailboat sits in the last slip in the marina.

The simple subject is *sailboat.*

What is the simple subject of the sentence below?

Three hundred passengers waited for the train.

Ask, "Who waited for the train?" The simple subject is *passengers.*

Circle the simple subject in each of your sentences in Exercise 5.5.

EXERCISE 5.6

The Three-Step Method of Finding Subjects

As you have already learned in this chapter, many sentences make statements. In most sentences that make statements, you can easily spot the subject if you follow these steps:

Step 1: Ask yourself the question "Who or what _____ ?" (Fill in this blank using key words from the sentence.)

Step 2: Locate the complete subject.

Step 3: Identify the simple subject.

Try this method with the following sentences:

The photographer at the wedding snapped the picture.

Step 1: Ask, "Who snapped the picture?"

Step 2: The complete subject is *The photographer at the wedding.*

Step 3: The simple subject is *photographer.* (Remember, the wedding did not snap the picture.)

My favorite snack is popcorn.

Step 1: Ask, "What is popcorn?"

Step 2: The complete subject is *My favorite snack.*

Step 3: The simple subject is *snack.*

Serious crime in my hometown has declined.

Step 1: Ask, "What has declined?"

Step 2: The complete subject is *Serious crime in my hometown.*

Step 3: The simple subject is *crime.* (Remember, the hometown has not declined; crime has.)

Subjects in Inverted Sentences

Note that in each example above, the complete subject appears at the beginning of the sentence. That is the case in most sentences. However, some sentences are inverted. *Inverted sentences* are turned around, and the subject does not appear at the beginning.

Inverted sentences often begin with the word *here* or *there:*

Here are the invitations to the reception.

There are too many customers waiting in line.

You can apply the same three steps to these sentences, but it will be easier if you reword the sentence so that the subject appears first, like this:

Here are the invitations to the reception.

The invitations to the reception are here.

Step 1: Ask, "What are here?"

Step 2: The complete subject is *The invitations to the reception.*

Step 3: The simple subject is *invitations.*

There are too many customers waiting in line.

Too many customers are waiting in line.

Step 1: Ask, "Who are waiting?"

Step 2: The complete subject is *Too many customers.*

Step 3: The simple subject is *customers.*

EXERCISE 5.7

In each sentence below, underline the complete subject, and circle the simple subject. **Hint:** Use the three-step method with each sentence.

1. My favorite Civil War hero is Confederate General Thomas Jonathan Jackson.

2. General Jackson's nickname was "Stonewall."

3. This fierce warrior was born in 1824 and died in 1863.

4. General Jackson studied at West Point but made poor grades.

5. He developed his furious fighting style in the Mexican War.

6. Prayer and fighting were a man's duties, according to Stonewall Jackson.

7. The men under his command respected him and fought by his side.

8. Jackson's strange habits led some to call him mad.

9. His own men shot him by mistake at the Battle of Chancellorsville in the Civil War.

10. Jackson had been riding out amid the fighting during a night attack.

11. His own soldiers mistook Jackson for a Union attacker.

12. There were two officers with Jackson that night.

13. These two officers were killed immediately.

14. The general was shot in the right hand and the left arm.

15. The doctors in the camp amputated his left arm.

16. General Jackson developed pneumonia and asked for his wife.

17. The doctors told his wife of her husband's death.

18. Many mourners, including General Robert E. Lee, cried over Jackson's death.

19. Jackson was buried at Virginia Military Institute in Lexington, Virginia.

20. Many monuments commemorate Jackson's bravery on the battlefield.

Subjects in Questions

Subjects in questions are sometimes difficult to spot.

Many questions begin with the word *who, what, when, where,* or *why.*

Who will be the president of the honor society?

When is the next committee meeting?

What is the location of the next game?

Questions (also called interrogative sentences) are inverted sentences, and the subjects of questions do not usually begin the sentence. To locate the subjects of questions with linking verbs, turn the questions around so that the subjects appear at the beginning of the sentence:

The president of the honor society will be who? (The complete subject is *The president of the honor society;* the simple subject is *president.*)

The next committee meeting is when? (The complete subject is *The next committee meeting;* the simple subject is *meeting.*)

The location of the next game is what? (The complete subject is *The location of the next game;* the simple subject is *location.*)

Now consider these questions:

Where will the family reunion be held?

Can you remember the teacher's name?

Did anyone in the class know the answer?

Again, to locate the subjects, turn the question around.

The family reunion will be held where? (The complete subject is *The family reunion*; the simple subject is *reunion*.)

You can remember the teacher's name. (The subject is *You*.)

Anyone in the class did know the answer. (The complete subject is *Anyone in the class*; the simple subject is *Anyone*.)

ESL TIP 5   **Questions**

When you write questions (interrogative sentences), be sure you include a subject, and watch the word order.

- You must include a **subject** in interrogative sentences.

    Error: Where is your **book?** Is in the car? (The subject **it** is missing.)

    Correct: Where is your **book?** Is **it** in the car?

- In questions, the action verb and subject frequently are inverted, and sometimes the complete verb is separated from the subject.

    Was the math assignment easy?
    What time **is** it?
    Where **are** you **studying** tonight?

- Questions beginning with the words *who* and *what* are followed by the main verb.

    Who <u>knows</u> the answer?
    What <u>are</u> the possibilities?

- Questions beginning with a **helping verb** are followed by the subject and then the <u>main verb</u>.

    May we <u>have</u> some tea?

EXERCISE 5.8

Underline the simple subject in each of the following questions.

1. Who asked the question?
2. When is the rehearsal?

3. What is the homework assignment?

4. Where will the dance be located?

5. What is the matter?

You can usually spot the subject in a question if you turn the question around. However, this method does not always work.

Look at these questions:

Who made the remark?

What scratched the door of my car?

Try turning these questions around.

The remark made **who?**

The door of my car scratched **what?**

These new questions do not make sense. In a case like this, the subject is *who* or *what*.

subject
Who has the scissors?

subject
What is making that noise?

Underline the simple subject in each of the following questions.

EXERCISE 5.9

1. Who made that cake?

2. Who will be the next class treasurer?

3. Who sounded the alarm?

4. What will happen next?

5. What is the price?

Subjects in Commands

The subject in a *command* sentence is always the reader or the listener.

Follow the directions.

Exit the room quietly.

Do not be late for class.

The subject of a command is the pronoun *you*. Even though the word *you* does not appear in the command, its meaning is understood. Therefore, subjects of commands are called "you understood" subjects.

(You) Follow the directions.

(You) Exit the room quietly.

(You) Do not be late for class.

EXERCISE 5.10

Fill in the blanks with complete subjects.

1. Where will _____ go for vacation next year?
2. _____ study carefully for the test.
3. When is _____ this year?
4. Will _____ go to the interview for the new job?
5. _____ proofread your papers thoroughly.
6. Where will _____ be held?
7. _____ be prepared for a medical emergency.
8. What should be _____?
9. Who will be _____?
10. _____ fill in the blanks completely.

EXERCISE 5.11

Underline the complete subjects. For each command, write **(You)** in front of the sentence.

_____ 1. When did the Civil War end?

_____ 2. Was President Lincoln assassinated before the end of the war?

_____ 3. Name the commanding generals of the Confederate and Union armies at the end of the war.

_____ 4. Where was the treaty of surrender signed?

_____ 5. Who signed the treaty?

_____ 6. What were the terms of the agreement?

_____ 7. How many soldiers lost their lives during the Civil War?

_____ 8. How did the soldiers get home?

_____ 9. Were all the slaves in the South set free?

_____ 10. Imagine a world without warfare.

Compound Subjects

Two or more simple subjects can appear in a single sentence. When more than one simple subject occurs in a sentence, the complete subject is called *compound*. Compound subjects are joined together by *and, or, either . . . or,* or *neither . . . nor.*

<u>My brother</u> **and** <u>sister</u> will be visiting our aunt and uncle next week.

<u>Dan</u> **or** <u>Gary</u> is driving to North Carolina this weekend.

Either <u>Carolyn</u> **or** <u>Beth</u> will be guests at the wedding.

Neither <u>John</u> **nor** <u>Mark</u> has been invited to the reunion.

The compound subjects in each sentence above consist of two one-word simple subjects joined together. However, compound subjects can be more complex.

Teresa and her friends were reviewing for the test. (Ask, "Who were reviewing for the test?" The complete compound subject is *Teresa and her friends*; the two simple subjects are *Teresa* and *friends*.)

Neither the actors nor the directors could have predicted the play's success. (Ask, "Who could have predicted the play's success?" The complete compound subject is *Neither the actors nor the directors*; the two simple subjects are *actors* and *directors*.)

Marco's table and desk were neatly organized. (Ask, "What were neatly organized?" The complete compound subject is *Marco's table and desk*; the two simple subjects are *table* and *desk*.)

Fill in the blanks with subjects. You may use one or more words in each blank.

EXERCISE 5.12

1. Either _____ or _____ will go to the football game next weekend.

2. _____ and _____ are coming over for dinner.

3. Neither _____ nor _____ attended the committee meeting.

4. Will _____ or _____ be in class this Friday?

5. Should _____ and _____ set a wedding date?

FOCUS ON VERBS: THE HEARTBEAT OF THE SENTENCE

If sentences are the heart of written and oral communication, then *verbs* are the heartbeat. Just as the heartbeat is vital to the life of your body, strong verbs are necessary for the functioning of your sentences. Consider these groups of words:

The student in the last row of the classroom

Alicia your new roommate

John F. Kennedy on November 22, 1963

What is missing from each of these word groups? Fill in these blanks:

The student _____ in the last row of the classroom.

Alicia _____ your new roommate.

John F. Kennedy _____ on November 22, 1963.

The words you wrote in the blanks are verbs. They give these sentences meaning. Here are some possibilities (your answers may vary):

The student **sat** in the last row of the classroom.

Alicia **is** your new roommate.

John F. Kennedy **was assassinated** on November 22, 1963.

Action Verbs

Action verbs tell what is happening in the sentence. For example, in the sentences

The student **sat** in the last row of the classroom.

John F. Kennedy **was assassinated** on November 22, 1963.

the verbs *sat* and *was assassinated* are action verbs.

You can easily identify *action verbs* because you can often visualize the action that the verb expresses. Here are some examples of action verbs. Try creating a visual image for each.

run	start	work	study	helps	talk
leap	finished	looks	jumped	bake	read

Notice that none of the action verbs in the box ends in *-ing*. (See ESL Tip 6.)

ESL TIP 6   **Simple Present Tense Verbs and *-ing* Verbs**

The following guidelines will help you know when to use a simple present tense verb and when to use an *-ing* verb.

- Use the **simple present tense**
  - To tell what usually happens

    I **eat** lunch with my sister every day.
  - To tell about a present condition

    I **feel** hungry now.

- To tell what is considered true

  The cafeteria **sells** sandwiches and salads.

- Use an *-ing* verb

  - To indicate that an action is in progress

    We **are eating** lunch now.

  - To indicate that an action is in progress, but not at that particular moment

    We **are meeting** by the picnic tables.

Write an action verb in each blank. **Hint:** Do *not* use an *-ing* ending.

EXERCISE 5.13

_____   _____   _____   _____

_____   _____   _____   _____

_____   _____   _____   _____

As a writer, you add life to your sentences when you use strong action verbs. Your sentences become more effective, and your reader is more likely to understand your message.

Here are some more action verbs. They are all related to the verb *walk*. Try visualizing each one.

walk, strut, march, trudge, stalk, pace, glide, stroll, saunter, dawdle

List other strong action verbs for these verbs. **Hint:** Do *not* use an *-ing* ending.

EXERCISE 5.14

1. talk   _____
2. sing   _____
3. eat   _____
4. sleep   _____
5. look   _____

Suppose you write the following sentence:

The employee shut the door behind her.

You decide you need a stronger verb, so you write

The employee slammed the door behind her.

How do these sentences differ? Why?

Change each verb in the sentences below to a livelier verb.

1. The supervisor **walked** into the office.

_____

2. My friend **talked** about her plans for summer vacation.

_____

3. The teacher **wrote** the homework assignment on the board.

_____

4. I **looked** at the new puppy in the store window.

_____

5. The sailboat **hit** the dock in rough winds.

_____

6. The raindrops gently **struck** the glass in the window.

_____

7. One of the students **entered** the classroom late.

_____

8. The doctor **told** me to lose weight.

_____

9. The photographer quickly **took** my picture.

_____

10. The car **moved** swiftly to avoid a collision.

_____

In each sentence below, circle the complete subject and underline the action verb.

1. My daughters, my husband, and I visited a number of Civil War battlefields last summer.

2. We stopped at Antietam National Battlefield.

3. The Battle of Antietam occurred on September 17, 1862, near Sharpsburg, Maryland.

4. Some 40,000 Confederates fought approximately 87,000 Union soldiers.

5. The battle began at dawn in a cornfield.

6. The Union soldiers exchanged fire with men under the command of Confederate General Stonewall Jackson.

7. Men died in this cornfield for nearly an hour.

8. Both sides suffered great losses.

9. Nearly 25,000 men lost their lives on this day.

10. A cornfield still grows today on this battle site.

Helping Verbs

Sometimes action verbs are used with *helping verbs* (also called *auxiliary verbs*). Helping verbs do what their name suggests. They help make clear what action is taking place and when it is occurring.

	helping verb	action verb	

Juan   **has**   **finished**   his homework. (Juan's homework is already complete.)

	helping verb	action verb	

Juan   **will**   **finish**   his homework. (Juan's homework is not yet completed.)

ESL TIP 7   **Helping Verbs**

Here are some tips on using helping (auxiliary) verbs in English:

- Use **helping verbs** with <u>action verbs</u>.
  - To add more meaning to the idea, for example, to add emphasis
    They **did** <u>buy</u> a new car.
  - To express a negative thought (*not* is not part of the verb)
    Unfortunately, the car **does** not <u>have</u> four doors.
  - To ask a question
    How **will** they <u>get</u> the baby in and out easily?
- Never use the basic form of a verb after any form of the helping verb *be*.

   Error: Yes, Mr. Smith is work late.

   Correct: Yes, Mr. Smith is <u>working</u> late.

   Correct: Yes, Mr. Smith <u>works</u> late.

- In negatives and past tense sentences, **helping verbs** change form while action verbs stay in basic form.
  - **Negatives:** Put the *s* for the third person singular only on the helping verb.

     Error: Alicia doesn't has any money today.

     Correct: Alicia **doesn't** <u>have</u> any money today.

- **Past tense:** Mark the past with the helping verb.

  Error: Tomas didn't ate the sandwich.

  Correct: Tomas **didn't** **eat** the sandwich.

The words below are common helping verbs. When you see one of these words in a sentence, look to see if it is accompanying an action verb.

be, been	may, might, must
am, is, are	can, could
was, were	shall, should
do, does, did	will, would

Here are some other examples:

Juan **did finish** his homework.

Juan **had finished** his homework.

Juan **has been finishing** his homework. (Notice that there can be more than one helping verb.)

Sometimes words can separate the helping verb from the action verb.

Juan **does** not always **finish** his homework.

Juan **will** usually **finish** his homework.

Juan **has** often **finished** his homework.

These words are not part of the verb:

not	never	also	usually	even
always	sometimes	often	generally	

ESL TIP 8   Avoiding Problems with Verbs

- **Negatives:** Put the *s* for the third person singular only on the helping (auxiliary) verb.

  Error: Andrea doesn't has any money today.

  Correct: Andrea **doesn't** **have** any money today.

- **Past tense:** Only the helping (auxiliary) verb marks the past.

  Error: Hakkim didn't ate the sandwich.

  Correct: Hakkim **didn't** **eat** the sandwich.

- **Modals:** Use only one modal with each basic form of a verb.

Error: We might could go to Six Flags Park on Sunday.

Correct: We **might** **be able to** go to Six Flags Park on Sunday.

| **ESL TIP 9** | **Verb Order** |

A helping (or auxiliary) verb is any verb used with the **basic form** of the verb. The most common helping verbs are the nine modals. **Modals** express ability (*can, could*), probability (*may, might, shall, will, would*), and necessity (*must, should*). When you use more than one verb in a sentence, you must place the verbs in the correct order.

auxilliary + basic form
Ann Marie **did send** the invitations for the party.

be + present participle
They **are making** the cake now.

have + past participle
Joe and Sue **have prepared** the sandwiches.

modal + basic form
The tables **should be** ready by now.

modal + *be* + present participle
Melon Band **will be playing** at midnight.

modal + *have* + past participle
Thien **would have gone** to the party.

modal + *have* + *be* + progressive
Everyone **must have been having** fun.

Fill in the blanks with helping verbs. Use a different helping verb in each sentence.

EXERCISE 5.17

1. Tomorrow I _____ ask my employer for a raise.

2. No one _____ forget to buckle his or her seat belt.

3. Shane _____ remember to pay his credit card bill on time.

4. Finally, we _____ arrived at our destination.

5. Jenny _____ elected president of the club.

6. I _____ dreaming about an island paradise.

7. The stock market _____ climbed to a new record.

8. My son _____ not always remember to complete his daily chores.

9. Tracy _____ thinking about moving into a new apartment.

10. The library _____ needed more space for many years.

In each sentence below, circle the complete subjects and underline the helping verbs and action verbs.

1. Our battlefield tour was not finished after our long visit to Antietam.

2. We had always wanted to visit the Gettysburg Battlefield and National Cemetery.

3. We were determined to drive to Gettysburg, Pennsylvania, the next day.

4. We had read a number of books about the Battle of Gettysburg.

5. This battle is usually considered the turning point of the Civil War.

6. General Robert E. Lee had been marching the Confederate Army into Northern territory.

7. The Union Army was following Lee's troops.

8. General Lee's army did not know the location of the Union Army.

9. Both sides were drawn into fierce fighting for three days.

10. More men were killed in this battle than in any other battle on North American soil.

Verbs in Questions

Action verbs occur frequently in questions. Helping verbs usually accompany action verbs in questions. Furthermore, the helping verb is generally separated from the action verb.

Do you **have** the answer?

Have you **finished** the project?

When **will** the packages **arrive?**

In the following sentences, fill in each blank with one or more helping verbs.

1. _____ you believe the rumor?

2. When _____ you complete your writing assignment?

3. _____ she study for the test?

4. When _____ the elections _____ held?

5. Who _____ swimming the first lap of the relay?

Underline the helping verbs and action verbs in each question.

1. Why did these two armies meet in such a small town?

2. How many men died at the Battle of Gettysburg?

3. How many soldiers are buried in Gettysburg National Cemetery?

4. Did Lincoln speak at the cemetery's dedication on November 19, 1863?

5. What made Lincoln's Gettysburg Address so famous?

Verbs in Commands

Some sentences issue commands. Generally, the action verb is the first word in a command.

Clean your room.

Repeat your question.

Answer quickly!

Sometimes, though, commands begin with other words.

always   never   please

These words are not part of the verb.

Always **study** for a test.

Never **procrastinate.**

Please **mop** the kitchen floor.

Commands can also begin with *-ly* words. These *-ly* words are not part of the verb.

Slowly **apply** the brakes.

Quietly **leave** the room.

Carefully **remove** the paint.

Helping verbs can sometimes appear in commands.

Do not **move** from this place.

Fill in the blanks with action verbs to complete the commands.

EXERCISE 5.21

1. Never _____ secrets about a friend.

2. Always _____ sure to lock the doors of your car.

3. _____ out for other drivers on the highway.

4. Please _____ your laundry.

5. Quietly _____ the door.

Underline the action verb in each command.

1.   Locate a copy of Abraham Lincoln's Gettysburg Address.

2.   Picture a crowd of nearly 6,000 on November 19, 1863, in Gettysburg, Pennsylvania.

3.   Imagine the restlessness of the audience.

4.   Notice the power of Lincoln's mere 269 words.

5.   Memorize the famous words "of the people, by the people, for the people."

Linking Verbs

Another type of verb is a linking verb. *Linking verbs* connect the subject in front of the verb to the words following the verb.

   What verb is missing from each of the following sentences?

   Dr. Martin Luther King, Jr., _____ a civil rights leader.

   Ms. Smith _____ senior class advisor.

   The bean soup _____ wonderful.

These sentences become complete with the addition of a linking verb:

   Dr. Martin Luther King, Jr., **was** a civil rights leader.

   Ms. Smith **is** senior class advisor.

   The bean soup **smells** wonderful.

   One purpose of linking verbs is to establish a time relationship. In the first sentence, the linking verb *was* establishes such a relationship between the subject, Dr. Martin Luther King, Jr., and the words following the verb, *a civil rights leader*. The reader can tell from the verb that Dr. King is no longer living.

   Another function of linking verbs is to show a relationship of equality.

   Ms. Smith = senior class advisor

In sentences like this one, the subject and the words following the linking verb are often interchangeable:

   senior class advisor = Ms. Smith

   In some sentences with linking verbs, the word or words following the verb describe the words before the verb.

   The bean soup smells wonderful.

In this example the word *wonderful* describes the smell of the soup.

The bean soup = wonderful

Some common linking verbs are

am, is, are	appear
was, were	become
be, been	smell
has been, have been, had been	taste
will be, would be	look
shall be, should be	sound
will have been, would have been	
shall have been, should have been	

Fill in each blank with a linking verb from the list above. Use a different linking verb in each sentence.

1. You _____ a guest in my house many times.

2. Denise _____ a good friend for many years.

3. The students _____ happy about the new computer lab.

4. Fresh bread just out of the oven _____ delicious.

5. In a few weeks Ms. Washington _____ the new chairperson of the board.

6. There _____ always _____ successful business entrepreneurs.

7. The flowers in the garden _____ sweet.

8. The subject of the lecture _____ microcomputer systems.

9. The financial management series _____ helpful for all attendees.

10. Air-conditioning _____ refreshing on a hot summer day.

Underline the linking verbs in each sentence.

1. One of the most fascinating figures of the Battle of Gettysburg was Joshua Chamberlain.

2. Before the war Joshua Chamberlain had been a teacher at Bowdoin College in Maine.

3. He became a friend of Harriet Beecher Stowe, author of *Uncle Tom's Cabin.*

4. During the Civil War, Chamberlain was commander of the Twentieth Maine, a group of farmers and seamen.

5. He seemed a born leader.

6. Later Chamberlain would be a hero of the Battle of Gettysburg and the Battle of Petersburg.

7. He should have been a casualty at the Battle of Petersburg, with bullet wounds in his hips and pelvis.

8. At eighty-four he appeared dignified at the fiftieth anniversary reunion of the Battle of Gettysburg.

9. Chamberlain was a scholar and a soldier.

10. He should be a role model for future generations.

Compound Verbs

When a sentence has more than one verb, the verbs are called *compound*.

> The bank teller **counted** the money and **put** it in the drawer.
>
> Jeff **went** to the bank, **bought** milk, and **mailed** the letter.
>
> **Can** you **take** the work home and **finish** it?

Like compound subjects, compound verbs are joined by certain connecting words:

and	She **is moving** to Texas <u>and</u> **getting** a job.
or	I **can walk** to school <u>or</u> **catch** the bus.
either, or	<u>Either</u> **do** your chores <u>or</u> **stay** home this weekend.
neither, nor	You **should** <u>neither</u> **spend** money foolishly <u>nor</u> **invest** money unwisely.

EXERCISE 5.25

Fill in the blanks with either action or linking verbs. You may use one or more words in each blank.

1. Either _____ by the rules or _____ the game.

2. The audience _____ and _____ during the play.

3. You must neither _____ nor _____ during the speaker's presentation.

4. Children _____ and _____ their parents.

5. _____ quietly or _____ the room.

6. _____ you _____ for the test today and _____ the answers to the questions?

7. _____ the president _____ forward and _____ his attackers?

8. The cats _____ inside or _____ outside.

9. The boat _____ and then _____ in rough seas.

10. _____ your résumé to the interview and _____ to answer questions.

Skill Check 1: Identifying Subjects and Verbs

Circle the complete subjects, and underline all verbs.

(1) My family continued our Civil War battlefield tour in Petersburg, Virginia. (2) During the Civil War, Petersburg was an important communications center for the Confederate Army. (3) By 1864, General Ulysses S. Grant had plotted its capture. (4) The Battle of Petersburg was the scene of one of the unusual events of the war. (5) In the summer of 1864, Union General George Meade approved a plan for a 500-foot tunnel under the Confederate lines. (6) Coal miners would pack it with several tons of gunpowder. (7) Many soldiers considered the plan impossible. (8) On July 30, 1864, the miners attempted to light the fuse. (9) This first attempt failed. (10) Later in the day, engineers lit the fuse successfully. (11) The earth shook. (12) The blast formed a crater nearly 80 yards long, 25 yards wide, and 10 yards deep. (13) Unfortunately, in the confusion many Union soldiers fell into the crater and could not get out quickly. (14) The Confederates gathered on the edge of the crater. (15) They fired on the soldiers inside the gaping hole. (16) Later that day, the Union soldiers in the crater would surrender. (17) The plot had failed. (18) Many of the Union troops in the crater were African American and were killed by the Confederate soldiers. (19) The siege of Petersburg would continue into 1865. (20) Today the crater is still a reminder of the horrors of war.

Skill Check 2: Identifying Subjects and Verbs

Circle the complete subjects, and underline all verbs.

(1) General Ulysses S. Grant and his Union officers were resting in a field on April 8, 1865. (2) A man on a horse approached and handed General Grant an envelope. (3) General Lee's offer of surrender was inside. (4) Only 100,000 men remained in the Confederate Army. (5) How many soldiers remained in the Union Army? (6) Neither General Lee nor his officers could fight any longer. (7) The Union cavalry under General Gordon had surrounded the Confederate Army. (8) General Robert E. Lee and General Ulysses S. Grant met in a house at Appomattox Court House, Virginia, on April 9, 1865. (9) Imagine the anxiety of these two great generals. (10) General Lee and his officers arrived first at the site of surrender. (11) General Lee's sword and clean uniform were striking. (12) Neither General Lee nor his officers could have predicted Grant's appearance.

(13) General Grant's boots and pants were muddy. (14) The terms of the surrender were straightforward. (15) The Confederate officers and their soldiers could keep their side arms and horses. (16) All the soldiers could go home without fear of capture. (17) Ely Parker, an Iroquois Indian on the staff of General Grant, prepared the written terms of surrender. (18) General Lee left the house and returned to his army. (19) A group of tearful soldiers met their general for the last time. (20) Then the soldiers went home to their waiting families.

FOCUS ON EDITING: AVOIDING FRAGMENTS

Your reader expects each of your sentences to form a complete thought. Therefore, you want to edit your paragraphs carefully for fragments. A *fragment* is a group of words that looks like a sentence but does not form a complete thought.

Look at this example:

At the back of the class near the window.

At first glance, this group of words appears to be a sentence. Like a sentence, it begins with a capital letter and ends with a period. However, this group of words has no subject and no verb. It is a fragment—only a piece of a sentence.

Think of a puzzle. When all the pieces of the puzzle are not together, you cannot see what the picture looks like. When a reader reads a fragment, the meaning of the sentence is unclear because the reader cannot see the whole picture.

Now read this group of words:

The student is reading quietly at the back of the class near the window.

Can you see the big picture? Yes, because this group of words has a subject, *student*, and a verb, *is reading*, and so its meaning is complete.

When you are checking for fragments, ask yourself these two key questions:

- Is there a verb?
- Is there a subject?

If the answer to both of these questions is no, then the group of words is a fragment.

Fragments with Missing Subjects

Suppose you write this group of words:

To complete my homework each day.

Is this group of words a sentence?

- **Is there a verb?**

  The words *to complete* do not form a complete verb.

- **Is there a subject?**

  Ask, "Who is completing my homework?" This group of words has no subject.

This group of words is a fragment.

Now consider this correction:

My challenge is to complete my homework each day.

- **Is there a verb?**

  Yes, the verb is the word *is*.

- **Is there a subject?**

  Yes, the subject is *My challenge*.

This correction forms a complete sentence.

Fragments with *-ing* Words

One common type of fragment is the *-ing* fragment. Consider this group of words:

Missing class on the day of the test review.

- **Is there a verb?**

  Sometimes students are confused because they think that any word ending in *-ing* is a verb. However, *-ing* words used as verbs have help- ing verbs. In the word group above, the *-ing* word *missing* does not have a helping verb with it. Therefore, it is not a complete verb, and the answer to this question is no.

- **Is there a subject?**

  Since there is no verb, there can be no subject.

Because the answer to both questions is no, *Missing class on the day of the test review* is a fragment.

Is the following group of words a fragment?

Missing class on the day of the test review was a mistake.

- **Is there a verb?**

  Yes, the verb is the word *was*.

- **Is there a subject?**

  Yes, the complete subject is *Missing class on the day of the test review*.

This group of words is a sentence.

Fragments with Missing Helping Verbs

Now look at this group of words:

Joan missing class on the day of the test review.

- **Is there a verb?**

  The word *missing* is not a complete verb because no helping verb is present.

- **Is there a subject?**

  No. Without a verb, there can be no subject.

To correct this fragment, you can add a helping verb.

Joan will be missing class on the day of the test review.

Another possible correction is to drop the *-ing* and then add a helping verb.

Joan will miss class on the day of the test review.

You can also change the *-ing* word to an *-ed* verb.

Joan missed class on the day of the test review.

EXERCISE 5.28

Write the letter **S** in the blank if the group of words forms a sentence. Write **F** in the blank if the group of words is a fragment.

_____ **1.** Taking good notes is critical to success in the classroom.

_____ **2.** To write key words from the lectures.

_____ **3.** Drawing pictures to represent key ideas is another helpful technique.

_____ **4.** Students summarizing the speaker's main ideas.

_____ **5.** Outlining can help organize lecture notes.

_____ **6.** Using Roman numerals for the teacher's main points.

_____ **7.** Using A, B, C, and so on for the supporting details for each main point.

_____ **8.** Copying material directly from the board.

_____   **9.**   It is important to leave space in the margins for additional notes.

_____   **10.**   Inserting questions marks beside difficult material.

_____   **11.**   Placing stars beside extra material is also helpful.

_____   **12.**   Exchanging class notes with others in the class can improve note-taking skills.

_____   **13.**   Reviewing lecture notes later in the day is a good idea.

_____   **14.**   Writing the class notes in paragraph form can also help students to retain information.

_____   **15.**   Practicing these skills regularly will result in improved grades.

Correct each of the fragments in Exercise 5.28. Then copy all the sentences (including your corrections) to form a paragraph. (Omit all the blanks and numbers.)

EXERCISE 5.29

Example Fragments

Sometimes a fragment occurs when the writer cuts off a supporting example from the point it illustrates. These fragments usually begin with *such as*, *for example*, or *for instance*.

Students can help keep their energy level high by engaging in physical activity. **Such as biking, swimming, dancing, or weightlifting.**

Effective readers mark their textbooks in several ways. **For example, underlining key ideas, writing notes in the margins, and circling key terms.**

When I finish an assignment, I like to do something fun. **For instance, going to the movies or meeting a friend for dinner.**

In each of these examples, a fragment lacking a subject and a verb follows a sentence. To correct the problem, join the fragment to the previous sentence.

Students can help keep their energy level high by engaging in physical activity, **such as** biking, swimming, dancing, or weightlifting.

Effective readers mark their textbooks in several ways, **for example,** underlining key ideas, writing notes in the margins, and circling key terms.

When I finish an assignment, I like to do something fun, **for instance,** going to the movies or meeting a friend for dinner.

Caution: The transitional phrases *for example* and *for instance* do not always begin fragments. Consider the following:

For example, important techniques for good readers include underlining key ideas, writing notes in the margins, and circling key terms.

- **Is there a verb?**

Yes, the verb of the sentence is *include.*

- **Is there a subject?**

Yes, the complete subject of the sentence is *important techniques for good readers.*

This group of words is a sentence.

EXERCISE 5.30

Write **S** in the blank if the group of words forms a sentence. Write **F** in the blank if the group of words is a fragment.

_____ 1. Marcus, Shaila, and I have formed a study group for this semester.

_____ 2. We are all taking the same classes.

_____ 3. Such as English, math, and reading.

_____ 4. Each time we have a test, we divide the work among us.

_____ 5. For example, creating a study sheet, defining key terms, and making a list of possible test questions.

_____ 6. Then we meet several times before the test.

_____ 7. Each of us has different strengths.

_____ 8. For example, Marcus has a talent for guessing which kinds of questions will appear on the test.

_____ 9. Such as multiple choice, true-false, and fill-in-the-blank.

_____ 10. Shaila usually creates a study sheet for each of us.

_____ 11. This study sheet includes several sections, such as definitions, key concepts, and an outline of the chapters.

_____ 12. Many times I have the task of defining key terms.

_____ 13. I gather these terms from a number of places.

_____ 14. For example, the list of key words at the end of the chapters and the glossaries in the back of the textbooks.

_____ 15. Working with this study group has helped to improve my test-taking skills as well as my grades.

EXERCISE 5.31

Correct each of the fragments in Exercise 5.30. Then copy all the sentences (including your corrections) to form a paragraph. (Omit all the blanks and numbers.)

WRITING ASSIGNMENT

Write a brief paragraph about a challenge you face when you take a test. Use the stages of the writing process. Write an experimental draft. Then revise, edit, and prepare a finished copy. Be sure to include a strong topic sentence and sufficient supporting details.

Writers as Spiders

The World Wide Web offers sites for more information about subjects, verbs, and fragments.

For more information about verbs, see

http://ecep1.usl.edu/ecep/english/b/b.htm

If you need more help with linking verbs, try

http://www.uottawa.ca/academic/arts/writcent/hypergrammar/link.html

For more practice identifying subjects, check

http://www.uottawa.ca/academic/arts/writcent/hypergrammar/subjpred.html#subject

For a review of fragments, read

http://www.lynchburg.edu/public/writcntr/guide/grammar/sentfrag.htm

You can find additional exercises on fragments at these locations:

http://www.hputx.edu/Academics/English/wlfragfr.htm

http://myst.hunter.cuny.edu/~rwcenter/writing/on-line/frgmnt-a.html

Web Exercise

Using a search engine, locate information about the role of women and/or African Americans in the Civil War. One such site is

http://scriptorium.lib.duke.edu/women/civilwar.html

Write a brief paragraph about one person who played an important role in the Civil War. In your first sentence, identify the person and the role he or she played. Then write about what that person actually did during the war. Be sure to use your own words. In the last sentence, state why you chose to write about this person.

Focus on the Sentence: Part II

As you learned in Chapter 5, a sentence carries a message from a writer to a reader. Writers construct their sentences with two basic building blocks.

1. **Phrases**

    A *phrase* is a group of words without a subject and a verb.

    in the classroom

    to see clearly

    playing baseball

2. **Clauses**

    A *clause* is a group of words with at least one subject and at least one verb. Not all clauses are complete sentences.

    S   V
    The students took the test.

    S   V
    Ellen won the most votes.

    S   V
    Because I stopped quickly

This chapter will help you use phrases and clauses to build effective sentences. In this chapter you will learn to

- Identify phrases
- Identify clauses
- Identify complete sentences

In order for their meaning to be clear, sentences also need punctuation. Punctuation helps the reader receive the writer's message. Two common punctuation marks are commas (,) and apostrophes ('). In this chapter you will learn

- Basic comma rules
- Apostrophe rules

Knowledge of phrases and clauses as well as punctuation will improve your confidence as a writer.

FOCUS ON PHRASES: THE MUSIC OF THE SENTENCE

Phrases are essential to the meaning of most sentences. *Phrases*—groups of words without subjects and verbs—can appear many places in the sentence: at the beginning, in the middle, and/or at the end.

Word phrases are like musical phrases. Imagine a song in which every note is the same length, the same tone, and in the same rhythm. You probably would not listen to the song for very long. A song needs musical phrases for expression. When you sing or play a musical phrase, you try to do so with one breath, making the music flow.

Sentences need word phrases for meaning and variety. Phrases consist of words related to each other in some way. When you read a sentence aloud, you should read the phrases as smoothly as possible. Read the following sentence aloud. Make every word distinct and pronounce each word in the same tone of voice.

The   student   sat   against   the   wall   in   the   back   row   of   class.

Does your voice sound like a robot's?

Now read the sentence as smoothly as possible. Group the words in phrases together.

	S V	phrase	phrase	phrase
	The student sat	against the wall	in the back row	of class.

Phrases give music to your sentences.

Prepositional Phrases

The most common type of phrase is the prepositional phrase. A *prepositional phrase* begins with a word known as a *preposition* and ends with a noun or pronoun called the *object of the preposition*.

Here are some examples of prepositional phrases:

Preposition	+	Object	=	Prepositional phrase
across	+	the lake	=	across the lake
in	+	the truck	=	in the truck
after	+	the party	=	after the party

Adjectives frequently appear between the preposition and the object.

Preposition	+	Object	=	Prepositional phrase
beneath	+	the clear water	=	beneath the clear water
without	+	your help	=	without your help

Many prepositions indicate direction or spatial relationships. You can remember these prepositions by thinking about anything a bird can do in relation to a tree.

prep. phrase
The bird sits **beneath the tree.**

prep. phrase
The bird flies **above the tree.**

prep. phrase
The bird nests **inside the tree.**

ESL TIP 10   Prepositions

Follow these tips when using **prepositions** in English:

- Use the prepositions *in, on,* and *at* carefully when referring to time and place.

Time

in a period of time	**in** a few days, **in** an hour
in a particular month or year	**in** June, **in** 1998
in a period during the day	**in** the morning
on a specific day	**on** Monday, **on** Sept. 24, **on** Veterans Day
on time	
at a definite time	**at** 9:00, **at** lunchtime

Place

in (inside) a specific place	**in** the desk drawer, **in** his pocket, **in** the room
at a specific place	**at** the park, **at** my mother's house
on top of something	**on** the desk, **on** the mountain, **on** my street

- Always include the **infinitive** marker *to* before the base form of a verb.

  I'd like **to** <u>return</u> to Saint-Germain **to** <u>see</u> my aunt and uncle.

Many different prepositions indicate direction or spatial relationships, including:

above	beneath	into	through
across	beside	near	throughout
against	between	off	toward
along	beyond	on	under
alongside	by	onto	underneath
around	down	out	up
behind	in	outside	upon
below	inside	over	within

Write a prepositional phrase in each blank. Use a different preposition in each phrase.

EXERCISE 6.1

_____   _____

_____   _____

_____   _____

_____   _____

_____   _____

Complete each sentence with a prepositional phrase. Use a different preposition in each sentence.

EXERCISE 6.2

1. The children played _____ .

2. Tamara parked her car _____ .

3. The couple walked _____ .

4. You must not walk _____ .

5. The park is located _____ .

Other prepositions indicate time relationships.

prep. phrase
Since last month Kesha has owned a bright red truck.

prep. phrase
Hugh lived in Atlanta **during the 1980s.**

prep. phrase
After the party the kitchen needed cleaning.

> These prepositions indicate time relationships:
>
> | | | | |
> |---|---|---|---|
> | about | before | past | until |
> | after | during | since | |

Write a prepositional phrase showing a time relationship in each blank. Use a different preposition in each blank.

_____   _____

_____   _____

Complete each sentence with a prepositional phrase indicating a time relationship.

1.   I will not be able to come visit you _____.

2.   _____ we are going out for pizza.

3.   No talking is allowed _____.

4.   The play will not end _____.

5.   We cannot leave for vacation _____.

Some prepositions are "little words." You will already recognize many of these words as prepositions.

> "Little word" prepositions include
>
> | | | | |
> |---|---|---|---|
> | as | for | like | to |
> | at | from | of | with |

Write a prepositional phrase in each blank. Begin the phrase with a "little word" preposition. Use a different preposition in each.

_____   _____

_____   _____

Complete each sentence with a "little word" prepositional phrase.

1.   I will be waiting _____.

2.   Who will be coming _____?

3.   My best friend is a native _____.

4.   We must rehearse _____.

5.   We can meet _____.

Underline the prepositional phrases in each sentence.

1. One of the largest rain forests in the world is in Brazil.

2. This rain forest is in the Amazon River basin.

3. Tropical rain forests occur in areas along the equator.

4. Rain forests are known for their humid climates.

5. Many rain forests receive more than sixty inches of rain during a year.

6. The abundant rainfall soaks through the trees to the ground.

7. Unfortunately, the large amount of rain in the rain forest drains minerals from the soil.

8. One-third of the world's plants grow within rain forests.

9. Many species of mammals also live in the trees of the rain forest.

10. Without rain forests, the world would lose a valuable natural resource.

Infinitive Phrases

Another common type of phrase is the infinitive phrase. An *infinitive phrase* is easy to spot; it begins with the word *to* followed by a verb.

to run	to believe	to look
to jump	to be	to teach

An infinitive phrase can also include a noun or a pronoun. This noun or pronoun is called an *object*.

Infinitive	+	Object	=	Infinitive phrase
to see	+	her	=	to see her
to write	+	a business letter	=	to write a business letter
to solve	+	a math problem	=	to solve a math problem

Many infinitive phrases include an *-ly* word. This word should end the infinitive phrase.

to see her clearly

to run quickly

to solve a problem correctly

Sometimes students confuse infinitive phrases with prepositional phrases beginning with the preposition *to*. Remember that in an infinitive phrase, the word *to* is followed by a verb.

to the store (prepositional phrase)

to write clearly (infinitive phrase)

EXERCISE 6.8   Fill in the blanks with infinitive phrases.

1. I am trying hard _____.
2. Jose wants _____.
3. The teacher asked her students _____.
4. The supervisor requires all employees _____.
5. Alicia's career goal is _____.

EXERCISE 6.9   Circle the prepositional phrases, and underline the infinitive phrases.

1. The rain forest is made of many layers of plant life.
2. The top layer is made of giant trees.
3. To reach the top, you would have to climb an enormous tree.
4. Monkeys like to jump from tree to tree in the highest layer of the rain forest.
5. Below this top layer is another of smaller trees.
6. In this layer parrots and other tropical birds come to gather food and to make their nests.
7. These two layers combine to form the canopy of the rain forest.
8. Underneath the canopy is an open space.
9. Monkeys and snakes frequently enter this space to find food.
10. The thick trees allow only a small percentage of the sunlight to reach this open space.
11. Beneath this open space of the rain forest is the floor.
12. Here termites and ants work to feed on the decomposing leaves on the ground.
13. The tree roots extend beneath the ground to form the last layer of the rain forest.
14. The plants and animals of the rain forest combine to form an important ecosystem.
15. Scientists must continue to study the fascinating rain forest.

-*ing* Phrases

Many word phrases begin with -*ing*. Two types of phrases beginning with -*ing* are

1. Present participle phrases

A present participle phrase begins with -*ing* and is used as an adjective.

present participle phrase
The bird   **chirping loudly**   is a mockingbird.

2. **Gerund phrases**
   A gerund phrase begins with *-ing* and is used as a noun.
   gerund phrase
   Winning the lottery is my dream.

Present Participle Phrases

Like other phrases, present participles can appear at the beginning, in the middle, and/or at the end of a sentence. Because they are adjectives, *present participles* answer the question "Which?" or "Which one?"

present participle phrase
The dog   **barking loudly**   is a nuisance. (The present participle phrase *barking loudly* answers the question "Which dog?")

present participle phrase
Answering the question correctly, the student smiled. (The present participle phrase *Answering the question correctly* identifies which student.)

present participle phrase
She was the supervisor **giving the instructions.** (The present participle phrase *giving the instructions* answers the question "Which supervisor?")

Writers sometimes confuse present participles with *-ing* verbs. For an *-ing* word to be the verb of a sentence, it must be used with helping verbs.

present participle phrase
Running swiftly, the sprinter won the race.

verb
The sprinter **was running** swiftly.

EXERCISE 6.10

Fill in the blanks with present participle phrases.

1. Mr. Pappas is the teacher _____ .
2. _____ , she narrowly escaped a car accident.
3. The toddler _____ demands attention.
4. _____ , the server greeted us at our table.
5. The president of the club is the one _____ .

Gerund Phrases

Gerund phrases are *-ing* phrases used as nouns. Gerunds are commonly used as subjects and objects of the preposition.

gerund phrase
Working long hours is mentally and physically exhausting. (Ask, "What is mentally and exhausting?" The gerund phrase *Working long hours* is the complete subject of the sentence.)

gerund phrase

Derek has hopes of **becoming a doctor.** (The gerund phrase *becoming a doctor* is the object of the preposition *of.*)

EXERCISE 6.11

Fill in the blanks with gerund phrases.

1. _____ was the goal of the team.

2. _____ is the household chore I dislike most.

3. The gifted athlete had hopes of _____.

4. _____ is essential for success in the classroom.

5. _____ is critical for success in the workplace.

EXERCISE 6.12

Skill Check: Phrases

Circle the prepositional phrases. Underline the infinitive phrases once, the gerund phrases twice, and the participle phrases three times.

1. Each year millions of acres of rain forest are destroyed by humankind.

2. Logging trees is one major threat to rain forests.

3. Slashing trees and burning them are techniques commonly used by loggers in rain forest areas.

4. Farmers then begin to plant crops on the burned ground.

5. Unfortunately, the top layers of soil have few nutrients for plant crops.

6. The farmers harvesting the crops can have success for only a few years.

7. Losing this precious resource is a constant threat, especially in Central and South America.

8. It is horrible to witness this destruction of the rain forests.

9. Working together, concerned students can become active in environmental organizations.

10. The delicate ecosystem of the rain forests must be preserved for future generations.

FOCUS ON CLAUSES: THE BACKBONE OF THE SENTENCE

Clauses—groups of words with at least one subject and at least one verb—form the backbone of sentences. Without clauses, sentences cannot function. Clauses provide written sentences with strength and durability.

There are two types of clauses:

  1. Independent (or main) clause
  An independent clause expresses a complete idea.

The homecoming dance will be held this weekend.

2. **Dependent (or subordinate) clause**
    A dependent clause must be joined to an independent clause in order for its meaning to be clear.

    Because the date of the test has been moved

Independent Clauses

Independent clauses—consisting of at least one subject, at least one verb, and any accompanying phrases—are complete sentences. They "stand alone." Many independent clauses form simple sentences. Simple sentences have just one independent clause.

Christopher wanted to come to the party.

He had a flat tire.

Writers can also join two independent clauses together to form a sentence.

Christopher wanted to come to the party, but he had a flat tire.

The process of joining together two independent clauses is known as *coordination*.

The most common way to join two independent clauses together is to use a comma followed by a coordinating conjunction (sometimes called FAN-BOYS—*For, And, Nor, But, Or, Yet, So*). These coordinating conjunctions are the only words used with a comma to connect two independent clauses. The comma before the coordinating conjunction is a signal to the reader that another subject and another verb will appear in the second part of the sentence.

Independent clause	, **for**	independent clause.
Independent clause	, **and**	independent clause.
Independent clause	, **nor**	independent clause.
Independent clause	, **but**	independent clause.
Independent clause	, **or**	independent clause.
Independent clause	, **yet**	independent clause.
Independent clause	, **so**	independent clause.

       S   **V**   **S**   **V**

The *picnic* <u>has been canceled</u>, **for** *rain* <u>is predicted</u> this weekend.

       S   **V**   **S** **V**

My *family* <u>is visiting</u> this weekend, **and** *we* <u>plan</u> to go to the beach.

S   V   V   S
Jessica <u>does</u> not <u>participate</u> in sports activities, **nor** <u>is</u> *she* a member of any clubs.

      S   V   S   V
Paul <u>was</u> late to class, **but** *he* <u>apologized</u> to the teacher.

        S   V   S   V
Either *you* <u>can come</u> with us now, **or** *you* <u>can join</u> us later.

      S   V   S   V
Fernando <u>does</u> not <u>read</u> music, **yet** *he* <u>plays</u> the piano well.

    S   V   S   V
We <u>have</u> not <u>picked</u> up our theater tickets, **so** *we* <u>must arrive</u> early.

Each coordinating conjunction shows a special relationship between the independent clauses that it connects. (See Table 6.1.)

TABLE 6.1	Coordinating Conjunctions and Their Meanings
Coordinating Conjunction	*Meaning*
for	express a cause of an action
and	add a closely related idea
nor	express a negative alternative
but	state a contrast
or	express an alternative
yet	express a contrast
so	state the result of an action

EXERCISE 6.13

Fill in the blanks with independent clauses. Be sure you have a subject and a verb in all blanks.

1. _____ , and _____ .
2. _____ , or _____ .
3. _____ , yet _____ .
4. _____ , for _____ .
5. _____ , but _____ .
6. _____ , so _____ .
7. _____ , nor _____ .

EXERCISE 6.14

Fill in each blank with a coordinating conjunction from Table 6.1. Be sure to place a comma before each coordinating conjunction. Do not use any conjunction more than once.

1. Tomorrow night is the concert _____ I hope you will come with me.

2. Either Michaela will fly to Boston this weekend _____ she will drive.

3. Paul will not be working this Monday _____ is he planning to work next week.

4. The committee planned to finish its report last week _____ the members could not agree about its contents.

5. The weather reporter promised rain this week _____ it hasn't rained at all.

6. I studied hard for the midterm _____ I should receive a good grade.

7. Juan will not be in class next week _____ he will be attending a meeting for student leaders.

Write **SS** in the blank next to each simple sentence (one independent clause). Write **IC/IC** in the blank if the sentence contains two independent clauses. **Hint:** If the sentence has two independent clauses, look for a comma before the coordinating conjunction and a subject and verb in each independent clause.

EXERCISE 6.15

_____ 1. One of the most interesting animals in the rain forest is the dart poison frog.

_____ 2. The dart poison frog measures one inch in length, and it is blue, orange, or yellow in color.

_____ 3. Perhaps the dart poison frog is a bright color to warn its enemies, for the poison is deadly.

_____ 4. The deadly poison is located in the frog's skin.

_____ 5. No animal would dare to eat the dart poison frog, and the frog eats only insects.

_____ 6. The effectiveness of the frog's poison is well known, and Native Americans sometimes use the poison on the darts for their blowguns.

_____ 7. The frogs make a buzzing sound to seek their mates, and the males call the females.

_____ 8. The mother dart poison frog carries her tadpoles on her back.

_____ 9. She carries them to a bromeliad plant growing in a tree, and then she enters the rainwater in the plant's center.

_____ 10. Finally, the tadpoles let go and begin life anew in the plant.

Dependent Clauses

Dependent clauses also have subjects and verbs. However, they cannot stand alone. A dependent clause must be attached to an independent clause for its meaning to be complete. Consider this dependent clause:

After the dinner had ended

This clause has a subject (*dinner*) and a verb (*had ended*), but it does not make sense by itself. What happened after the dinner had ended? The reader can only wonder.

       DC   IC
After the dinner had ended, the guests left for home.

Now the dependent clause is followed by an independent clause (subject = *guests*, verb = *left*), and the meaning is complete.

 You could also write the sentence this way:

     IC   DC
The guests left for home after the dinner had ended.

A dependent clause can either introduce or follow an independent clause.

 The process of joining dependent clauses to independent clauses is known as *subordination.* Two subordination patterns are

1. **DC, IC**

   Because she wants to major in business, she is taking a computer course.

2. **IC, DC**

   She is taking a computer course because she wants to major in business.

Dependent clauses generally begin with words known as *subordinating conjunctions.*

sub. conj.   DC   IC
After the dinner had ended, the guests left for home.

Subordinating conjunctions are powerful words because they have the task of joining dependent and independent clauses. A subordinating conjunction is the only word that distinguishes a dependent clause from an independent clause.

The dinner had ended. (independent clause, no subordinating conjunction)

sub. conj.
After the dinner had ended (dependent clause)

Some subordinating conjunctions, such as *after* or *before*, indicate a time relationship. Dependent clauses beginning with these subordination conjunctions answer the question "When?"

sub. conj.   DC   IC
When the game ended, the team celebrated its victory. (Ask, "When did the team celebrate its victory?" When the game ended.)

          IC   sub. conj.   DC
I need to review the chapters **before** I take the test. (Ask, "When do I need to review the chapters?" Before I take the test.)

These subordinating conjunctions demonstrate time relationships:

after	once	when
as	since	whenever
before	until	while

Note that some of the words in the box above can also be prepositions. Remember that dependent clauses have subjects *and* verbs.

after the dinner (prepositional phrase)

after the dinner had ended (dependent clause)

EXERCISE 6.16

Fill in each blank with a dependent clause. Begin each dependent clause with a subordinating conjunction from the list above. Circle the subject and underline the verb in each dependent clause.

1. The job supervisor praised the employees _____.

2. _____, he was late for the meeting.

3. _____, she feels nervous.

4. I cannot remember _____.

5. _____, I review my class notes.

Other subordinating conjunctions contrast the idea expressed in the dependent clause and the idea expressed in the independent clause.

sub. conj.
Although I wanted to go to the movies, I had too much homework.

                                        sub. conj.
Maria became a doctor **even though** at first she wanted to be a teacher.

These subordinating conjunctions can be used to contrast ideas:

although	even though
as though	though

You can also use subordinating conjunctions to state a conditional relationship. Dependent clauses beginning with these subordinating conjunctions answer the question "Under what condition?"

sub. conj.

If   John does not have to work Saturday, he will come to the wedding. (Ask, "Under what condition will John come to the wedding?" If he does not have to work Saturday.)

sub. conj.

Mary will try out for the play **even if** she is nervous. (Ask, "Under what condition will Mary try out for the play?" Even if she is nervous.)

These subordinating conjunctions can state a condition:

as if   if   even if   unless   whether   as long as   provided that

EXERCISE 6.17   Fill in each blank with a dependent clause. You may use any of the conditional subordinating conjunctions.

1. _____ , I will have to stay up late tonight.

2. Frank will be able to go with us _____.

3. Mr. Leopold will give the class a homework assignment _____

   _____.

4. You must decide _____.

5. _____ , then Alyssa must find another job.

Two subordinating conjunctions indicate location. These subordinating conjunctions are *where* and *wherever.*

sub. conj.

Wherever you go, I will follow.

sub. conj.

Laura cannot remember   **where**   she left her keys.

Two commonly used subordinating conjunctions are *so that* and *because.* The subordinating conjunction *so that* shows purpose. Dependent clauses beginning with *so that* answer the question "Why?"

sub. conj.

She will join the club **so that** she can make new friends.

sub.conj.

Jonathan will finish his science lab **so that** he can complete the course.

The subordinating conjunction *because* shows a cause-and-effect relationship. The cause appears in the dependent clause, and the effect appears in the independent clause.

sub. conj.

Because the student had studied hard for the math test, she made an A. (The cause is *the student studied hard for the math test.* The effect is *she made an A.*)

sub. conj.

I could not attend class **because** I was sick with the flu. (The cause is *I was sick with the flu.* The effect is *I could not attend class.*)

> These subordinating conjunctions can state location or introduce a cause:
>
> where   wherever   so that   because

Fill in the blanks with dependent clauses. Use any of the subordinating conjunctions from the list above.

EXERCISE 6.18

1.   I will attend class _____.

2.   _____ , I could not keep the doctor's appointment.

3.   Lynn will leave the party early _____.

4.   Do you know _____?

5.   Trevor will make an A in his English course _____.

A memory technique can help you recall some of the most common subordinating conjunctions. Just remember BU BU IS WA WA WA (pronounced "boo boo is wah wah wah"). Each letter of these strange-sounding words is the first letter of a subordinating conjunction.

> **B**ecause
> **U**nless
> **B**efore
> **U**ntil
> **I**f
> **S**o that
> **W**hen
> **A**fter
> **W**henever
> **A**s
> **W**here
> **A**lthough

EXERCISE 6.19 Underline the independent clauses once and the dependent clauses twice. **Hint:** Not every sentence contains a dependent clause.

1. Because the rain forest offers a place for animals to hide, many species call the rain forest home.

2. One of these animals is the jaguar.

3. The jaguar is considered a threatened species because it faces danger from hunters and environmental changes.

4. Although jaguars were once found in the United States, they now live in the rain forests of Central and South America.

5. Adult jaguars are approximately five to seven feet long, and they can weigh up to three hundred pounds.

6. Jaguars roam the undergrowth of the rain forests so that they can capture their prey.

7. Jaguars generally hunt on the ground at night even though they are good swimmers.

8. When the jaguar hunts, its prey includes almost any animal.

9. After the jaguar reaches sexual maturity, it lives with its mate during the mating season.

10. As loggers destroy more rain forests, the jaguar's existence will be constantly threatened.

Dependent clauses can also begin with words known as relative pronouns. *Relative pronouns* refer to people or things. Like subordinating conjunctions, relative pronouns serve two functions. They

1. **Introduce dependent clauses**

2. **Join dependent clauses to independent clauses**

rel. pronoun
She is the sprinter **who** won the race.

rel. pronoun
Joe is the supervisor to **whom** I report.

rel. pronoun
The letter **that** the company sent me was lost in the mail.

rel. pronoun
Whoever answers the question will win a prize.

rel. pronoun
Durango, Colorado, **which** is my favorite vacation spot, is a charming town.

Notice that relative pronouns appear immediately after the noun to which they refer.

These relative pronouns can begin dependent clauses:

who	whom	which	whose
whoever	whomever	whichever	that

Fill in the blanks with dependent clauses. Use the relative pronoun in parentheses to begin the dependent clause.

1. *(which)* On the bathroom shelf is the prescription medicine, _____

    _____.

2. *(whom)* The letter began "To _____."

3. *(that)* I appreciate the gift _____.

4. *(who)* He is the basketball player _____.

5. *(whomever)* You can invite to the party _____.

Skill Check: Clauses

Identify each sentence as two independent clauses **(IC/IC)**, a dependent clause followed by an independent clause **(DC/IC)**, or an independent clause followed by a dependent clause **(IC/DC)**. Underline coordinating conjunctions. Circle subordinating conjunctions.

_____ **1.** The monkeys of the rain forest are wonderful acrobats as they leap from tree to tree.

_____ **2.** The spider monkey is a large mammal of the tropical rain forest, and the marmoset is a much smaller monkey.

_____ **3.** Because its tail is so strong, the spider monkey can pick up objects with its tail.

_____ **4.** The spider monkey got its name because it hangs on tree limbs like a spider.

_____ **5.** When a spider monkey hangs in a tree, it is usually upside down.

_____ **6.** Spider monkeys are tree dwellers, but they can be found in any layer of the rain forest.

_____ **7.** They live in groups with approximately thirty other monkeys, and they feed on fruits and seeds.

_____ **8.** Whereas most monkeys have five fingers, including a thumb, some spider monkeys have no thumb.

_____ **9.** Spider monkeys are a threatened species, for they have long been hunted for their fur.

_____ **10.** Although spider monkeys can weigh up to twenty pounds, the tiny marmoset can sit in a human hand.

_____ **11.** Marmosets do not have opposable thumbs, so they use their long fingers to grasp food.

_____ **12.** Marmosets have a distinct smell that they use to communicate with other monkeys.

_____ **13.** Marmosets are very small, so their diet is critical.

_____ **14.** If marmosets do not eat for several days, they can die.

_____ **15.** Marmosets dwell in trees where they feed on fruit and insects.

_____ **16.** A marmoset's tail can be twice the length of its body, and in some species the tail is black with white rings.

_____ **17.** Whenever marmosets want to "talk" to other monkeys, they chirp like birds.

_____ **18.** While spider monkeys have sharp fingernails, marmosets have nails that look more like claws.

_____ **19.** Animals such as spider monkeys and marmosets may become extinct unless we act to preserve our rain forests.

_____ **20.** We need to study all the mammals of the rain forests, yet acres of rain forest are destroyed each day.

FOCUS ON EDITING: DEPENDENT CLAUSE FRAGMENTS

In Chapter 5, you learned about fragments. Now that you can recognize phrases and clauses, you are ready for more information about this topic.

One of the most common types of fragments is a *dependent clause fragment.* This type of fragment happens when a writer uses a dependent clause but fails to connect it to an independent clause. A dependent clause must be connected to an independent clause in order to form a sentence.

Suppose you write this group of words:

Because I was nervous during the test.

- **Is there a subject?**

Yes, the subject is *I.*

- **Is there a verb?**

Yes, the verb is the word *was.*

When the answers to these two questions are both yes but you still suspect you have written a fragment, you need to ask a third question:

- **Is there a subordinating conjunction?**

  Yes, the word *because* is a subordinating conjunction.

If the answer to all three questions is yes, then the group of words is a fragment unless it is connected to an independent clause.

You can correct this fragment as follows:

Because I was nervous during the test, I had difficulty concentrating.

I had difficulty concentrating because I was nervous during the test.

What happened because you were nervous? You had difficulty concentrating. Now that you have connected the dependent clause to an independent clause, your reader can see the complete picture—not just a puzzle piece.

Fragment: Before I take a test

Independent clause: I visualize a beautiful, calm place.

Dependent clause followed by an independent clause: Before I take a test, I visualize a beautiful, calm place.

Independent clause followed by a dependent clause: I visualize a beautiful, calm place before I take a test.

Notice that you can correct the fragment by placing the dependent clause either before or after the independent clause.

Write **S** in the blank if the group of words forms a sentence. Write **F** in the blank if the group of words is a fragment.

EXERCISE 6.22

_____	**1.**	When I was in high school.
_____	**2.**	I rarely studied for tests.
_____	**3.**	When I took my first college test, I was in shock.
_____	**4.**	Because I had spent a few minutes looking over the material, I expected to do well on the test.
_____	**5.**	After my instructor returned my test.
_____	**6.**	I knew that my study habits needed to change.
_____	**7.**	After I checked out a book on study skills from the library.
_____	**8.**	I learned that short-term memory differs from long-term memory.

_____ **9.** When I hear a lecture, the information enters my short-term memory.

_____ **10.** Unless I do something to send the information into my long-term memory, I will lose the information within a day or so.

_____ **11.** When I want to move some information into long-term memory, I have to review it, recite it, and repeat it.

_____ **12.** If I wait too long to review the material, I will have to re-learn it.

_____ **13.** Because I do not often have several hours of uninter-rupted time for study.

_____ **14.** I try to review the class material as soon as possible.

_____ **15.** Since I have begun these daily reviews, my test grades have improved.

EXERCISE 6.23

Correct each of the fragments in Exercise 6.22. Then copy all the sentences (including your corrections) to form a paragraph. (Omit all the blanks and numbers.)

EXERCISE 6.24

Skill Check: Fragments

Underline the fragments in the paragraph below. Then draw an arrow from each fragment to the independent clause to which it should be connected.

(1) Although the human population of the rain forests is decreasing each year. (2) Many tribes still live in rain forests around the world. (3) Some tribespeople are hunters and gatherers. (4) Surviving by fishing, hunting, and gathering fruits and nuts. (5) These people hunt animals such as squirrels, wild pigs, and monkeys. (6) Using primitive weapons including poisoned darts and blowpipes. (7) Because these tribes depend on hunting and gathering for their food. (8) They are nomads. (9) Moving from place to place. (10) Other tribes are farmers. (11) Most of the soil is poor. (12) Because the plants in the forest have removed most of the nu-trients from the soil. (13) To improve the quality of the soil. (14) Farmers burn the plants to create ash. (15) The ash then becomes fertilizer. (16) To plant seeds. (17) The farmers use a simple stick. (18) Because the burnt

soil is soft. (19) When the rain forests disappear. (20) What will happen to these tribes?

Editing Tip

Some students write fragments because they are worried about their sentences being too long. However, cutting off part of a sentence just confuses the reader.

To check for fragments, read your paragraph *backwards,* checking each word group for completeness. If possible, read your paper aloud and listen to your thoughts. Is every sentence complete?

FOCUS ON PUNCTUATION: THE BREATH OF THE SENTENCE

While phrases give music to the sentence and clauses provide a foundation for sentence construction, punctuation is necessary to carry the sentence's meaning to the reader. Punctuation marks are used to connect phrases to clauses, clauses to clauses, and sometimes words to words. Good readers use punctuation marks as a guide to help them know what words to stress and when to take a breath. Correct use of punctuation helps the sentence to "breathe."

Commas

The most frequently used punctuation mark is the comma. The comma is also the most frequently misused. In fact, students ask more questions about commas than about any other form of punctuation.

The following comma rules cover the ordinary uses of the comma. Becoming familiar with these rules can help build your confidence.

Comma Rule 1: Use a comma before a coordinating conjunction (*for, and, nor, but, or, yet, so*) joining two independent clauses (each with a subject and a verb).

> Debra does not know how to use a computer, **but** she is willing to learn.
> The play starts next weekend, **so** I have to buy my tickets soon.

You were introduced to this rule earlier in this chapter. Remember that the comma before the coordinating conjunction (FANBOYS) signals the reader that a subject and verb will follow. The words before the comma form a complete thought, and so do the words after the coordinating conjunction.

No comma is needed before a conjunction that is not followed by an independent clause.

Debra does not know how to use a computer, **but** <u>she</u> is willing to learn. (The comma is needed because a subject, *she*, and a verb, *is*, follow the coordinating conjunction.)

Debra does not know how to use a computer **but** is willing to learn. (No comma is needed because no subject appears after the coordinating conjunction *but*.)

EXERCISE 6.25

Insert commas where they are needed. **Hint:** Not all sentences will require commas.

1. My supervisor wants me to work more hours but I have too much homework.

2. Disciplining children is difficult but necessary.

3. Joe plans to attend college next year and he is completing his application this week.

4. Christopher has finished college and is working at a computer firm.

5. Joan wants to major in political science yet she is unsure of her career plans.

Commas are often used after words, phrases, or clauses that introduce the main idea of a sentence.

Comma Rule 2: Use a comma following words or phrases that introduce the main idea of the sentence.

Moreover, the homicide rate in New York City is continuing to decline.
During the last two weeks of October, tourists crowd the roads in western North Carolina.
Singing her solo, the child looks serene.
To complete the task, the employee must work overtime.

A comma is optional if only one short prepositional phrase opens the sentence.

After the test the class quickly left the room.

A comma is also optional if the sentence begins with *also*, *then*, or *next*.

Then we went out for pizza.

Comma Rule 3: Use a comma to separate an introductory dependent clause from the independent clause that follows it.

Because the airfares are low, the couple is planning a vacation to Paris.

If college students want to succeed, they must organize their time effectively.

Note that the comma in each sentence above follows the dependent clause.

Insert commas where they are needed.

1.   If my sisters cannot come with us I will not be able to go.

2.   During the months of November and December many students leave campus to visit their families.

3.   To make a good homemade pizza you need a pizza stone.

4   Furthermore we need more parking spaces on campus.

5.   When students need help with homework they can visit the learning support center.

Writers also use commas to set off words, phrases, or clauses that interrupt the flow of the sentence.

Comma Rule 4:   Use commas to set off words or phrases that interrupt the main idea of the sentence.

> The essay, **however,** is not due until next week.
> The personal computer, **for example,** was not invented until the 1970s.
> Some students, **therefore,** will not be able to attend the lecture.
> Johnny, **on the other hand,** is outgoing.

Comma Rule 5:   Use commas to set off clauses that begin with *who* or *which* and are not essential to the meaning of the sentence.

> Richard Nixon, **who was the thirty-seventh President of the United States,** resigned from office.
> My red 1997 truck, **which I bought new,** is a joy to drive.

In the first example, the clause *who was the thirty-seventh President of the United States* is not essential to the meaning of the sentence. Although this clause adds information about Richard Nixon, it is not needed to identify him. This clause is a *nonessential clause.* Commas set off a nonessential clause from the rest of the sentence.

In the second example, the truck is identified without the clause *which I bought new.* This clause is also nonessential and is set off with commas.

Sometimes the words in the clause are essential for the meaning of the sentence. In that case, no commas are needed.

She was the student who was in my class last semester.

The clause *who was in my class last semester* is necessary to identify the student. Therefore, no commas appear.

EXERCISE 6.27   Insert commas where they are necessary.

1. Leonardo da Vinci who was a famous Renaissance artist painted the beautiful mural called *The Last Supper.*

2. Leonardo moreover was a child prodigy.

3. *The Last Supper* which is located in an Italian monastery was nearly destroyed in a bombing raid in World War II.

4. Leonardo's experimentation with paint however was devastating to this famous mural.

5. Today this mural which is peeling away from the wall is still a symbol of Renaissance art.

Comma Rule 6: Use a comma to separate three or more items in a series.

I have lived in **South Carolina, Texas, Georgia, and Florida.**
A flavorful spaghetti sauce needs **onion, garlic, and Italian seasoning.**

Comma Rule 7: Use a comma to separate items in dates and addresses.

My sister was born on **Tuesday, February 1, 1953,** in **Augusta, Georgia,** at noon.
Hugh, Karen, George, and Frances live at **4555 Mountain Road, Calais, Vermont.**
Angela moved from **Buffalo, New York,** to **Tampa, Florida,** last year.

Be careful to use a comma after the last item if the address or date appears in the middle of the sentence. No comma is needed before a zip code.

Comma Rule 8: Use commas to separate units of three within numbers.
Venus' diameter is approximately **7,600** miles.
The earth moves in its orbit at **66,600** miles per hour.

EXERCISE 6.28   Place commas where they are needed.

1. Light travels at 186300 miles per hour.

2. Michelangelo Buonarroti was born on March 6 1475 in Caprese Italy.

3. Pizza lasagna and manicotti are my favorite Italian foods.

4. William of Normandy invaded the British Isles on October 14 1066 at Hastings England.

5. The mountains on the ocean floor can range from 10000 to 13000 feet high.

Skill Check: Commas

Insert commas where they are needed.

1. Scientists estimate that more than 30 million species of plants and animals live in the rain forest and most of them live nowhere else.

2. In addition to jaguars and monkeys other animals such as the giant armadillo iguana and bearded pig make the rain forest their home.

3. The giant armadillo which is covered with bony plates digs a hole in the forest floor.

4. When an armadillo is hungry it digs for termites ants and snails to eat.

5. Even though many iguanas live in deserts they also thrive in the trees of rain forests.

6. Iguanas which can grow up to six feet long eat flowers fruits and tree leaves.

7. The bearded pig is known for its whiskers narrow body and bristly hair.

8. The bearded pig eats fruits but it also feasts on insects and roots.

9. Because these animals are quick to sense danger they have survived in the rain forests.

10. Their survival in future generations however is at risk with as many as 40 million acres of rain forest being destroyed each year.

Apostrophes

Many students omit apostrophes from their writing because they are unsure how to use these punctuation marks. Here are the rules for using apostrophes.

Rule 1:   Use an apostrophe to form a contraction.

would not = wouldn't

The words *would not* are contracted, or shortened, to form *wouldn't*. The apostrophe indicates where a letter has been omitted.

Other contractions are

I am = I'm	is not = isn't	we have = we've
he is = he's	are not = aren't	you have = you've
she is = she's	was not = wasn't	they have = they've
it is = it's	do not = don't	he will = he'll
we are = we're	will not = won't	she will = she'll
you are = you're	did not = didn't	
they are = they're	should not = shouldn't	

EXERCISE 6.30 Insert apostrophes as needed.

1. Im planning a trip to Key West next winter.

2. Didnt she tell you about her promotion?

3. Hes unsure whether theyll go with us this weekend.

4. Its been a long time since weve been able to visit our parents.

5. Wont you agree that Angela hasnt finished her chores?

> **Rule 2:** Use an apostrophe on a noun to show possession. Add *'s* if the noun representing the owner does not end in *-s*.
>
> John's room

The apostrophe shows that the room belongs to John. Because the noun *John* does not end in *-s*, an apostrophe followed by an *s* is added to show that John is the owner.

Owner	+	What is owned	=	Possessive
children	+	toys	=	children's toys
teacher	+	computer	=	teacher's computer
student	+	textbook	=	student's textbook
men	+	room	=	men's room

If the noun representing the owner already ends in *-s*, then add just an apostrophe.

Owner	+	What is owned	=	Possessive
players	+	soccer ball	=	players' soccer ball
teachers	+	computers	=	teachers' computers
students	+	textbooks	=	students' textbooks
ladies	+	room	=	ladies' room

Remember that pronouns that show possession (*my, mine, your, yours, his, her, hers, its, our, ours, their, theirs*) do not need an apostrophe. Also, not every noun that ends in *-s* requires an apostrophe. There must be an owner and something that is owned.

Fill in the blanks using apostrophes where they are needed.

Owner	+	What is owned	=	Possessive
1. Sarah	+	car	=	_____
2. women	+	clothes	=	_____
3. employees	+	time sheets	=	_____
4. truck	+	driver	=	_____
5. director	+	plans	=	_____

Add apostrophes where they are necessary.

1. The Smiths station wagon was involved in an accident last week.

2. Please remember that all students lockers must be emptied by next week.

3. I just finished decorating the childrens room.

4. The jurys verdict in the murder trial was "Not guilty."

5. The classes field trip to the museum was successful.

Skill Check: Punctuation

Add the missing punctuation marks to the sentences below.

1. In addition to the many animal species found in the rain forest millions of plant species thrive there.

2. The rain forests climate is ideal for many plants.

3. The humidity is generally between 75 and 90 percent and the temperature is between 75 and 85 degrees Fahrenheit.

4. Over 1500 types of bromeliads grow in tropical forests.

5. Bromeliads which are also called air plants have broad leaves.

6. Air plants grow on other plants such as trees and they get most of their nutrients from the air.

7. The base of a bromeliads leaves forms a holding area for water.

8. Frogs tadpoles and salamanders can be found in these holding tanks.

9. Other air plants growing in the rain forest include ferns mosses and orchids.

10. More than 20000 species of orchids grow in the wild.

11. Orchids grow on rocks tree trunks and tree branches.

12. An orchid plants size can range from less than 1 inch to more than 80 feet.

13. Although orchids grow in many different regions they thrive in wet areas.

14. One form of orchid is a wildflower called ladys slipper.

15. Its not widely known that more than one-fourth of the worlds medicines come from rain forest plants.

16. Quinine for instance comes from the cinchona tree.

17. Many of the worlds fruits can be found in rain forests including bananas sugar cane pineapples and peanuts.

18. Furthermore chocolate comes from the seeds of the cacao tree which also grows in the rain forest.

19. Its been estimated that the rain forests plants might even offer a possible cure for cancer.

20. Shouldnt scientists continue to study the vast resources of the worlds rain forests?

WRITING ASSIGNMENT

Read about a plant or animal that lives in the rain forest. Then write a short paragraph about this plant or animal. What does it look like? Where in the rain forest does it live? Why are you interested in this plant or animal?

Use the stages of the writing process. Write an experimental draft. Then revise, edit, and prepare a finished copy. Be sure to include a topic sentence and sufficient supporting details.

Writers as Spiders

The World Wide Web has many fascinating sites related to the rain forest. You can find one of these sites at

http://www.ran.org

Web Exercise 1

Using a search engine or the address above, locate a web site on the rain forest. Use the information at this site to complete the writing assignment above.

Additional Help

Many online writing centers offer assistance with punctuation, including help with commas and apostrophes.

For more work with commas, see

http://www.grammarbook.com/punctuation/commas.html

To review apostrophes and take a quiz, visit

http://www.grammarbook.com/punctuation/apostro.html

Focus on Narration

Now that you have reviewed paragraph and sentence structure, you are ready to learn to write different kinds of paragraphs. Chapters 7 through 11 each introduce a different type of paragraph. Practicing these paragraph types will help you improve your writing and prepare you for success in the classroom and workplace.

What Is Narration?

One of the oldest forms of writing is narration. *Narration* is storytelling. Our earliest ancestors told stories to entertain each other and to teach young people the beliefs and customs of the tribe. Here, for example, is a tale told by the Inuit:

> Long ago a sister and her brother lived in a village. In this village was a house where the children of the village loved to play. One night when the sister was playing in the house, all the lamps in the house went out, and a stranger entered the door. She was frightened. She placed her hands in soot and marked the man's back. When she relit the lamps, she discovered the stranger was her brother. She ran away from him, grabbed a piece of brightly burning wood, and rushed out the door. Her brother seized another piece of burning wood. Then the brother fell down, and the light of the wood nearly went out. It had only a weak glow. Suddenly, the brother and sister were lifted to run from each other in the sky. The sister became the sun and the brother the moon.

A narrative can be short (a joke) or long (a novel). It can be real (what happened at a party over the weekend) or fictional (such as a situation comedy on television or the screenplay of a movie).

All narratives have a beginning, a middle, and an end. Because narratives are stories, they are organized according to time order (see Chapter 4). They unfold one event at a time until the story ends.

This chapter focuses on the personal narrative. When you write a personal narrative, you recall an experience you have had. A personal narrative can be a recent event or, as in the example that follows, a memory from childhood.

> I could not believe that this day had finally arrived. I had waited all year for the chance to pitch for my sixth grade softball team. Finally, it was my turn. I stood before the batter and stared him in the eyes. The distance between him and me seemed more like a mile than a few yards. How would I ever be able to throw the ball that hard? Sucking in my breath, I took my first pitch. Wham! I heard the bat crack the ball. Suddenly, I felt myself flying backward. I hit the ground and felt something gooey running out of my nose. Then the pain began. The ball had hit me squarely in the nose. I was out for the rest of the game. My excitement turned to tears.

A narrative can be humorous or serious. The following paragraph is a combination of the two—something that could have been a terrible accident has a happy ending.

> One night a few summers ago while I was cooking supper, I heard a strange noise coming from the laundry room. Thump! Rrrrr! Thump! Rrrr! Worried, I quickly ran into the laundry room and looked around. Then I went back to working in the kitchen. The sound began again. Thump! Rrrr! Thump! Rrrr! What could it be? This time I opened the dryer door. My eight-year-old cat, Snowball, staggered out of the dryer. He was dizzy and couldn't walk straight. He was also panting. I ran for some water and held him until he calmed down. He had crawled into the dryer, which was filled with towels, and settled in for a nap. Unfortunately, I came in soon after and turned on the dryer. Fortunately, Snowball was all right. I learned a valuable lesson. Always look in the dryer before pressing the start button.

When you write a personal narrative, keep two points in mind:

- Tell your story in a lively, interesting way.
- Follow a logical order so that you do not confuse your reader.

EXERCISE 7.1

Write the letter **N** in the blank if the example would be told in narrative form. Write the letter **X** in the blank if the example would not be told in narrative form.

_____ **1.** A shopping list for the grocery store

_____ **2.** A movie about the search for alien life on Earth

_____ **3.** A description of the top ten restaurants in New York City

_____ **4.** A diary of a runaway slave on the Underground Railroad

_____ **5.** A story about reaching the top of Mt. Everest

_____ **6.** A list of the one hundred best movies

_____ **7.** An account of the assassination of President Abraham Lincoln

_____ **8.** A diagram of a computer hard drive

_____ **9.** A floor plan of a condominium

_____ **10.** A joke about the last presidential campaign

CHOOSING A TOPIC

As you learned in Chapter 3, an effective paragraph has a clearly focused topic. When you write a personal narrative paragraph, you must keep a sharp focus. Otherwise, your story will ramble. Suppose, for example, that you are going to write about a time when you had some bad luck. You can narrow this topic by using any of the methods you have already learned—brainstorming, clustering, freewriting, or journal writing. (See Chapter 2.)

A time when I had bad luck

Automobile accidents

My first automobile accident

Here is another example:

A vacation experience

My family's trip to Myrtle Beach

Going to the amusement park

Riding my first wooden roller coaster

Narrow each of the following topics so that you could write about it in a paragraph. When you fill in a blank, be sure to limit the topic more specifically than in the previous blank. (Add blanks as necessary to narrow your topic.)

1. <u>A holiday memory</u>

_____

_____

2. <u>An unforgettable experience</u>

_____

_____

_____

3. <u>A conflict I had with a family member or a friend</u>

_____

_____

4. <u>A time when I had good luck</u>

_____

_____

5. <u>A humorous childhood experience</u>

_____

_____

Organizing a Personal Narrative

Like all good paragraphs, a personal narrative is organized around three key elements:

- Topic sentence
- Supporting details
- Concluding sentence

The Topic Sentence

As you learned in Chapter 3, your reader should discover the focus of your paragraph in your topic sentence. Are you recalling a memory from childhood? Are you telling about something that happened to you at work last week? What is the focus of your narrative?

One of the keys of writing a good narrative is to create suspense, so you do not want to give away the ending in the topic sentence. However, you do want to set the stage for the story ahead. A sharp focus helps your reader zoom in on the topic while preparing for what is to come.

Topic: A time when I had good luck

Topic sentence: One night last summer at a college track meet, I won the race of my life.

The focus of this topic sentence is clear—the good fortune of winning a race. However, some suspense remains. What happened during the race? How was winning the race good luck? If your topic is clearly focused, you should be able to write fully about your topic in a single paragraph.

Topic: A vacation experience

Unfocused: My camping trip over the Fourth of July weekend was a disaster. (How can this writer discuss an entire camping trip in a single paragraph?)

Focused: I spent last Fourth of July in a tent at Beach Park listening to the rain pound on the canvas and wishing for sunshine. (This topic sentence is more manageable because the writer is focusing on the disappointing weather.)

Topic: An unforgettable experience

Unfocused: Last summer I spent an unforgettable week in New York City. (Is it possible to discuss a week of vacation in the Big Apple in one paragraph?)

Focused: I will never forget my first look at the Statue of Liberty last summer. (This topic sentence is more workable for a single paragraph.)

EXERCISE 7.3

Read each of the following sentences. Place a check mark in the blank to the left of each sentence that would make a good topic sentence. If the sentence is unfocused, place an **X** in the blank.

_____   **1.**   My birthday party was great.

_____   **2.**   Last October at my birthday party, I received an unforgettable present.

_____   **3.**   My senior year in high school was remarkable.

_____   **4.**   I can still remember the shouts of my family and friends as I walked across the stage at my high school graduation.

_____   **5.**   When I received an A on my midterm exam, I knew I had accomplished an important goal.

In Chapter 3, you learned that a topic sentence has two parts. It states the topic, and it makes a comment about the topic. In the topic sentence for your narrative paragraph, you must also give some basic information to set the stage for your story.

Think about the reporter's questions you learned in Chapter 4. In a narration paragraph, the topic sentence should answer these key questions:

- Who was involved in the event?

- What is the focus of the story?

- When did the event happen?

- Where did the event happen?

Who was involved in the event? You are telling the story, so use first person singular pronouns (*I, me, my*) in your topic sentence or first person plural pronouns (*we, us, our*) if others are involved.

What is the focus of your story? The topic sentence should state the focus of your narrative. Are you writing about a holiday memory? Are you recalling an unforgettable experience? Although your topic sentence should announce the focus, you may want to create some suspense by withholding the outcome until later in the paragraph.

When did the event occur? Establishing the time of the event helps the reader experience the event from your point of view. You should let the reader know if the event occurred recently or years ago. Your reader will also probably expect you to remember more details if you are recalling a recent memory.

Where did the event happen? Where an event occurred is often as important as *when* it happened. Stating clearly in the topic sentence where the event happened will help your reader picture the scene you are creating.

Keep the reporter's questions in mind as you read this topic sentence:

On a cold October night six years ago at a dinner with my best friend, I learned a valuable lesson about the meaning of friendship.

Who was involved in the event? The writer and her best friend.

What will be the focus of the narrative? A valuable lesson.

When did the event occur? On a cold October night six years ago.

Where did the event happen? At dinner.

EXERCISE 7.4

Read each of the following topic sentences. Each sentence is missing one or more answers to the questions "Who?" "Where?" "When?" and "What?" Place an **X** in the blank if a topic sentence is missing that answer.

1. I will never forget my climb to the top of Bald Mountain.

Who? _____ What? _____ When? _____ Where? _____

2. My sister and I learned a valuable lesson.

Who? _____ What? _____ When? _____ Where? _____

3. An incredible surprise happened last Saturday afternoon.

Who? _____ What? _____ When? _____ Where? _____

4. On my first day of work, I made an embarrassing mistake.

Who? _____ What? _____ When? _____ Where? _____

5. Winning the championship football game in eleventh grade was a thrill.

Who? _____ What? _____ When? _____ Where? _____

EXERCISE 7.5

Write a topic sentence for each of your narrowed topics in Exercise 7.2.

1. A holiday memory

Narrowed topic: _____

Topic sentence: _____

2. An unforgettable experience

Narrowed topic: _____

Topic sentence: _____

3. A conflict I had with a family member or a friend

Narrowed topic: _____

Topic sentence: _____

4. A time when I had good luck

Narrowed topic: _____

Topic sentence: _____

5. A humorous childhood experience

Narrowed topic: _____

Topic sentence: _____

Supporting Details

In a narration paragraph, you will arrange your supporting details using time order (see Chapter 4). You want to re-create the experience for your reader, so you need to present the details in the order in which they occurred. Sometimes this is difficult because human memory is unreliable. You have to work hard to remember all the details in the order in which they occurred. To help yourself recall the event in detail, try making a flow chart, filling in the details as they occur to you.

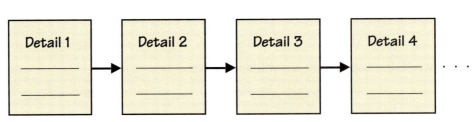

You can add as many boxes as you need. Here is a flow chart for a narration paragraph about high school graduation:

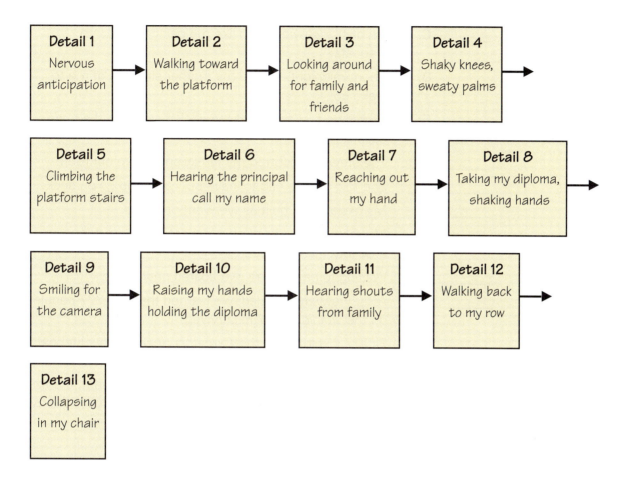

When you have finished your flow chart, check to be sure each detail leads smoothly into the next. If you find a detail that does not support your topic sentence, remove it. Details that are irrelevant to your experience are distracting and frustrating for your reader. You may also discover that you have omitted some key details. If so, just add them as needed.

EXERCISE 7.6

Develop a flow chart for any one of the topics from Exercise 7.5 or for some other topic of your choice.

EXERCISE 7.7

The following paragraph is based on a survivor's account of the sinking of the *Titanic,* but the sentences are not in the correct order. Place each detail in time order by writing the appropriate number in the blank.

Topic sentence: I will never forget the fateful night of April 14, 1912, that changed my life forever.

_____ **A.** After supper, I fell asleep, exhausted from my exciting day aboard the great ship.

_____   **B.**   On a bright spring day in 1912, my mother and I bought tickets in Southampton, England, for the maiden voyage of the "unsinkable" ship, the *Titanic*.

_____   **C.**   On deck, I saw children like me being forced into lifeboats.

_____   **D.**   About midnight, I heard my mother shouting at me to wake up.

_____   **E.**   When we first arrived at the dock, I stared at the huge ocean liner.

_____   **F.**   The steward escorted my family and me to our room.

_____   **G.**   She told me we had to leave our cabin and go on deck.

_____   **H.**   My excitement built as we went on board.

_____   **I.**   My mother and I entered a lifeboat and were soon lowered into the black sea.

_____   **J.**   Waiting to be rescued, we floated until dawn.

_____   **K.**   After we were rescued, we learned that of 2,227 people on the *Titanic*, only 705 survived.

_____   **L.**   Finally, a ship called the *Carpathia* picked up our lifeboat.

EXERCISE 7.8

Below is a brief account of another tragic and unforgettable event, the explosion of the space shuttle *Challenger*. Place each detail in time order by writing the appropriate number in the blank.

Topic sentence: On January 28, 1986, as I sat in my third grade classroom, I stared at the television.

_____   **A.**   After the walkway was removed, the countdown began.

_____   **B.**   The shuttle had taken off!

_____   **C.**   When the *Challenger* crew was in place, the walkway was pulled away from the shuttle.

_____   **D.**   The countdown continued, and the minutes ticked away.

_____   **E.**   With my classmates, I watched Christa McAuliffe, a civilian teacher and mother, and six astronauts board the space shuttle *Challenger*.

_____   **F.**   "T minus seven minutes, thirty seconds and counting."

_____   **G.**   Then followed "Four . . . three . . . two . . . one . . . and liftoff."

_____   **H.**   Then the horror came.

_____   **I.**   "T minus ten seconds . . . nine . . . eight . . . seven . . . six . . . five. . . . We have main engine start."

_____   **J.**   *Challenger* exploded in a fireball.

The Concluding Sentence

Your narrative paragraph will not be complete without a concluding sentence. Your reader will want to know not only what happened to you but also your reaction to the event.

When you write your concluding sentence, you should answer the question "So what?" What is the point of your narrative? Why was this event significant? Did you learn a lesson? Has your reader likely experienced a similar event?

Your concluding sentence should reinforce in the reader's mind the main idea of your narrative. Notice that the narratives in Exercises 7.7 and 7.8 lack concluding sentences. The author who wrote about the *Titanic* disaster ended the supporting details with a count of the survivors. But what is the rest of the story? Readers will probably be curious about what happened to the remains of the great ship. Here are two possible concluding sentences:

The "unsinkable" *Titanic* had disappeared in the water and was not seen again until 1985.

Our trip on the ship of dreams had turned into a nightmare for my family.

The first possible concluding sentence adds drama to the narrative and helps explain why this disaster still fascinates the public. The second ends on a personal note as the writer reflects on the meaning of the journey for her family. There is no single way to end a story. What is essential is that the concluding sentence be logical, based on the events of the narrative.

The narrative in Exercise 7.8 is told from the viewpoint of an adult remembering an experience in elementary school. What did the child witnessing the space shuttle explosion learn that day? The concluding sentence makes this point:

In just 73 seconds, my classroom and the rest of the nation learned how quickly joy can turn into sorrow.

Write a concluding sentence for each of your narrowed topics in Exercise 7.5.

EXERCISE 7.9

1. <u>A holiday memory</u>

Narrowed topic: _____

Topic sentence: _____

Concluding sentence: _____

2. <u>An unforgettable experience</u>

Narrowed topic: _____

Topic sentence: _____

Concluding sentence: _____

3. A conflict I had with a family member or a friend

Narrowed topic: _____

Topic sentence: _____

Concluding sentence: _____

4. A time when I had good luck

Narrowed topic: _____

Topic sentence: _____

Concluding sentence: _____

5. A humorous childhood experience

Narrowed topic: _____

Topic sentence: _____

Concluding sentence: _____

TRANSITIONS IN NARRATIVE PARAGRAPHS

Using transitions will help your reader follow the details in your story. Transitional words and phrases connect the sentences in your paragraph so that your ideas will flow smoothly. (See Chapter 4.)

These transitional words are commonly used in narrative paragraphs:

first	suddenly	then
previously	soon	later
next	eventually	afterward
meanwhile	gradually	finally

EXERCISE 7.10

The following exercise features pairs of sentences. In each blank, write an appropriate transitional expression from the list above. Do not use the same transitional expression more than once.

1. Before I received my grades this semester, I was nervous about my math grade. _____ , I felt relief.

2. The car pulled slowly into the driveway. _____ , the doorbell rang.

3. When I first started walking for exercise, I could walk only twenty minutes without feeling exhausted. _____ , I built up my endurance.

4. After the interview, I waited anxiously to hear if I had gotten the job. _____ , the manager called.

5. This semester I am attending Young Harris College. _____ , I attended St. Petersburg Junior College.

6. First, we need to finish studying for our English test. _____ , we'll go out for pizza.

7. I am waiting to register for my classes next semester. _____ , I am meeting with a counselor to review my transcript.

8. Each session I sign up for only two classes. _____ , next semester I plan to quit work and attend school full-time.

9. I've been working since eight o'clock this morning. _____ , I'll be able to leave for the day.

10. To prepare homemade lasagna, I first gather all the necessary equipment. _____ , I check to be sure that I have the ingredients in my cupboard.

Underline the transitional words in the following narrative.

EXERCISE 7.11

On a dark, lonely road one summer night, fear turned to laughter. I was on my way home from work and ready to turn into my street when I saw the flashing of police lights in my rearview mirror. Suddenly, I panicked. Why were the police stopping me? Was I speeding? Gradually, I brought my car to a stop. Then I waited for the patrol officer to come to my window. "Can I see your license?" he growled. "OK," I responded as I groped for my wallet. "Did you know you were going fifty-five in a forty-mile zone?" he demanded. I said, "See the sign right there. It says fifty-five miles per hour." "I'll be back," he snarled as he returned to his car. I waited impatiently for him to return. Finally, he came back to my window. "Ma'am, I cannot give you a speeding ticket." My heart was pounding rapidly as I heard him speak these words. "The computer in my patrol car is down," he said. Afterward, I pulled into my driveway with a great sigh of relief and a smile on my face.

FOCUS ON DICTION

Strong verbs are the heartbeat of a lively story. They carry the action of each sentence and hold the reader's attention.

Using Lively Verbs

Suppose you wrote the following sentence in your narrative:

The actor danced across the stage.

What picture comes to your mind when you read the verb *danced?* Is the person *twirling, leaping,* or *tapping?*

The five-year-old ran across the street.

Did the child *sprint, jog,* or *race?* Make your action verbs as specific as possible to help your reader visualize the events as they unfold.

Here are some possibilities:

The dancer **quickly twirled** across the stage.

The dancer **tapped loudly** across the stage.

The five-year-old **raced heedlessly** across the street.

Notice that the action verb in each sentence is accompanied by an *-ly* word. With each verb and *-ly* word, the meaning of the sentence changes. You can use *-ly* words either before or after the verb to make your writing more energetic.

EXERCISE 7.12

Edit the sentences below by changing the verbs in bold print and adding *-ly* words. You may use a dictionary and/or a thesaurus. Be ready to explain how your changes affect the sentence's meaning.

1.   I **watched** the woman as she **walked** along the beach.

   _____

2.   The bride and groom **left** the church.

   _____

3.   The boat **moved** through the waves as the storm **came.**

   _____

4.   The students **wrote** notes while the teacher **spoke** in class.

   _____

5.   As the child **ran** through the store, her mother **called** her name.

   _____

EXERCISE 7.13

Replace each of the verbs in bold print with another action verb. Add *-ly* words when possible.

On a crisp fall evening of my junior year in college, I became a campus hero. I was a receiving back on our football team, and our opponent had not been scored on for the entire season. Our goal that night was to (1) **make** at least one touchdown and to (2) **beat** the other team. Our coach had (3) **planned** the perfect play. The quarterback would move out to the right and (4) **place** the ball into my hands downfield. Then I would (5) **run** to the goal line. Fortunately, I caught the ball. Unfortunately, two huge players from the other team (6) **threw** me to the ground. Back I went into the huddle. This time we (7) **ran** the play to the right. Miraculously, I (8) **passed** the tackles and (9) **went** for the touchdown. After I returned to the bench, the coach (10) **said,** "Now just do that one more time!" That never happened; we lost the game 56 to 6. However, the next morning the newspaper headlines read, "Williams Scores One Touchdown!" It didn't matter that we lost. I was a hero—at least until the next game.

FOCUS ON REVISING: UNRELATED DETAILS

When you have arranged your ideas and written your first draft, you are ready to revise. Revising is a critical stage in the writing process. (See Chapter 2.) To revise is to *see again* (*re* = "again," *vise* = "to see")—that is, you reread your paragraph from the reader's viewpoint rather than your own.

One of your tasks in the revising process is to eliminate any ideas that are unrelated to your topic. Have you ever listened to someone tell a story and start to ramble, relating unnecessary details so that the story drags on and on? Unrelated details also throw the reader off track, so be sure to check that each major point is clearly related to your focus.

Read the following paragraph. Then reread it and cross out all the sentences that are off the topic.

EXERCISE 7.14

(1) Two summers ago, my boyfriend, Mike, and I decided to hike the Panther Creek Nature Trail in the Blue Ridge Mountains. (2) We started our three-mile hike early so that we could avoid the afternoon sun. (3) Last summer at the beach I got a terrible sunburn. (4) My skin finally healed, but it took days. (5) The trail began beside a beautiful creek. (6) We watched the water roll gently over moss-covered rocks. (7) Taking off our shoes, we crossed the creek. (8) On the other side, the trail grew steeper. (9) My legs began to ache. (10) Fortunately, our backpacks were light—just a few essentials such as water, crackers, and insect repellent—so we did not carry much extra weight. (11) I remember when my father used to pack my school backpack so full that I could hardly get on the bus. (12) After an hour of hiking through a beautiful forest of pines

and hardwoods, Mike decided to take a shortcut through a creek bed. (13) Ignoring signs saying "Do Not Leave Trail," he scurried off. (14) Why does Mike always have to look for an easier way to do something? (15) I'll never understand why he is so stubborn. (16) Suddenly, I heard him warn, "Don't move!" (17) "What's wrong?" I cried. (18) By then I had almost caught up with him. (19) "There's a rattlesnake beside my hand," he answered, his voice quavering. (20) He had grabbed a rock to steady his balance and nearly touched a rattler! (21) Then Mike said, "I think it's sleeping. (22) I'm going to move my hand slowly and hope the snake doesn't wake up!" (23) Inch by inch, Mike backed away until he reached me. (24) The rattler never moved. (25) We both looked at each other with a sigh of relief. (26) That unforgettable trail was truly a nature hike!

REVISING TIP: WRITING WITH A COMPUTER

Before computers, writers had to handwrite or type each draft, starting from the beginning each time and taking care not to make a mistake. Too many typing errors meant starting all over again. Today, writers can create computer files that can be changed easily. As a result, many writers do much of their revision work on the computer.

Cut and Paste

One of the most useful revising tools on the computer is cut and paste. This feature allows you to select a portion of text and move it to a different location in the same document or to another document. When you cut and paste, you delete the text from its original location. If you make a mistake with cut and paste, use the undo feature, which allows you to reverse your decision on the next keyboard stroke.

Suppose you are revising your narration paragraph and discover some details that are out of order. You can use the cut and paste feature to move the details to the desired location.

EXERCISE 7.15

Type either Exercise 7.7 or Exercise 7.8 onto your computer screen (omit the blanks, but keep the sentence letters). Save this file on your hard drive or on a disk. Then use the cut and paste feature to arrange the sentences in the correct order. Finally, renumber the sentences and put them in paragraph form. Be sure to indent at the beginning. Save your revised file.

FOCUS ON EDITING

After you have revised your paragraph, you are ready to edit. Editing means reading your work over to strengthen your word choice and to correct spelling, grammar, capitalization, and punctuation. This section concentrates on those errors that are likely to appear in a narration paragraph.

Avoiding Run-ons

A *run-on sentence* (sometimes called a *fused sentence*) happens when a writer runs together two independent clauses (sentences) with no punctuation to connect them. In narrative paragraphs, run-on sentences sometimes occur because the writer is in a hurry to tell the story and forgets to end one sentence before beginning another.

Run-on: The quarterback threw the ball gracefully down the field the receiver scored a touchdown.

Run-on: Sue hoped for an A on the exam she made a B.

A run-on is like two cars colliding head-on. There is nothing to stop the sentences from running together, yet the reader must stop to determine where one independent clause ends and another begins in order to understand what is being said.

When you find a run-on sentence in your writing, you can correct it using one of four methods.

Method 1: Separate the independent clauses with a period, and capitalize the word following the period.

> ✔   IC.   IC.

The quarterback threw the ball gracefully down the field. The receiver scored a touchdown.

Sue hoped for an A on the exam. She made a B.

When you place a period between two independent clauses, you provide a traffic signal for the reader. A period brings the reader to a full stop, avoiding head-on collisions. Perhaps this is why in England a period is called a full stop!

Place a slash mark (/) where each run-on occurs. Then correct the run-on by using method 1.

EXERCISE 7.16

1. Miguel has to work Saturday he cannot go with us to the beach.

_____

2. The basketball team won the game they set a new school win-loss record.

_____

3.   I need to go buy some new clothes at the mall I have to wait for my sister.

_____

4.   You can go to the movies later you can wait until the second showing.

_____

5.   We'll stop at Manny's house we'll go to Roxanna's house afterward.

_____

Method 2: Connect the independent clauses with a comma followed by a coordinating conjunction.

The coordinating conjunctions are *for, and, nor, but, or, yet,* and *so* (FANBOYS). (See Table 6.1.) **Hint:** A comma alone will *not* correct a run-on; the comma must be followed by a coordinating conjunction.)

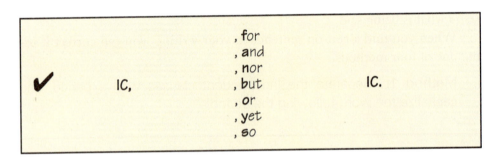

The quarterback threw the ball gracefully down the field, **and** the receiver scored a touchdown.

Sue hoped for an A on the exam, **but** she made a B.

This method corrects run-ons by using coordination. *Coordination* is the process of joining independent clauses that are equal in importance (co = "equal," *ord* = "order"). In Chapter 6, you learned how to join two independent clauses together using coordinating conjunctions (FANBOYS). Using a coordinating conjunction is a common way to correct run-on sentences.

Remember that when you use a comma before a coordinating conjunction, you signal the reader that a subject and a verb will appear in the next clause. (See Comma Rule 1 in Chapter 6.)

               S   **V**

The quarterback gracefully threw the ball down the field, **and** the

      S   **V**

receiver scored a touchdown.

     S **V**   **S** **V**

Sue hoped for an A on the exam, **but** she made a B.

EXERCISE 7.17

Place a slash mark (/) where each run-on occurs. Then correct the run-on by using method 2.

1. Miguel has to work Saturday he cannot go with us to the beach.

   _____

2. The basketball team won the game they set a new school win-loss record.

   _____

3. I need to go buy some new clothes at the mall I have to wait for my sister.

   _____

4. You can go to the movies later you can wait until the second showing.

   _____

5. We'll stop at Manny's house we'll go to Roxanna's house afterward.

   _____

 IC; IC.

Method 3: Connect the independent clauses with a semicolon.

The quarterback gracefully threw the ball down the field; the receiver scored a touchdown.

Sue hoped for an A on the exam; she made a B.

You should use a semicolon, which is more powerful than a comma, when the two clauses are closely related in meaning. A semicolon has the same strength as a period or a comma followed by a coordinating conjunction (FANBOYS).

EXERCISE 7.18

Place a slash mark (/) where each run-on occurs. Then correct the run-on by using method 3.

1. Miguel has to work Saturday he cannot go with us to the beach.

   _____

2. The basketball team won the game they set a new school win-loss record.

   _____

3. I need to go buy some new clothes at the mall I have to wait for my sister.

   _____

4.   You can go to the movies later you can wait until the second show-ing.

_____

5.   We'll stop at Manny's house we'll go to Roxanna's house afterward.

_____

Method 4:   Connect the independent clauses with a semicolon fol-lowed by a conjunctive adverb.

Common conjunctive adverbs are *however, nevertheless, conse-quently, therefore, thus, otherwise, instead, then, meanwhile, more-over, furthermore, also,* and *in addition* (See Table 7.1.) Use a comma following a conjunctive adverb of more than four letters.

 IC;   *conjunctive adverb,* IC.

The quarterback gracefully threw the ball down the field**; then** the receiver scored a touchdown.

Sue hoped for an A on the exam**; however,** she made a B.

TABLE 7.1 Conjunctive Adverbs and Their Meanings	
Meaning	*Conjunctive Adverb*
to contrast	however nevertheless
to express a result	consequently therefore thus
to present an alternative	otherwise instead
to indicate time	then meanwhile
to add a closely related idea	moreover furthermore also in addition

EXERCISE 7.19   Place a slash mark (/) where each run-on occurs. Then correct the run-on by using method 4.

1.   Miguel has to work Saturday he cannot go with us to the beach.

_____

2. The basketball team won the game they set a new school win-loss record.

   _____

3. I need to go buy some new clothes at the mall I have to wait for my sister.

   _____

4. You can go to the movies later you can wait until the second showing.

   _____

5. We'll stop at Manny's house we'll go to Roxanna's house afterward.

   _____

Method 5: Change one independent clause to a dependent clause by using a subordinating conjunction. (See Table 7.2.) The dependent clause can come first or second.

 (Sub. conj.) **DC, IC.**

After the quarterback gracefully threw the ball down the field, the receiver scored a touchdown.

Even though Sue hoped for an A on the exam, she made a B.

TABLE 7.2   Subordinating Conjunctions and Their Meanings

Meaning	*Subordinating Conjunctions*	
to indicate time	after	since
	as	until
	before	when
	once	whenever
		while
to indicate contrast or condition	although	even though
	as if	though
	as though	unless
	if	whether
	even if	
to indicate location	where	
	wherever	
to indicate purpose	in order that	that
	so that	
to indicate cause and effect	because	
	since	

When the dependent clause comes first, you must insert a comma between the two clauses.

✔   *IC*   (sub. conj.)   **DC.**

The receiver scored a touchdown **after** the quarterback gracefully threw the ball down the field

Sue made a B **even though** she hoped for an A on the exam.

When you subordinate, you place the idea of lesser importance in a dependent clause and the idea of greater importance in the independent clause (*sub* = "under").

EXERCISE 7.20

Place a slash mark (/) where each run-on occurs. Then correct the run-on by using method 5.

1.   Miguel has to work Saturday he cannot go with us to the beach.

Dependent clause first: _____

Dependent clause last: _____

2.   The basketball team won the game they set a new school win-loss record.

Dependent clause first: _____

Dependent clause last: _____

3.   I need to go buy some new clothes at the mall I have to wait for my sister.

Dependent clause first: _____

Dependent clause last: _____

4.   You can go to the movies later you can wait until the second showing.

Dependent clause first: _____

Dependent clause last: _____

_____

5.   We'll stop at Manny's house we'll go to Roxanna's house afterward.

Dependent clause first: _____

Dependent clause last: _____

EXERCISE 7.21

Write **RO** in the blank if the sentence is a run-on, **C** if the sentence is correct. Then use any of the methods to correct the run-ons. Use each method at least once.

_____ 1. Last summer my friend Maria and I set out on a thrilling white-water rafting trip on the San Juan River in Colorado.

_____ 2. That morning we arrived early soon afterward we met our guide, Rudy.

_____ 3. Rudy showed us our eight-person raft then we met the other rafters.

_____ 4. We couldn't wait to get on the river we quickly put on our life jackets.

_____ 5. As Rudy shouted the safety instructions, we listened to the white water roaring in the river beside us.

_____ 6. Maria and I headed to the front of the raft for the best view.

_____ 7. Soon we were surrounded by the white-water rapids of the beautiful San Juan.

_____ 8. The landscape flew by quickly we headed into deep water.

_____ 9. Suddenly our guide yelled at us to hold on tightly a difficult rapid was quickly approaching.

_____ 10. I grasped Maria's hand and then grabbed the side of the raft.

_____ 11. The front of the raft leaped into the air like a gymnast on a trampoline we splashed hard into the river.

_____ 12. I was soaking wet it was so exciting.

_____ 13. Everyone was safe no one had tumbled out of the raft.

_____ 14. Fortunately, the next set of rapids was easier to navigate our heartbeats returned to normal.

_____ 15. After about forty-five minutes of easy rapids, our guide warned us to stay alert.

_____ 16. The end of our journey was approaching first we had to go over a small waterfall.

_____ 17. We all had to paddle furiously; our raft might capsize in the river.

_____ 18. Suddenly, we were free-falling in foam as our raft dove into the waterfall.

_____ 19. Our raft regained its position we all shouted in relief.

_____ 20. For an unforgettably thrilling experience, white-water rafting is the greatest!

Avoiding Comma Splices

Another sentence error commonly found in narrative paragraphs is the comma splice. A *comma splice* happens when the writer uses *only* a comma to separate two independent clauses. **Note:** Not every misused comma is a comma splice. A comma splice occurs *only* between independent clauses.

> **Comma splice:** I had to work late yesterday, I was still on time to class.

> **Comma splice:** Mr. Hardin wants his students to succeed, he tutors them outside class.

A comma is not a strong enough punctuation mark to prevent a head-on collision of two independent clauses. Your reader needs a stronger traffic signal. You can correct comma splices using the same alternatives you use to correct run-ons.

Method 1: Separate the independent clauses with a period, and capitalize the word following the period.

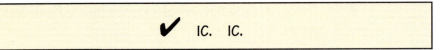

I had to work late yesterday. **I** was still on time to class.

Mr. Hardin wants his students to succeed. **He** tutors them outside class.

The period brings the reader to a full stop at the end of the first independent clause. This strong traffic signal keeps the clauses from being spliced together.

Method 2: Connect the independent clauses with a comma followed by a coordinating conjunction.

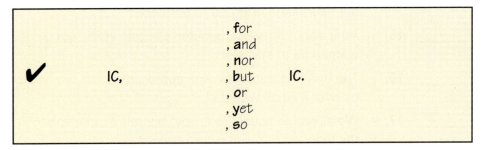

I had to work late yesterday, **but** I was still on time to class.

Mr. Hardin wants his students to succeed, **so** he tutors them outside class.

Method 3: Connect the independent clauses with a semicolon.

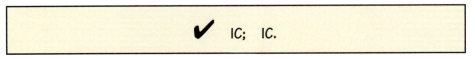

I had to work late yesterday; I was still on time to class.

Mr. Hardin wants his students to succeed; he tutors them outside class.

Method 4: Connect the independent clauses with a semicolon followed by a conjunctive adverb. (See Table 7.1.)

>   IC; *conjunctive adverb,* **IC.**

I had to work late yesterday; **however,** I was still on time to class.

Mr. Hardin wants his students to succeed; **consequently,** he tutors them outside class.

Method 5: Change one independent clause to a dependent clause by using a subordinating conjunction. (See Table 7.2.)

>   *(Sub. conj.)* **DC, IC.**

Even though I had to work yesterday, I was still on time to class.

Because Mr. Hardin wants his students to succeed, he tutors them outside class.

Remember to insert a comma between the two clauses if the dependent clause comes first. No comma is needed if the dependent clause follows the independent clause.

>   IC *sub. conj.* **DC.**

I was still on time to class **even though** I had to work yesterday.

Mr. Hardin tutors his students outside class **because** he wants them to succeed.

Correct the comma splices below using each method. Rearrange the words as needed.

EXERCISE 7.22

1. Kwan wants to buy a sports car, she is looking for a job with a high salary.

Method 1: _____

Method 2: _____

Method 3: _____

Method 4: _____

Method 5: _____

2. The actor was extremely believable in her part, she was nominated for an Academy Award.

Method 1: _____

Method 2: _____

Method 3: _____

Method 4: _____

Method 5: _____

3. I want to pick up some books at the library, I have to pay my fines.

Method 1: _____

Method 2: _____

Method 3: _____

Method 4: _____

Method 5: _____

4. The mayor can ask the council to vote tonight, he can also delay the vote for a week.

Method 1: _____

Method 2: _____

Method 3: _____

Method 4: _____

Method 5: _____

5. We had finished our homework, we ate some lunch.

Method 1: _____

Method 2: _____

Method 3: _____

Method 4: _____

Method 5: _____

EXERCISE 7.23

Write **CS** in the blank if the sentence is a comma splice or **C** if the sentence is correct. Then use any of the methods to correct the comma splices. Use each method at least once.

_____ **1.** Last year on a scorching August afternoon, I witnessed the incredible corn dance at the Santo Domingo pueblo in New Mexico.

_____ **2.** Every August 4, the pueblo celebrates the feast day of St. Dominic, he founded the Dominican order of Catholic friars.

_____ 3. I was excited, this was my first trip to the Santo Domingo pueblo.

_____ 4. I reached the plaza late in the morning, the crowd filled every street of the pueblo.

_____ 5. I could not believe my eyes, nearly 500 dancers filled the plaza.

_____ 6. The brightly costumed dancers were of all ages, ranging from small children to the elderly.

_____ 7. The sun's heat did not disturb the dancers' concentration, they danced in perfect unison.

_____ 8. The dancers lifted their right legs together, then they pounded the earth.

_____ 9. Their movements were as quick as lightning, the noise was like thunder.

_____ 10. Suddenly, the drummers changed the beat; the dancers shifted rhythm.

_____ 11. Then the drumming paused, and the dancers stopped.

_____ 12. Once again, the drummers began their insistent beating, the dancers started to move.

_____ 13. As they moved around the plaza, the dancers formed a snake-like line.

_____ 14. Sometimes the line broke into overlapping lines, the dancers still moved in unison.

_____ 15. Their knees would bend, and their bodies would lean toward the ground.

_____ 16. As they danced, the stamping of their feet never stopped.

_____ 17. Then they would straighten their bodies, and they would raise their arms to the sky.

_____ 18. The dancing lasted all day, dancers would leave and rejoin the line.

_____ 19. Rain showers arrived at the end of the day, the rain was a blessing to the dancers and to the crowd.

_____ 20. For the Pueblo Indians, corn represents life, this dance is a celebration of the joy of life.

Skill Check: Run-ons and Comma Splices

EXERCISE 7.24

Write **RO** in the blank if the sentence is a run-on or **CS** if it is a comma splice. Write **C** in the blank if the sentence is correct. Then use any of the five methods to correct each run-on and comma splice.

_____	1.	Late on a hot July afternoon, my friend, Dan, and I took a fascinating ride into the heart of Navajo country.
_____	2.	Around six o'clock we arrived at the tourist center at Monument Valley, New Mexico, then we saw the "Closed" sign on the door.
_____	3.	We were disappointed, we had been looking forward to our visit.
_____	4.	Just then, we saw a sign advertising a sunset tour, we eagerly signed up.
_____	5.	Our driver was a young Navajo woman; her name was Irene.
_____	6.	She took us to an old yellow Jeep, soon we were on our way into the valley.
_____	7.	The valley is desert country with large buttes, enormous rock formations jutting toward the sky.
_____	8.	After about fifteen minutes of driving on desert roads, our Jeep came to a sudden stop.
_____	9.	Our guide explained the problem the radiator was out of water.
_____	10.	Irene filled the radiator, and we were again on our way.
_____	11.	The valley was beautiful; the red buttes glowed in the late afternoon sun.
_____	12.	Irene stopped at a hogan a hogan is a circular house made of mud and logs.
_____	13.	When Irene asked if we wanted to meet her grand-mother, we said that we did.
_____	14.	Irene took us inside her grandmother greeted us.
_____	15.	Inside the hogan were an iron stove and a weaving loom Irene's grandmother is a rug weaver.
_____	16.	After a brief visit, we continued our tour.
_____	17.	The sun was quickly setting, so our guide stopped in front of a large butte called Left Mitten.
_____	18.	The sun was setting the rays of the sun lit the butte.
_____	19.	We quickly snapped a picture, we wanted to preserve this memory.
_____	20.	Our visit to Monument Valley began with disappoint-ment, but it ended in beauty.

Editing Tip

A great way to check for run-ons and comma splices is to read your papers aloud. (Reading aloud can also help you with the exercises in this textbook.) Read aloud this run-on from Exercise 7.24:

Our guide explained the problem the radiator was out of water.

You can hear your voice drop after the word *problem.* If your voice drops after a word, you are probably reading a run-on sentence or a comma splice. It's as if your voice knows there is a sentence error that needs correction. Once you hear the problem, check to see whether there is an independent clause on either side. If you find a run-on or comma splice, correct the error using one of the five methods you have learned.

FOCUS ON PEER REVIEW

In a writing classroom, you are part of a community of learners. As a member of this community, you can show your drafts not only to your instructor but also to other members of the community— your peers. When you share your drafts with another student or a group of students, you are participating in *peer review.*

Peer reviewing your papers will benefit you in many ways. You have the opportunity to submit your drafts to a reader on a trial basis before you present the final draft to your instructor. Using peer review questions, your reader and you can think through your paper together, evaluating its strengths and weaknesses. You can then make your revisions and editing corrections as you prepare your final draft.

You may feel uncomfortable at first about peer review. You may ask yourself, "How can I help someone else revise and edit when I have trouble finding mistakes in my own papers?" You may also not want to make any comments that are critical of another student's work.

1. Remember that it is often easier to read someone's paper than to read your own.

2. Peer review is a learning experience, and, as with any learning experience, practice is the key.

3. Give praise as well as criticism.

Each of the following chapters provides peer review questions. Use these questions not only to peer review someone else's paper but also to guide you through the stages of the writing process as you write your own compositions.

Use these guide questions to revise, edit, and peer review your narrative paragraph:

GUIDE QUESTIONS

1. Does the topic sentence of the paragraph focus on a specific event? Tell why or why not.

2. Does the topic sentence answer the reporter's questions? (Who was involved? When did the incident occur? Where did the incident happen?) If not, which of the reporter's questions is missing?

3. Is any information missing from the topic sentence? Will this lack of information affect the reader's understanding of the paragraph?

4. Does the writer use first person (*I, me, my, mine, myself, we us, our, ourselves*) consistently? If the writer uses second person (*you, your, yourself, yourselves*), indicate by circling each use. Can this narrative be rewritten in first person?

5. Check the development of the paragraph. Are the events in logical order? If not, what changes need to be made?

6. Does the writer include any details that are not directly related to the paragraph's focus? If so, where does the writer get off track?

7. Does the concluding sentence reinforce the focus of the paragraph? Does the concluding sentence satisfy the reader?

8. List the transitional expressions the writer uses.

9. List four or five action verbs in the paragraph.

10. Are there any fragments in the paragraph? If so, how could they be corrected?

11. Are there any comma splices or run-ons? Indicate where they occur.

12. Note any misspelled words or punctuation problems. Write **sp** (spelling) or **punc** (punctuation) at the end of each line with an error.

13. The strengths of this paragraph are _____.

14. These areas need more work: _____.

EXERCISE 7.25

Form a small group and use the guide questions to analyze the following personal narrative paragraph written by a student.

Student Sample

On June 20, 1998, another scorching Saturday afternoon, I was ringing up groceries at the local Winn-Dixie. I was unaware of what was happening around me. I was more concerned about an elderly customer's complaint about the shortage of strawberry-flavored drumsticks. Suddenly, I heard the piercing noise that still rings in my head. Beep! Beep! Beep! As the store's security device sounded, a slender, unclean man ran like an Olympic track star into the parking lot and then to the mobile home park next door. The store's managers sprinted after the robber soon to be known as the pork chop thief. As I gazed into the crowded parking lot, I watched our diminutive but powerful manager pull the man back into the store. As the head cashier called the police, the thief presented the manager with a large package of boneless pork chops from the front of his red drawstring sweatpants. I kept thinking, "Will he pull out a gun? Will he try to hurt anyone?" When a burly police office barreled through the door five minutes later, he arrested the thief, who, fortunately, did not resist. I was relieved that no one was harmed. I was also surprised that someone could be so desperate for food that he would stick raw meat down his pants and expect to get away with it!

—Michelle Pinciotti

WRITING ASSIGNMENT

Use the steps of the writing process to write a personal narrative paragraph. You may want to develop one of the topics from Exercise 7.2. Here are some other possible topics:

- A time when you were proud of yourself for reaching a goal
- An experience you had on your first job
- A time when you were caught telling a lie
- A birthday memory
- A first date

You can also choose your own topic.

Writers as Spiders

Many World Wide Web sites are preserving historical and personal narratives. Some of these narratives include slave narratives, war narratives, and personal interviews. One fascinating site features interviews with achievers in a wide variety of areas, including sports, science, business, and public service. The address of this site is

http://www.achievement.org/autodoc/pagegen/galleryachieve. html

Web Exercise 1

Choose one of the categories in the column labeled "Gallery of Achievers." Read an interview with one of the people listed. Then return to the address above and choose a category under "Steps to Success." Again, read one of the narratives.

Choose your favorite interview or an individual story. Then answer the following questions:

1. What is the focus of this memory or event?

2. Who is involved in the story?

3. What happens in this story?

4. What is the person's attitude toward this experience?

5. How do you think this experience helped the person achieve success?

Web Exercise 2

Choose one of your family members or friends whom you consider an achiever. Ask him or her to tell you a story that led to success. Write this person's story using narrative paragraph form.

Additional Help

To review run-ons, check out

http://webster.commnet.edu/hp/pages/darling/grammar/ runons.htm

Many online writing centers offer help with fragments, run-ons, comma splices, and other sentence errors. One address featuring comma splice exercises is

http://karn.wright.edu/~sq–ysu/csrev.htm

For an online thesaurus, see

http://www.thesaurus.com

CHAPTER 8

Focus on Description: Part I

WHAT IS DESCRIPTION?

Description begins with observation. The writer observes an object, an animal, a person, or a place and then uses words to communicate this observation to a reader. You will find many examples of description in everyday life. Here, for instance, is a description of a new truck from an advertisement in a local newspaper:

> This sleek new truck with V-8 engine just arrived at our showroom. The interior offers comfortable bucket seats available in a wide variety of colors. Other features include power windows and locks, a stereo radio with CD, and a cell-phone tray under the armrest. The exterior design is sturdy yet attractive with its aerodynamic build and 16-inch aluminum wheels. The safety package includes dual air bags and antilock brakes. This truck is available for lease or sale.

Whether a description is written for specialized readers (advertisements or catalog descriptions) or general readers (descriptions of places or people in books), the goal of description is to create a lively picture in the reader's mind.

Below is one writer's description of an object familiar to her but not to her reader:

> The Norwegian troll doll stands guard on the bookcase shelf. Approximately six inches in height, the witch-like doll has wild, purple-gray hair that stands out from her head as if she has just been struck by lightning.

Underneath this shocking hair is a small, elongated face with wrinkled brow, bulging brown eyes outlined in black, rosy cheeks, open mouth with one tooth exposed, and a sharp chin. In the middle is a half-inch Pinocchio nose with a pink tip. Her olive green dress has long sleeves with an orange, one-pocket apron. She leans forward. One of her arms is extended with the hand grasping a walking stick. The other arm is behind her back with her hand resting on her left hip. Her apron is tied in the back around her waist. Two bare feet peek out from her dress. This troll looks ready to gobble up any unwanted intruder.

Even though the reader may never have seen a Norwegian troll doll, the descriptive details such as *purple-gray hair*, *wrinkled brow*, and *orange, one-pocket apron* allow the reader to see the object in the mind's eye.

Like all paragraphs, a good descriptive paragraph has a beginning, a middle, and an end. Descriptive paragraphs are generally organized according to spatial order—from left to right, top to bottom, back to front, and so on. In the above description, the writer first notes the troll's overall appearance and then presents the details from top to bottom. When you write a description, you should present the details in a clear order so that you do not confuse your reader.

When you write a descriptive paragraph, be sure to

- Relate your description using specific, interesting details
- Use spatial order

Choosing a Topic

To write a good descriptive paragraph, you must narrow the focus of your observation. When you write a description, you are acting as a photographer. If you try to fit too much into your picture, you will not be able to complete your description in a single paragraph. Instead, you should zoom in and limit your focus to a single object. You can narrow your topic using brainstorming, clustering, freewriting, or journal writing.

Suppose you are writing about an interesting animal. Here is one student's freewriting on this topic:

Yesterday at the zoo I saw this funny-looking animal swimming in a water tank. It had a small head and a huge body. It's so large that I can't imagine how it can swim so easily through the water. Someone called it a

➡️

sea cow. That's the strangest name I ever heard. I sure wouldn't want anyone to call me that! Later I saw it is called a manatee. This creature's having lunch. I'm hungry, but I don't think I'd like to eat water plants for lunch. I want to learn more about this fascinating animal.

EXERCISE 8.1   Do a freewriting (3–5 minutes) on each of the following topics. When you finish your freewriting, underline a sentence that you might use to develop a descriptive paragraph.

1. A prized possession
2. A familiar household object
3. An interesting animal
4. A car, truck, or bike
5. A favorite poster

Organizing a Descriptive Paragraph

Like a personal narrative, a descriptive paragraph has three key parts:

- Topic sentence
- Supporting details
- Concluding sentence

The Topic Sentence

As in all paragraphs, the topic sentence of a descriptive paragraph announces the paragraph's focus to the reader. The focus must be narrow enough so that the description seems complete in one paragraph.

Topic: A prized possession

Unfocused topic sentence: One of my prized possessions is my collection of family photographs.

Focused topic sentence: The photograph of my mother and me at last year's family reunion is a prized possession.

The first attempt at a topic sentence is unfocused because the writer would have a difficult, if not impossible, task trying to describe all the photographs in the collection. The second topic sentence is more manageable because only two figures are in the picture.

Read each of the following sentences. Place a check mark in the blank by each focused topic sentence. Place an **X** in the blank by each unfocused sentence.

   _____ **1.** A battered Little League baseball bat hangs in the back of my brother's bedroom closet.

   _____ **2.** The tiny kitten, purring loudly, snuggles in my arms.

   _____ **3.** The rap group's last three CD covers are all similar in style.

   _____ **4.** The paintings hanging in the large art gallery are big and abstract.

   _____ **5.** The plate of Mexican food looks inviting to the eye and appeals to the taste buds.

The topic sentence of a descriptive paragraph should answer these questions:

- What did the writer observe?
- What impression did the observation make on the writer?

Look again at the topic sentence from the description at the beginning of this chapter:

The Norwegian troll doll stands guard on the bookcase shelf.

- What is the focus of this description?

  The writer focuses on a prized possession—a Norwegian troll doll.

- What impression did the observation make on the writer?

  The troll doll is guarding the room and watching for intruders.

This topic sentence is effective because it makes the reader wonder how and why a troll doll is standing guard. As in a narrative paragraph, the topic sentence in a descriptive paragraph should attract the curiosity of the reader without giving too much away.

Write a topic sentence for each topic from Exercise 8.1. For item 6, add a topic of your own choosing. In each topic sentence, underline your focused topic and circle the impression of the topic you want to communicate to your reader.

1. Topic: A prized possession

Topic sentence: _____

2. Topic: A familiar household object

Topic sentence: _____

3. Topic: An interesting animal

Topic sentence: _____

4. Topic: A car, truck, or bike

Topic sentence: _____

5. Topic: A favorite poster

Topic sentence: _____

6. Topic of your choice: _____

Topic sentence: _____

Supporting Details

The most successful descriptive paragraphs are rich in sensory details. A *sensory detail* is something you can observe with your five senses. It is a sight, sound, touch, smell, or taste associated with the object.

Here are some questions to help you get started collecting sensory details:

Sensory detail: Sight
- What is its size?

  How tall is it?
  How long is it?
  How wide is it?
  How much does it weigh?

- What is its shape?

  Is it round?
  Is it square or rectangular?
  Is it symmetrical?
  Is the shape normal or unusual?
  Does its shape change?

- What color or colors is it?

Is its color typical or surprising?

How are the colors arranged?

- What else looks like it?

Sensory Detail: Sound
- What sound or sounds are associated with it?
- When does it make a sound?
- Does it make a loud or soft sound?
- Is the sound repetitive?
- Is the tone of the sound high, medium, or low?
- Is the sound surprising?
- Does it sound like something else?

Sensory Detail: Touch
- How does it feel to the touch (soft, hard, furry, smooth, etc.)?
- Does it feel different from one part to the next?
- Does it feel as you would expect?
- Does it feel like something else?

Sensory Detail: Smell
- How does it smell (sweet, sour, sweaty, etc.)?
- Does this smell ever change?
- Does it smell like something else?
- Is this smell surprising in any way?

Sensory Detail: Taste
- How does it taste (bitter, sweet, sour, salty, etc.)?
- Does the taste ever vary?
- Does it taste like something else?
- Is the taste typical or unexpected?

Of course, not every question will apply to every object you observe. The purpose of these questions is to help you gather the kinds of physical details that will help your reader to picture the animal or object you are describing.

EXERCISE 8.4

Use the questions above to gather details about the topics in Exercise 8.1. List the answers to your questions. Do not worry about the order of your answers.

1.   Topic: A prized possession

Topic sentence: _____

Sensory detail 1: _____

Sensory detail 2: _____

Sensory detail 3: _____

2.   Topic: A familiar household object

Topic sentence: _____

Sensory detail 1: _____

Sensory detail 2: _____

Sensory detail 3: _____

3.   Topic: An interesting animal

Topic sentence: _____

Sensory detail 1: _____

Sensory detail 2: _____

Sensory detail 3: _____

4.   Topic: A car, truck, or bike

Topic sentence: _____

Sensory detail 1: _____

Sensory detail 2: _____

Sensory detail 3: _____

5.   Topic: A favorite poster

Topic sentence: _____

Sensory detail 1: _____

Sensory detail 2: _____

Sensory detail 3: _____

6.   Topic of your choice: _____

Topic sentence: _____

Sensory detail 1: _____

Sensory detail 2: _____

Sensory detail 3: _____

Note taking can also help you gather specific sensory details. Carefully observe the object for at least five minutes. While you observe, take notes that you can use later to write your descriptive paragraph. These notes do not have to be in complete sentences.

One way to set up your notes is to divide a piece of paper into two columns and write the word *objective* at the head of one column and the word *subjective* at the head of the other. On the objective side, use the sensory detail questions above to record the physical details of the animal or object: what you see, hear, touch, smell, and taste. Also be sure to record any changes that occur during your observation. In the subjective column, note your feelings or opinions about what you are observing. Does the subject of the observation remind you of something else? What are your impressions of what you are observing?

Suppose you were asked to write a description of your pet. Here is one writer's observation of her sleeping cat, Sammy:

Observation 1: Sammy

Objective	Subjective
Adult male cat (8 years old) named Sammy	Seems like yesterday that he was a kitten
Mostly black with white paws	
About 13 inches long (not including tail)	
Tail nearly 10 inches long	Tail almost as long as body
Approximately 12 pounds	
Soft to touch	Feels like soft cotton
Smooth, short fur	
Lying on back	How can he sleep like that?
Belly of white fur	
Legs in air	Looks funny in this position
Head turned to right side	
Tail extended from body	What is he dreaming about?

Notice that this writer has more notes on the objective side than on the subjective side. You do not need to take an equal number of notes on each side. How many notes you take will depend on the subject of your observation.

You may also need to make more than one observation. If you are observing an animal, it will change positions and activities many times during a single day. If you are observing an object, it may look different depending on the light. You will want to note these changes. Also, you may miss some important details during your first observation.

When this writer observes the cat again, he is awake. The writer includes some physical details omitted from the first observation.

| **Observation 2: Sammy** | |
Objective	Subjective
Sits looking at me with four feet on floor	What he is thinking?
Green eyes with large black pupils	Intelligent eyes
Frequently makes high-pitched, short meows	Is he trying to tell me something?
More white hair than I thought	
White hair coming out of ears	
White whiskers	
White hair under and above nose	
Ears up, set far apart on head	He's alert, ready to play.
I call his name.	What a smart cat!
Sammy meows and moves forward to greet me.	

Use your notes to help you collect the specific details you will need to write a strong descriptive paragraph.

EXERCISE 8.5

Complete observation notes on one of the topics in Exercise 8.1. You may need to do more than one observation.

After you have collected enough details, you must arrange them. Because you are trying to create a picture in the mind of your reader, you must present your ideas in a methodical way. Most descriptions are arranged spatially. Here are some possibilities:

- Left to right, right to left
- Top to bottom, bottom to top
- Front to back, back to front
- Near to far, far to near
- Inside to outside, outside to inside

Choose the order that you think will be most helpful to your reader. For example, some of the objective details about Sammy the cat can be arranged from his head to his tail:

- Sits upright looking at me with four feet on the floor
- Ears up, set far apart on head
- White hair coming out of ears

- Green eyes with large black pupils
- White whiskers
- White hair under and above nose
- Belly of white fur
- Tail extended from body

Study the objective details from your observation notes in Exercise 8.5. Using spatial order, arrange as many objective details as possible.

EXERCISE 8.6

The Concluding Sentence

Your descriptive paragraph needs a strong ending. Your reader should know not only what you have observed but also your reaction to your observation. What overall impression do you want to leave in the mind of your reader?

Before you write your concluding sentence, read your topic sentence again. Your concluding sentence should lead your reader back to where you began. Here is the topic sentence of the descriptive paragraph at the beginning of the chapter:

The Norwegian troll doll stands guard on the bookcase shelf.

The concluding sentence, like the topic sentence, refers to the troll's "guard" appearance:

This troll looks ready to gobble up any unwanted intruder.

Thus the concluding sentence reinforces the impression that the writer wants to leave with the reader.

Write a concluding sentence for each of your topic sentences in Exercise 8.3.

EXERCISE 8.7

1. Topic: A prized possession

   Topic sentence: _____

   Concluding sentence: _____

2. Topic: A familiar household object

   Topic sentence: _____

   Concluding sentence: _____

3. Topic: An interesting animal

   Topic sentence: _____

   Concluding sentence: _____

4. Topic: A car, truck, or bike

   Topic sentence: _____

   Concluding sentence: _____

5. Topic: A favorite poster

    Topic sentence: _____

    Concluding sentence: _____

6. Topic of your choice: _____

    Topic sentence: _____

    Concluding sentence: _____

TRANSITIONS IN DESCRIPTIVE PARAGRAPHS

Use transitional words and phrases to make your description easy for your reader to follow.

These transitional expressions are often found in descriptive paragraphs:

here	below	near	in the center	inside
there	beyond	beside	in the back	outside
above	behind	next to	at the bottom	to the right
at the top	further	opposite	at the front	to the left

EXERCISE 8.8

In each blank, write an appropriate transitional expression from the list above. Do not use the same transitional expression more than once.

1. To the left is a woman in formal dress. _____ is her companion in a tuxedo.

2. At the top of the chalkboard are the homework assignments for this week. _____ is the date of the next test.

3. Inside the computer is the central processing unit. _____ are the keyboard and mouse.

4. In the front of the painting stands a woman. _____ are her three children.

5. _____ are the stars in the brightly lit sky. Below is the city skyline.

EXERCISE 8.9

Underline the transitional words and phrases in the following descriptive paragraph.

My view of Ship Rock on the Navajo Reservation in New Mexico is stunning. At the bottom, rainwater has gathered to form a small stream. Here desert grasses in many shades of green and brown form small clumps in the water. Above, the brown earth stretches out from the stream to the base of Ship Rock. Beyond rises the powerful Ship Rock, a rock formation named for its resemblance to a sailing ship. This "ship" looks gray-black in the morning sun. Ship Rock is so gigantic that it serves as a landmark for desert wanderers. Next to Ship Rock are several rolling hills topped with smaller rock formations. Above is the expansive western sky. Puffy white clouds are mixed with patches of blue. This mixture of rock and water and sky is unforgettable.

FOCUS ON DICTION

To create lively images in your readers' minds, choose your adjectives and adverbs carefully.

Adjectives: The Color of the Sentence

Adjectives give your sentences color. *Adjectives* are used before nouns (names of persons, places, or things) or following linking verbs such as *is, are, was,* or *seems.* (For a list of linking verbs, see Chapter 5.)

Adjectives used before nouns answer three questions:

- **What kind of?**

   puffy white clouds (*Puffy* and *white* are adjectives answering the question "What kind of clouds?")

   expansive western sky (*Expansive* and *western* answer the question "What kind of sky?")

- **Which?**

   this mixture (The adjective *this* answers the question "Which mixture?")

   The words *a, an,* and *the* (called *articles*) are adjectives answering the question "Which?"

   a landmark

   the top

   Possessive words such as *my, our, his, her, your, its,* and *their* are also adjectives.

   our family

   my bike

   its food

- **How many?**

   many shades

   several rock formations

Other adjectives that can answer the question "How many?" include *few, most, some, that, this, these, each,* and *both.* Numbers appearing before nouns are also adjectives.

two teachers

twenty-five students

Adjectives are critical to your reader because they make more specific the meaning of the noun they accompany. Notice the difference between these two phrases:

adj.	noun
a	cat

adj.	adj.	adj.	adj.	noun
a	black-and-white	adult	male	cat

The use of specific adjectives is critical to the success of your descriptive paragraph.

EXERCISE 8.10

Underline the adjectives in the following sentences taken from the writing samples in this chapter. Use the first sentence as an example. **Hint:** Remember that *a, an,* and *the* are *always* adjectives. Prepositions (see Chapter 6) are *not* adjectives.

1. <u>The Norwegian troll</u> doll stands guard on <u>the bookcase</u> shelf.
2. Her olive green dress has long sleeves with an orange, one-pocket apron.
3. Her apron is tied in the back around her waist.
4. One of her arms is extended with the hand grasping a walking stick.
5. The witch-like doll has wild, purple-gray hair.
6. The other arm is behind her back with her hand resting on her left hip.
7. Yesterday at the zoo I saw this funny-looking animal swimming in a water tank.
8. It had a small head and a huge body.
9. At the bottom, rainwater has gathered to form a small stream.
10. Next to Ship Rock are several rolling hills topped with smaller rock formations.

Adjectives can also appear after linking verbs (see Chapter 5). Adjectives that follow linking verbs describe the subject of the sentence.

The water looks **cold.** (*cold* water)

The jazz band sounds **great.** (*great* jazz band)

The melon smells **fresh.** (*fresh* melon)

The trip has been **wonderful.** (*wonderful* trip)

Underline the adjectives in the following sentences. **Hint:** Some of these adjectives follow a linking verb.

1. The abstract painting is colorful.
2. My new truck is bright red with thin blue stripes around the bed.
3. The three-cheese lasagna tastes great.
4. The speakers for my new computer system are large.
5. The fresh bread smells wonderful.
6. The new teacher is nervous.
7. The cover for my English textbook is lively.
8. The grand piano looks small on the stage.
9. The political cartoon in the newspaper is funny.
10. The directions on the city map are helpful.

Adverbs: The Energy of the Sentence

Adverbs energize your sentences. *Adverbs,* which can appear anywhere in a sentence, answer four questions:

- **When?**

    Some adverbs that answer the question "When?" include *today, yesterday, tomorrow, hourly, daily, weekly, now, then, often, recently,* and *later.*

    Our plane leaves **tomorrow.**

    Maggie checks her e-mail **often.**

    Recently, I have been exercising **daily.**

    Finally, the subway train arrived at the station.

- **Where?**

    These adverbs include *here, there, anywhere, nowhere, everywhere, nearby, forward,* and *backward.*

    The children are playing **here** this afternoon.

    There is the new computer.

    I left my keys **somewhere.**

    Jonathan can go **everywhere** with us.

- **How?**

  Many adverbs that answer the question "How?" end in *-ly*. These adverbs are too numerous too list.

  Answer the question **carefully.**

  Quickly exit the room.

  David scores home runs **consistently.**

  The dog walks **painfully** on his injured leg.

- **How much?**

  Adverbs that answer the question "How much?" include *too, very, really, greatly, completely, entirely, partly,* and *partially.*

  The supervisor is **too** protective of his employees.

  My father is a **very** good cook.

  Adults should be **completely** responsible for their actions.

  Her writing skills have **greatly** improved this semester.

EXERCISE 8.12

Fill in each blank with an adverb answering the question in parentheses.

1. The tiger is (*how much?*) _____ quick in its movements.
2. The sleeping child lies (*how?*) _____ on the pillow.
3. The cuckoo clock chimes (*when?*) _____ each hour.
4. Dents, rust spots, and scratches cannot be found (*where?*) _____ on the body of the car.
5. The moon shines (*how much?*) _____ (*how?*) _____ on the surface of the water.

EXERCISE 8.13

Underline the adverbs in the following sentences. **Hint:** Some sentences contain more than one adverb.

1. Recently, I discovered an old photograph of two children playing happily in the sand.
2. Behind them, the waves gently break against the shoreline.
3. The children are too busy to notice that the waves will reach them soon.
4. The sun must have been shining very brightly on this morning.
5. Light green water completely fills the top of the photograph.

6. The child sitting on the left is nearly six years old.

7. She is turned to the side, and her right arm stretches playfully toward the sand.

8. She is concentrating intently on the sand castle in front of her.

9. There on the right side of the photograph is her four-year-old helper.

10. Her assistant is cautiously pouring water from an orange bucket onto the sand.

11. Slowly the sand castle is taking shape.

12. Four towers have been carefully formed.

13. A newly dug hole forms the center of the castle.

14. The sand castle will disappear soon with the waves quickly coming.

15. The happiness of children is a very great gift.

FOCUS ON REVISING: USING A THESAURUS

Using lively adjectives and adverbs can greatly improve your writing. But what if you cannot think of the word you need to express your idea clearly? Or what if you have repeated an adjective or an adverb too many times in your paper? Consider using a thesaurus, a special dictionary of synonyms. A *synonym* is a word with the same meaning as another word. For example, a synonym for *nice* is *kind*. A word can have more than one synonym. The word *quickly* has these synonyms, among others: *hurriedly, fast, rapidly, hastily,* and *lickety-split.*

You can locate a thesaurus in several ways:

- In book format such as *Webster's Thesaurus* or *Roget's Thesaurus*
- As a feature of some handheld spell checkers or translators
- As part of the grammar checker of some word processors

Caution: Be sure that the synonym you use has the meaning you intend. If you are not sure of the meaning of a synonym, look it up in a dictionary.

Use a thesaurus to find synonyms for the common adjectives below. Write at least four synonyms for each word.

EXERCISE 8.14

1. beautiful _____

2. important _____

3. young _____

4. kind _____

5. bad _____

EXERCISE 8.15

Write a sentence using one of the synonyms you found for each adjective in Exercise 8.14. Underline the synonym you use. Be sure to place the synonym before a noun or after a linking verb. Use the first sentence as a model.

1. (*beautiful*) The view from the top of the mountain was <u>breathtaking</u>.

2. (*important*) _____

3. (*young*) _____

4. (*kind*) _____

5. (*bad*) _____

EXERCISE 8.16

Use a thesaurus to find at least four synonyms for each of the common adverbs below. **Hint:** If your thesaurus gives you the adjective form of the synonym, you may need to add *-ly*.

1. rudely _____

2. softly _____

3. surely _____

4. often _____

5. now _____

EXERCISE 8.17

Write a sentence using one of the synonyms you found for each adverb in Exercise 8.16. Underline the synonym you use. Be sure to place the synonym before a noun or after a linking verb. Use the first sentence as a model.

1. (*rudely*) I heard the new supervisor speak <u>harshly</u> to an employee.

2. (*softly*) _____

3. (*surely*) _____

4. (*often*) _____

5. (*now*) _____

Revising Tip: Using a Thesaurus

Many word processing programs include a thesaurus. In some programs, the thesaurus is part of the grammar checker; in others, the thesaurus is a separate tool. The thesaurus will suggest a list of synonyms for a word you select. If you do not know the meaning of a particular synonym, the thesaurus may be able to give you some definitions.

FOCUS ON EDITING

When you write a descriptive paragraph, you want your reader to share your observation. Therefore, you may choose to use the present tense of verbs. If so, you should follow the principles of subject-verb agreement.

Subject-Verb Agreement

The grammatical term *tense* refers to the time of the action expressed in the verb. *Present tense* means that the action is happening in the present time. In the present tense, subjects agree with their verbs when the correct verb form is used. The principle of *subject-verb agreement* states that verbs must agree with their subjects in number.

◆ If the subject of a sentence is *he*, *she*, *it*, or any singular subject, the verb (in the present tense) must also be singular (representing *one*).

Here is the singular present tense for the verb *walk:*

Singular		Subject	Verb
First person		I	walk
Second person		you	walk
Third person		he, she, it	walks
		boy	walks
		woman	walks
		tiger	walks

Notice that the first person and second person subjects are pronouns (*I* and *you*). The third person subject can be a singular pronoun (*he, she, it*) or a singular noun (*boy, woman, tiger*).

Note: A singular verb in the present tense ends in the letter *s*. Many students are confused because they associate the letter *s* with plural words. However, an -*s* ending on a verb *always* indicates a singular verb.

TABLE 8.1	**Present Tense Endings: Subjects and Verbs**
Singular Subject: no -s	*Singular Verb (third person):* -s
athlete	is
tiger	walks

EXERCISE 8.18   In each sentence below, underline the simple subject. Then underline the correct verb in parentheses.

1.   The white Bengal tiger (*lies, lie*) on the green grass in its zoo home.

2.   This animal (*is, are*) not an albino.

3.   It (*has, have*) distinct features.

4.   One distinct feature (*is, are*) its blue eyes.

5.   Another (*is, are*) its pink nose.

6.   Furthermore, each stripe (*is, are*) chocolate brown in color.

7.   This animal (*appears, appear*) about three yards long.

8.   It (*weighs, weigh*) about four hundred pounds.

9.   The white tiger (*does, do*) require special breeding.

10.   Only a zoo (*houses, house*) this rare breed.

◆   If the subject of a sentence is *we, they,* or any plural noun, the verb (in the present tense) must also be plural (representing *more than one*).

Here is the plural present tense for the verb *walk*:

Plural		Subject	Verb
First person		we	walk
Second person		you	walk
Third person		they	walk
		boys	walk
		women	walk
		tigers	walk

Again, the first and second person subjects are pronouns (*they* and *we*). The third person subject can be a plural pronoun (*they*) or a plural noun (*boys, women, tigers*).

Note: A plural verb *never* ends in the letter -*s*.

TABLE 8.2	**Present Tense Endings: Subjects and Verbs**
Plural Subject: -s	*Plural Verb (third person): no* -s
athletes	are
tigers	walk

For each verb in parentheses, underline the simple subject. Then underline the correct verb in parentheses.

1. In addition to the white Bengal tigers, typical orange-striped tigers also (*lives, live*) in this zoo.

2. In the tiger exhibit, two tigers (*roams, roam*) the area.

3. These tigers (*is, are*) not Bengals; only a few Bengal tigers (*resides, reside*) in North American zoos.

4. Instead, they (*is, are*) Siberian tigers, originally found in Russia.

5. They (*looks, look*) tame as they (*enters, enter*) the shade of a rock formation.

6. Both animals (*lies, lie*) down in the shade, protected from the afternoon sun.

7. Their paws (*stretches, stretch*) out in front of them.

8. Soon each animal's head (*rests, rest*) on its paws.

9. Their tails (*curls, curl*) around the powerful hindquarters of their bodies.

10. Captive breeding programs (*is, are*) helping to preserve this endangered species.

The subject can be hard to spot in some instances. In the following cases, the subject can be difficult to find and the correct verb difficult to determine. In each case, the verb is in the present tense.

Case 1: The subject of a sentence is never found in a prepositional phrase. The subject, not an object of a preposition, determines the verb.

You learned about prepositional phrases in Chapter 6. Prepositional phrases sometimes come between the subject and the verb. Here is an example:

subject	prep. phrase(s)	verb
The employees	in the training program	work hard.

Subjects are *not* found in prepositional phrases. Therefore, to expose the subject, cross out the prepositional phrase, and then ask yourself the question "Who or What _____?"

The employees in the training program work hard.

In this case, ask yourself, "Who or what works hard?" *Employees* is the subject. *Employees* is plural; therefore, the verb *work* does not end in *-s*.

To check for subject-verb agreement in this case, follow these three steps:

- Cross out prepositional phrases.
- Find the subject (ask, "Who" or "What?").
- Make sure the subject and verb agree (both are singular or both are plural).

Examine the following sentence:

One of the best players on the team (*is, are*) on first base.

Apply the three steps:

- Cross out prepositional phrases.

  One ~~of the best players on the team~~ (*is, are*) ~~on first base~~.

- Find the subject.

  Ask, "Who is on first base?" *One.*

- Make sure the subject and verb agree (both are singular or both are plural).

  The subject *one* is singular. Because the verb is singular (ends in *-s*), the verb must be *is*.

EXERCISE 8.20

Use the three-step method to determine the verb. (You may want to review the list of prepositions in Chapter 6.) In each sentence, underline the simple subject, and underline the correct verb in parentheses.

1. One of the members of the band (*is, are*) late.
2. Brian along with Matt (*plans, plan*) to go this weekend.
3. The students in the back of the classroom (*listens, listen*) carefully.
4. The dancer on the stage (*twirls, twirl*) quickly.
5. The coach of the swimming team (*encourages, encourage*) the team members.
6. The performers in the play (*is, are*) nervous.
7. All ten of the student government leaders (*is, are*) attending the convention next weekend.
8. The advertisements before the movie (*is, are*) annoying.
9. The interior of both cars (*is, are*) charcoal gray.
10. The new styles for fall (*resembles, resemble*) the 1970s styles.
11. Both of my aunts (*teaches, teach*) math.
12. One of my coworkers (*calls, call*) in sick every week.
13. Only two of my last three jobs (*has, have*) paid minimum wage.

14. Several old friends from high school (*is, are*) visiting town next week.

15. Both cars in the showroom (*is, are*) luxury sports cars.

Case 2: When the word *and* links two or more subjects, the subjects are usually considered plural. Therefore, the verb must also be plural (no -*s*).

subject + **subject** **verb**
Beth and **Carolyn** <u>enjoy</u> math courses.

The word *and* is like an addition sign:

one subject + one subject = two subjects = plural verb

The same rule applies in the examples below:

English and science <u>are</u> my two favorite subjects.

The lead **actor** in the play and the **director** of the play <u>are</u> cousins.

If the two subjects joined by *and* act together as a single unit, they are singular.

Rock and roll from the 1970s <u>is</u> my favorite music.

Bacon and eggs <u>is</u> a great breakfast.

Underline the correct verb in each sentence.

EXERCISE 8.21

1. Peanut butter and jelly (*is, are*) Robert's favorite sandwich.

2. Both faculty and administration (*is, are*) busy during final exam week.

3. Spring rolls and Chinese fried rice (*is, are*) two foods I enjoy.

4. The movie *Frankie and Johnny* (*is, are*) one of my favorites.

5. Walking and swimming (*provides, provide*) excellent exercise.

6. Fishing and playing football (*is, are*) my favorite pastimes.

7. Both Ms. Rodriguez and Mr. Roche (*plans, plan*) field trips each year.

8. The student in the back row and the student in the front row (*works, work*) together in the cafeteria.

9. Long life and good health (*is, are*) important to me.

10. Both my teacher last semester and my teacher this semester (*tutors, tutor*) students.

Case 3: When subjects are joined by *or, nor, either . . . or,* or *neither . . . nor,* the verb agrees with the closest subject.

If the subject closest to the verb is singular, then the verb is singular (ends in -*s.*)

Cory *or* **Barbara** <u>works</u> on Saturday. (singular)

If the subject closest to the verb is plural, then the verb is plural (does not end in -*s*).

Cory *or* his **friends** <u>work</u> on Saturday. (plural)

Look how the verb changes in the following cases:

Either the coach *or* the **captain** <u>calls</u> the play. (singular)

Either the coach *or* the **co-captains** <u>call</u> the play. (plural)

Neither Jan *nor* **Carolyn** <u>attends</u> the class. (singular)

Neither Carolyn *nor* her **friends** <u>attend</u> the class. (plural)

Notice that the subject in bold letters determines whether the verb is singular or plural.

Writers sometimes confuse case 2 and case 3. Remember that the conjunctions *or* and *nor* do not have the same meaning as the conjunction *and.* The word *and* between two subjects makes the subjects plural, but when the conjunction *or* and *nor* joins two subjects, the subject closest to the verb will control the verb.

EXERCISE 8.22

Underline the simple subject closest to the verb. Then underline the correct verb in parentheses.

1. Neither the president nor the vice-president of the club (*has, have*) plans to attend next month's meeting.

2. Either the supervisor of the factory or his representatives (*plans, plan*) to meet with the union leader next week.

3. Biology lab or anatomy lab (*is, are*) offered on Tuesdays next semester.

4. Walking or swimming (*provides, provide*) excellent exercise.

5. Neither Fred nor his coworkers (*is, are*) expecting a raise.

6. Either Traci or Bonnie (*wants, want*) to come over to study.

7. Neither the scientists nor government officials (*has, have*) determined the cause of the accident.

8. Either the local government or the state government (*is, are*) expected to raise taxes next year.

9. Neither the judge nor the lawyer (*believes, believe*) the defendant.

10. Fruit salad or soup (*makes, make*) an excellent appetizer.

Case 4: These subjects are always singular:

either (of)	neither (of)
each (of)	one (of)

The words *either*, *each*, *neither*, and *one* are often followed by a prepositional phrase beginning with *of*. In this case, the verb is singular.

Each of the girls **plays** the clarinet. (singular)

Neither of the team members **has** won a championship. (singular)

One of the students **writes** in a journal every day. (singular)

Case 5: The following subjects are always singular.

any**one**	any**body**	any**thing**
every**one**	every**body**	every**thing**
some**one**	some**body**	some**thing**
no **one**	no**body**	no**thing**

Notice that most of these words end in *one* and *body*. *One* is singular, and so is *body* (*bodies* = plural). So all these words take singular verbs.

Anybody **enjoys** going to the movies.

Something in this room **smells** musty.

Everyone **likes** to visit new places.

In each sentence, underline the simple subject, and underline the correct verb in parentheses.

EXERCISE 8.23

1. Each of the students (*is, are*) expecting to do well on the midterm exam.

2. Neither of the players (*was, were*) chosen for the all-star team.

3. Either of the actors (*is, are*) competing for the lead in the play.

4. Each of us (*has, have*) questions for the instructor.

5. One of the students (*works, work*) in the learning center.

6. Someone (*forgets, forget*) my birthday every year.

7. Everybody (*needs, need*) a parking permit.

8. Everyone (*is, are*) willing to volunteer at the elementary school.

9. Either of the employees (*works, work*) evening hours.

10. Neither of the athletes (*is, are*) playing at a professional level.

Case 6: The words *there* and *here* cannot be the subject of a sentence.

In many sentences beginning with *there* or *here*, the subject following the verb controls whether the verb is singular or plural.

There <u>go</u> the **runners.**

Here <u>is</u> the winner of the **competition.**

To determine the correct verb, turn the sentence around so that the subject comes before the verb:

The **runners** <u>go</u> there.

The **winner** of the competition <u>is</u> here.

EXERCISE 8.24

Rearrange each of the following sentences so that the subject comes before the verb. Write your rearranged sentences in the blanks. Then underline the simple subjects and circle the verbs.

1. Here are next week's homework assignments.

_____

2. Here are the plans for next week's meeting.

_____

3. There are the new textbooks for the course.

_____

4. There is an old lookout tower on top of the mountain.

_____

5. Here is the list of vacation days for this year.

_____

EXERCISE 8.25

Skill Check: Subject-Verb Agreement

In each sentence, underline the subject, and underline the correct verb in parentheses.

1. Fascinating sea creatures (*lives, live*) underneath the ocean's surface.

2. One of the most fascinating of these creatures (*is, are*) the shark.

3. There (*swims, swim*) two hammerhead sharks in the tank in front of me.

4. Each of these hammerheads (*is, are*) a bottom feeder.

5. Coral reefs and the ocean bottom (*is, are*) its habitat.

6. The most noticeable feature of this hammerhead shark (*is, are*) its T-shaped head.

7. Scientists (*believes, believe*) that the head (*acts, act*) as a rudder.

8. A powerful group of muscles (*provides, provide*) motion.

9. The shark's brain (*is, are*) not as impressive as its teeth.

10. Even large sharks such as those in the tank (*has, have*) tiny brains.

11. The eyesight of these sharks (*is, are*) probably poor.

12. Most sharks (*relies, rely*) on their sense of smell rather than their sense of sight.

13. The teeth of this hammerhead (*is, are*) sharp.

14. Several rows of teeth (*helps, help*) the shark feed on its prey.

15. Fortunately, neither of these sharks (*seems, seem*) hungry.

16. A powerful tail (*is, are*) noticeable on each shark.

17. A slap of a shark's tail (*is, are*) often deadly.

18. The tails of sharks (*is, are*) covered with sharp scales.

19. Sharks often (*swipes, swipe*) their tails against their prey before they attack.

20. Everyone (*seems, seem*) amazed by these creatures of the deep.

Two Problem Verbs: *Be* and *Do*

The most commonly used verb in the English language is the verb *be*. Here is the present tense of the verb *be:*

Singular		Plural	
First person	I am	**First person**	we are
Second person	you are	**Second person**	you are
Third person	he, she, it (*or any singular noun*) is	**Third person**	they (*or any plural subject*) are

Watch for these errors in the third person:

✗ He be coming over this weekend.
✔ **He is** coming over this weekend.

✗ They be late for class every day.
✔ **They are** late for class every day.

Another problem verb is *do*. Below are the correct forms of this verb:

Singular		Plural	
First person	I do	**First person**	we do
Second person	you do	**Second person**	you do
Third person	he, she, it (*or any singular noun*) does	**Third person**	they (*or any plural subject*) do

Again, watch for problems when you are using the third person:

✘   She do everything right.
✔   **She _does_** everything right.

Beware also of using *don't* ("do not") with *he, she, I,* or *it*:

✘   He don't want to go with us.
✔   **He _doesn't_** want to go with us.

✘   It don't matter to me.
✔   **It _doesn't_** matter to me.

EXERCISE 8.26

Write **C** in the blank if the verb in bold type is correct. If the verb is incorrect, write the correct form in the blank.

_____   **1.**   Jack **don't** like to ask questions in class.

_____   **2.**   Tonya **be** studying two hours every day.

_____   **3.**   That solution to the problem **does** work.

_____   **4.**   She **be** the first in line.

_____   **5.**   That test score **don't** affect my grade in the class.

_____   **6.**   My parents **do** encourage me to make good grades in my classes.

_____   **7.**   That cake **do** look good.

_____   **8.**   They **be** waiting for us around the corner.

_____   **9.**   It **don't** matter as long as you say you're sorry.

_____   **10.**   Joanne **does** her best on every test.

 ## Using Past Tense

In the English language, verbs are either regular or irregular.

Regular Verbs

Regular verbs add *-ed* to form the past tense and past participle. The *past tense* indicates action that has previously occurred. The *past participle* expresses action that happened in the distant, rather than the recent, past.

Present	Mary **walks** home.
Past	Mary **walked** home.
Past participle	Mary **has walked** home.
	We **have walked** home.
	They **had walked** home.

Notice that the past participle form requires a helping verb—*has, have,* or *had.* Below are just a few of the many regular verbs in the English language:

Regular Verbs

Present	Past	Past Participle (*has, have, had*)
talk	talked	talked
roar	roared	roared
listen	listened	listened
push	pushed	pushed
tackle	tackled	tackled

Change each boldfaced present tense verb to past tense. Write the past tense form in the blank.

EXERCISE 8.27

1. The red car **races** through the intersection. _____
2. The chefs carefully **prepare** each entrée. _____
3. Dane **starts** the job on Monday. _____
4. Caroline **works** the late shift on weekends. _____
5. My family **lives** in Buffalo, New York. _____
6. The twins **crawl** on the living room floor. _____
7. Many shoppers **crowd** the mall on weekends. _____
8. The student **listens** carefully to the instructions. _____
9. The drops of dew **glisten** on the grass. _____
10. The lion **roars** in its cage. _____

Change each present tense verb in bold type to the past participle form. **Hint:** Use *has, have,* or *had* as a helping verb.

EXERCISE 8.28

1. The red car **races** through the intersection. _____
2. The chefs carefully **prepare** each entrée. _____
3. Dane **starts** the job on Monday. _____
4. Caroline **works** the late shift on weekends. _____
5. My family **lives** in Buffalo, New York. _____

6. The twins **crawl** on the living room floor.   _____

7. Many shoppers **crowd** the mall on weekends.   _____

8. The student **listens** carefully to the instructions. _____

9. The drops of dew **glisten** on the grass.   _____

10. The lion **roars** in its cage.   _____

Irregular Verbs

Irregular verbs form the past tense and past participle in many different ways. That's why they are called irregular. Here is a common irregular verb:

Present	George **writes** letters.
Past	George **wrote** letters.
Past participle	George **has written** letters.
	We **have written** letters.
	They **had written** letters.

Again, notice that the past participle form requires a helping verb.

There are many irregular verbs in English. The most common irregular verb is *be*. Here is the past tense form of *be*:

Singular	**Plural**
I was	we were
you were	you were
he, she, it (*or any singular noun*) was	they (*or any plural noun*) were

Following is the past participle form of *be*:

Singular	**Plural**
I have (*or had*) been	we have (*or had*) been
you have (*or had*) been	you have (*or had*) been
he, she, it (*or any singular noun*) has (*or had*) been	they (*or any plural noun*) have (*or had*) been

EXERCISE 8.29

In each blank, write the correct form of the verb *be*.

1. It _____ a pleasure working with the team last week.

2. You _____ the first to finish the test yesterday.

3. Until his sister left for college this week, Juan _____ the first college student in his family.

4. The runners _____ exhausted from their marathon race last Wednesday.

5. Since last September, we _____ employees of a local computer company.

6. They _____ lucky enough to win the lottery last weekend.

7. Kate _____ my friend since sixth grade.

8. I _____ on time to every class this semester.

9. We _____ pleased with the car we bought last September.

10. It _____ a long time since I first started my diet.

Here are some other irregular verbs:

Present	Past	Past Participle (use with *has, have,* or *had*)
become	became	become
begin	began	begun
blow	blew	blown
break	broke	broken
bring	brought	brought
buy	bought	bought
catch	caught	caught
choose	chose	chosen
come	came	come
do	did	done
draw	drew	drawn
drink	drank	drunk
drive	drove	driven
eat	ate	eaten
fall	fell	fallen
fight	fought	fought
fly	flew	flown
forget	forgot	forgotten
forgive	forgave	forgiven
get	got	gotten
give	gave	given
go	went	gone
have	had	had
hide	hid	hidden
know	knew	known
lay	laid	laid
lie	lay	lain

make	made	made
meet	met	met
ride	rode	ridden
ring	rang	rung
rise	rose	risen
run	ran	run
see	saw	seen
shake	shook	shaken
sing	sang	sung
sit	sat	sat
speak	spoke	spoken
spring	sprang	sprung
swim	swam	swum
take	took	taken
tear	tore	torn
understand	understood	understood
win	won	won
write	wrote	written

You can also use a dictionary to look up the past tense and past participle forms of irregular verbs.

EXERCISE 8.30

In each sentence, use the list above to fill in the correct form of the verb in parentheses. **Hint:** If a helping verb is present, use the past participle form.

1. (*come*) I have _____ to the aquarium to observe the fish.

2. (*forget*) You may have _____ to give me your new phone number.

3. (*meet*) John _____ his old girlfriend for dinner last week.

4. (*shake*) The dog _____ off his leash and ran away.

5. (*rise*) The sun has just _____ over the horizon.

6. (*speak*) Mrs. James has _____ to her supervisor about a raise.

7. (*take*) The flight _____ off an hour late.

8. (*sing*) The country western band has _____ together for years.

9. (*go*) Josh _____ to pick up a loaf of bread and some milk.

10. (*write*) Many writers have _____ about love.

In each sentence, fill in the correct form of the verb in parentheses. If a helping verb is present, use the past participle form.

1. (*see*) He has _____ many Broadway shows.
2. (*win*) The team has _____ three state championships.
3. (*hide*) The child _____ the money under the mattress.
4. (*forgive*) Sean has _____ me.
5. (*lay*) The teacher _____ the book on the desk.
6. (*drink*) The cats have _____ all the milk.
7. (*drive*) Have you _____ downtown lately?
8. (*become*) Mr. Johnson _____ president of the company last year.
9. (*run*) Susan _____ for class treasurer but lost.
10. (*eat*) Had the child _____ breakfast yet?

Skill Check: Past Tense

Change each of the words in bold type to the past tense form of the verb.

The huge manatee **swims** gracefully in the sea-green water, despite its gigantic size. Usually found in the warm waters of the Gulf of Mexico and the Caribbean, this creature **is** confined to a water tank at the zoo. The manatee, otherwise known as a sea cow, **is** eating a lunch of water plants. As I **watch** the gray animal swim across the tank, I **notice** its large body. It **appears** to be about eight feet long and **weighs** approximately a thousand pounds. Amazingly, there **are** no hind flippers, but the animal **has** a large, flat tail that **helps** it move smoothly through the water with its two companions—another adult manatee and a baby. At the front of its body **are** two well-developed flippers located close to the head. As the manatee **turns** to face me, I **notice** its laughably small head. Why **does** such a large animal have such a small head? Its two eyes **look** intelligent, and I **wonder** what the manatee **is** thinking of me. When Christopher Columbus saw the manatee, he thought it was a mermaid. This manatee **moves** with the grace of a mermaid, but it **does** not have a mermaid's body!

> **Editing Hint**
>
> Working with verbs can be tricky. Here is a suggestion. If you know that the subject is singular and masculine, read the sentence substituting the pronoun *he*. This will make it easier for you to choose the correct verb.
>
> **The man on the street** (*is, are*) waiting for a cab.
>
> **He is** waiting for a cab.
>
> If the subject is singular and feminine, read the sentence substituting *she*. If the subject is plural, substitute the pronoun *they*.
>
> Use this tip to edit your papers for correct verb usage.

FOCUS ON PEER REVIEW

When you have finished drafting a descriptive paragraph, you are ready to participate in peer review. Use the following questions to guide you:

1. Does the topic sentence limit the focus to a specific object?

2. Does the topic sentence state an overall impression of the object?

3. Does the writer include sensory details so that reader can share the observation? List at least three sensory details the writer uses.

4. What order does the writer use to organize the details in the body of this paragraph? Is this order logical and appropriate for the topic?

5. Is the concluding sentence effective? Why or why not?

6. List any transitional words or phrases in the paragraph.

7. List at least five adjectives the writer uses to describe the object.

8. List at least three adverbs in the paragraph.

9. Are there any errors in subject-verb agreement in the paragraph? If so, list them.

10. What verb tense does the writer use? Is this verb tense used throughout the paragraph?

11. Are there any fragments in the paragraph? If so, how could they be corrected?

12. Are there any comma splices or run-ons? If so, where do they occur?

13. Make a list of any errors in spelling or punctuation.

14. What I like most about this description is _____

    _____.

15. This area needs more work: _____

    _____.

In the following description, the writer assumes the role of a common household object. Form a small group and use this paragraph to answer the peer review questions.

EXERCISE 8.33

Student Sample

I am a familiar household appliance that works all day long. I have at least one door—and sometimes two or three. My exterior can be any color—designer white, contemporary almond, basic black, avocado green, harvest gold, shell pink, or electric turquoise. On a hot day, I chill out, especially if the air conditioner is on vacation. People of all ages put their sweaty faces on my cool, smooth outside and say, "Ah, that feels good." Since I am good-natured, I go about my daily business, humming to myself. When it comes to thirst, no problem! With the necessary equipment, I can fill a glass with crunchy cubes of crystal-clear ice floating on chilled water. Inside me, all kinds of goodies are stashed on gleaming chrome-and-glass shelves. In the center today is yesterday's pizza, loaded with extra cheese and juicy mushrooms, carefully packaged to microwave into a warm, gooey snack. To the left are yesterday's cupcakes, with tempting dark fudge icing dripping with butter. Yes, I'm always here, a cool friend—the refrigerator.

—Patricia Montgomery Smith

WRITING ASSIGNMENT

Write a descriptive paragraph focusing on an object or an animal. Follow the steps of the writing process in Chapter 2. You can choose one of the topics in Exercise 8.1. Some other possible topics include

- An unusual piece of furniture
- A CD (or book) cover
- An advertisement from a magazine
- A cartoon
- A musical instrument

Writers as Spiders

You will find many colorful images of objects on the World Wide Web. Using these images, you can practice writing descriptive paragraphs.

Web Exercise 1

Suppose you want to buy a new or used car. Using a search engine such as Ask Jeeves <http://www.askjeeves.com> or Dogpile <http://www.dogpile.com>, ask for information about a specific car (give the model year and the name of the car). Then locate a web site recommended by the search engine. Find a picture of the car you want to buy, and write a paragraph describing the exterior features of this car.

Web Exercise 2

Many of the graphical images you see on the web are digital photographs. One site featuring a huge number of photographs is

http://www.photovault.com

At this site you will find pictures of a wide range of animals, including amphibians, birds, fish, insects, mammals, and reptiles.

Locate one of these pictures. You can select and enlarge an image so that you can study it more closely.

Write a paragraph about this picture as if you were describing it to someone who could not see it.

Additional Help

To review the rules of subject-verb agreement, see

http://leo.stcloud.msus.edu/grammar/subverag.html

You can practice subject-verb agreement at this site:

http://www.hputx.edu/Academics/English/wlsvagfr.htm

For more information about regular versus irregular verbs, consult

http://97.com/pi/writing._center/83.html

This site offers a list of irregular verbs:

http://owl.english.purdue.edu/Files/75.html

CHAPTER 8

Focus on Description: Part II

This chapter focuses on describing a person or a place. To find descriptions of people and places, look no further than your local newspaper. Many "Help Wanted" ads, for instance, describe a type of person:

> Our company has an immediate need for an accounting assistant. The ideal candidate for this job likes working with details and has at least two years experience in the field. We need someone who has strong time management skills and familiarity with accounting software. We especially want someone who can work independently and is willing to take on challenging responsibilities and special projects. The candidate for this job will receive opportunities for professional growth as well as a competitive salary and benefits.

The classified ads also feature descriptions of places. Here is a description of a luxury home in a beach community:

> This beautiful pool home is one of a kind. It offers three bedrooms, two baths, a family room, a study, a formal living room, and a game room. Special features include vaulted ceilings, a gas fireplace, a security system, a central vacuum system, and ceramic tile floors. A wet bar complements the pool and spa. This unique house is just five minutes from the beach.

Whether you are describing a person or a place, the purpose is to use words to create a lively picture in the mind of the reader. The reader can then share your thoughts.

DESCRIBING PEOPLE

How often do you take the time to notice the people around you? Writing a physical description of a person gives you a chance to develop a "writer's eye" and observe things you may never have noticed about the people with whom you come in contact.

A description of a person, however, does not have to be limited to appearance, as the "Help Wanted" ad demonstrates. You can also observe a person's actions, as in the following paragraph:

> The professional baseball player is confident as he steps up to home plate. With three runners on base, two outs, two strikes, and three balls, the pressure is intense. Twice, he taps the bat on the far side of home plate. As he digs the cleats of his shoes into the dirt, he looks like a bull preparing to charge a matador. He looks for a moment at the ground. Maybe he is praying for good luck. As he raises his chin, he glares at the pitcher and adjusts his helmet, proudly displaying the team's logo. He raises his bat at the proper angle and swings a few times, daring the pitcher to throw a strike. Then he awaits the ball, knowing he will have only a fraction of a second to decide whether to swing at the object traveling toward him at more than ninety miles per hour. Anyone observing this athlete can see the intensity of his focus. This confident athlete never gives the pitcher, his teammates, or the crowd a sign that he is anything but sure of himself.

Not only does this descriptive paragraph *tell* us about the player, but it also *shows* us the player in action.

DESCRIBING PLACES

When you describe a place, you create a mental image so your reader can also visit that place. The following is an example:

> My favorite picnic spot is a large boulder in the middle of a rushing mountain stream. Across the stream, large evergreens hug the edge of the water. Even at noon these woods look dark, mysterious, and uninviting. The ➡

stream, however, glimmers in the light of the noon sun. In this part of the stream are huge gray boulders with flat tabletops. They jut above the water, forcing the stream to make its way around them. The tops of the boulders are large enough for four people to spread out a tablecloth for a picnic. This picnic, however, will be noisy. Standing on the bank of the stream, I hear the constant roar of the water. Fortunately, the bank beside the river road is not very steep. A few well-placed steps lead to the water's edge. Small rocks in the river create stepping-stones for picnickers. This marriage of rock and water creates an excellent scene for a picnic.

Descriptive paragraphs of people and places, like the examples above, have topic sentences, supporting details, and concluding sentences. Most, like the paragraph observing the picnic spot, are organized according to spatial order. The description of the mountain stream starts across the water and ends at the water's edge. A descriptive paragraph of a person emphasizing action, such as the example of the baseball player, can also be organized using time order.

In Chapter 8, you learned to use lively details to describe objects. A descriptive paragraph focusing on a person or place also depends on interesting details to

- Attract the reader's attention
- Paint a "word picture" for the reader

Choosing a Topic

As in all paragraphs, you need to limit the focus when you describe a person or a place. Before she made her observation, the writer who described the baseball player used brainstorming to list the kinds of details she wanted to observe. She did not worry about using complete sentences but just jotted down the ideas as fast as she could.

Batter at the plate

How many runners on base

How many strikes and balls

How many outs

Batter's movements

Batter's attitude

Waiting for the pitch

A brainstorming list helps you think through the kinds of details you should observe. As you observe, you can, of course, collect notes about anything not on the list. However, having a list ahead of time will help you get more out of the time you spend observing.

Brainstorm a list of things to observe about each of the following topics.

EXERCISE 9.1

1. A favorite relative
2. A talented athlete
3. A child at play
4. A room in my home
5. A favorite restaurant

ORGANIZING A DESCRIPTION OF A PERSON OR A PLACE

Like a description of an object (see Chapter 8), a descriptive paragraph focusing on a person or place has all three key elements of any successful paragraph:

- Topic sentence
- Supporting details
- Concluding sentence

The Topic Sentence

In your topic sentence, your reader should discover

- The focus of your observation
- Your overall impression of the person or place

As you learned in Chapter 8, the topic sentence of a descriptive paragraph should announce the focus of your paragraph and also state the impression the observation made on you, the writer. In other words:

Topic sentence = Focused topic + Overall impression

The first part of the topic sentence is the focused topic. Limit your topic so that you can finish the description in a single paragraph. For example, if you want to write on the topic "a child at play," you can limit your description to a particular child, as in the following:

Topic: A child at play

Focused topic: My four-year-old niece, Frances, playing an imaginary game

You might limit another topic this way:

Topic: A talented athlete

Focused topic: A professional baseball player

EXERCISE 9.2

For each of the following topics, write a focused topic.

1. Topic: A favorite relative

Focused topic: _____

2. Topic: A talented athlete

Focused topic: _____

3. Topic: A child at play

Focused topic: _____

4. Topic: A room in my home

Focused topic: _____

5. Topic: A favorite restaurant

Focused topic: _____

Writers often use adjectives and adverbs to state the dominant impression in the topic sentence. Consider the following topic sentence:

My four-year-old niece, Frances, happily plays an imaginary game.

- **What is the focus of this description?**

  A four-year-old niece, Frances, playing

- **What is the writer's impression?**

  The writer uses an adverb, *happily*, to state an overall impression.

In the paragraph about the professional baseball player [earlier in this chapter], the topic sentence is

The professional baseball player is confident as he steps up to home plate.

- **What is the focus of this description?**

  The writer has limited the focus to *a professional baseball player*.

- **What is the writer's impression?**

  The adjective *confident* conveys the writer's dominant impression to the reader.

Write a topic sentence for each topic in Exercise 9.2. Circle the words that present the focus of your observation. Underline the word or words that express the dominant impression.

1. Topic: A favorite relative

   Focused topic: _____

   Topic sentence: _____

2. Topic: A talented athlete

   Focused topic: _____

   Topic sentence: _____

3. Topic: A child at play

   Focused topic: _____

   Topic sentence: _____

4. Topic: A room in my home

   Focused topic: _____

   Topic sentence: _____

5. Topic: A favorite restaurant

   Focused topic: _____

   Topic sentence: _____

Supporting Details

Descriptive paragraphs depend on lively sensory details—especially sights, sounds, and smells. Here are some questions to help you get started gathering details.

Description of a person (personal appearance)

Sensory Detail: Sight
- How old is the person?
- What is the person's gender?
- How tall is he or she?
- What is the person's body build (average, thin, lanky, etc.)?
- What is the person's position (sitting, standing, etc.)?
- What is the person's hair color?
- How long is the person's hair?
- What is the hair texture (curly, thick, thin, etc.)?
- What is the shape of the person's head?
- What is the person's eye color?
- What are the other distinctive facial characteristics (forehead, nose, cheeks, chin, etc.)?
- What are the other distinguishing body characteristics?

- How is this person dressed?
- What colors is the person wearing?

Sensory Detail: Sound
- Is the person making any sound?
- Does this sound resemble anything else?

Description of a person (physical action)

Sensory Detail: Sight
- What is the person doing?
- What are the person's facial expressions?
- What movement is the person making?
- What changes in movement are occurring?
- When do changes in movement occur?
- Why do changes in movement occur?
- Do the movements remind you of something else?

Sensory Detail: Sound
- What sounds are associated with the movement?
- Are there any changes in the sounds?
- Do these sounds resemble something else?

Description of a place

Sensory detail: Sight
- What is the location?
- What size is the place?
- What shape is the place?
- Is the shape normal or unusual?
- What colors are associated with the place?
- Do the colors ever change? If so, how?

Sensory detail: Sound
- What sounds are associated with the place?
- When do the sounds occur?
- Are the sounds repetitive?
- Are the sounds soft or loud?
- Are the sounds surprising in any way?

Sensory Detail: Smell
- What smells are associated with the place?
- Do these smells ever change?

You do not need to answer every question for every observation you make. However, these questions will help you collect the details you will need to write the body of your paragraph.

Read the following paragraph. Then answer the questions below.

   An old man sleeps, nestled comfortably in an armchair. His white hair curls gently around his high forehead and above his ears. His silver-rimmed eyeglasses look as if they are about to slide off the end of his large nose. His wrinkled brow is relaxed, probably because he is napping. His smooth, rosy cheeks are surprising. They look youthful instead of old. Resting on his chest is his heavy chin. From his mouth, slightly open, comes a sound like the purring of a cat. Slumped shoulders give way to a sunken chest. A long-sleeved blue sweater is draped over a white shirt, and navy polyester pants held up by red suspenders lead to white socks and brown shoes. Maybe his body has been weighted down over the years by the burdens he has carried. Today, though, his aged body looks peacefully at rest.

1.   What is the writer's overall impression of this person?

   _____

2.   List five sensory details related to sight.

   A.   _____

   B.   _____

   C.   _____

   D.   _____

   E.   _____

3.   List a detail related to sound.

   _____

   In addition to asking questions about the five senses, you can take notes to record your observations. Here is student Anne Nero's observation of her weeks-old baby:

Objective	Subjective
Sleeping quietly	Sleeping angel
Eyes open slowly	Wants to make sure he is not missing anything
Eyes roll to back of head	Imagines himself falling
Eyes closed tightly	Lullaby music playing
Jerking body as a door slams	
Swinging hands	Time to eat!

Anne not only notes the physical movements of her sleeping infant (objective column) but also records what she is thinking as she makes the observation (subjective column).

Below is the paragraph Anne Nero wrote using her observation notes. Underline all sentences containing sensory details.

Even though my son is only three weeks old, he has a distinct personality all his own. Today he looks peaceful and content as he rests in his crib. He is not really asleep, though. His eyes slowly open to peek as if he wants to make sure he is not missing anything. I tiptoe a few steps back to sneak out of his view for fear he might see me and wake up all the way. He is fighting to stay awake. His eyes roll to the back of his head as his eyelids struggle to stay open. A few minutes later his eyes are closed tightly. Is it the lullaby music playing that makes him sleep? I know it cannot be the racket in the house. I can hear cabinets banging in the kitchen. Dishes clink together as dinner is being prepared for the rest of the family. Although the house is bustling with activity, the baby is sleeping like an angel. Someone slams a door, and the baby reacts by jerking his body and swinging his hands. Perhaps he is imagining himself falling. Maybe he is dreaming about swinging in his swing on the deck by the water. Finally, the lullaby stops, and the family finishes eating dinner. The baby begins to cry loudly for his supper. Big, grayish-blue eyes stare at me. This waking-sleeping-waking goes on all day and through the night.

—Anne Nero

Prepare observation notes on one of the topics in Exercise 9.1. Use the following guidelines:

1. Divide a piece of paper into two columns.
2. Identify your notes with your name, the date, the time of day, and the subject of your observation.
3. Record your objective observations in the left-hand column.
4. Note your subjective observations in the right-hand column.
5. Do not worry about sentence structure. Informal notes are fine.

The Concluding Sentence

End your descriptive paragraph on a strong note. Your concluding sentence should echo the topic sentence by reminding the reader of the focus of your observation and the overall impression it made on you.

For example, the description of the professional baseball player at the beginning of this chapter has this topic sentence:

> The professional baseball player is confident as he steps up to home plate.

In the concluding sentence, the writer repeats the key word *confident* and reinforces this impression with these words:

> This confident athlete never gives the pitcher, his teammates, or the crowd a sign that he is anything but sure of himself.

Similarly, the paragraph describing a favorite picnic place ends on a strong note. The topic sentence is

> My favorite picnic spot is a large boulder in the middle of a rushing mountain stream.

The concluding sentence reinforces the importance of both rock and water in this special place.

> This marriage of rock and water creates an excellent scene for a picnic.

Writing an effective concluding sentence takes practice. If you are not satisfied with your first attempt to end the paragraph, keep trying. You want to end your paragraph with as much strength as possible.

EXERCISE 9.7

Write a concluding sentence for each of your topic sentences in Exercise 9.3.

1. Topic: A favorite relative

   Topic sentence: _____

   Concluding sentence: _____

2. Topic: A talented athlete

   Topic sentence: _____

   Concluding sentence: _____

3. Topic: A child at play

   Topic sentence: _____

   Concluding sentence: _____

4. Topic: A room in my home

   Topic sentence: _____

   Concluding sentence: _____

5. Topic: A favorite restaurant

Topic sentence: _____

Concluding sentence: _____

TRANSITIONS IN DESCRIPTIVE PARAGRAPHS

Although using transitional words and phrases is the most common way to provide transitions in a paragraph, it is not the only way. In a descriptive paragraph featuring a person, you can use personal pronouns to link the ideas in your paragraph.

A *pronoun* is a word that substitutes for, or takes the place of, a noun. *Personal pronouns* substitute for

- A noun representing a person (*professional baseball player*)
- A name of a person (*Frances*).

Personal pronouns are

First person	I, me, my, mine, myself, we, us, our, ours, ourselves
Second person	you, your, yours, yourself, yourselves
Third person	he, him, his, himself, she, her, herself, it, its, itself, they, them, their, theirs, themselves

For writers, pronouns provide a shortcut. Without personal pronouns, writers would have to repeat the noun. Read this version:

> **The professional baseball player** is confident as he steps up to home plate. . . . Twice, **the professional baseball player** taps the bat on the far side of home plate. As **the professional baseball player** digs the cleats of **the professional baseball player's** shoes into the dirt, **the professional baseball player** looks like a bull preparing to charge the matador.

Repeating the noun is dull for the both the writer and the reader. Fortunately, you have pronouns to provide transition, or movement, from one idea to the next.

> The professional baseball player is confident as **he** steps up to home plate. . . . Twice, **he** taps the bat on the far side of home plate. As **he** digs the cleats of **his** shoes into the dirt, **he** looks like a bull preparing to charge a matador.

This use of pronouns is economical (the passage is shorter), and the description is unified by the use of the third person pronouns *he* and *his*.

Underline each personal pronoun in the following paragraph.

My four-year-old niece, Frances, happily plays an imaginary game. She is sitting on the floor with her legs tucked under her body and her arms moving back and forth. In front of her are two of her favorite dolls. She leans toward the doll as if they are sharing a secret. She whispers words that I cannot understand. Then she tosses back her head of long, curly brown hair and laughs. The joyful sound of her laughter fills the room.

In a paragraph describing a place, you will use transitional words that indicate direction. These are the same words you used in Chapter 8 to describe an animal or object:

here	below	near	in the center	inside
there	beyond	beside	in the back	outside
above	behind	next to	at the bottom	to the right
at the top	further	opposite	at the front	to the left

Underline the transitional words and phrases in the following paragraph.

The small city park is deserted on a rainy day. In the center is a large, lonely oak tree. At the bottom of the tree, someone has planted flowers that are drowning in the heavy rain. To the left is an area about ten feet wide and fifteen feet long. Here grass grows in uneven clumps as it stretches toward the city sidewalk. To the right is another grassy area that includes a few brown cement park benches. In front of the tree someone has dumped the remains of a picnic—a bag from a fast-food place and a soda can. Otherwise, the park is clean except for cigarette butts near the benches. Beyond, the tall buildings of the city stretch toward the sky, dwarfing the small park on this dreary morning.

FOCUS ON DICTION

As you learned in Chapter 8, lively diction (word choice) is essential to an effective descriptive paragraph. You can use a number of techniques to strengthen your observations.

Using Lively Adjectives and Adverbs

Using adjectives and adverbs can greatly improve your writing, but these adjectives and adverbs must be specific and exact—not vague.

Some adjectives have been used so many times that they have lost their effectiveness. Avoid overused words in your descriptive paragraphs. Some of these words are

good	pretty	okay	bad
nice	beautiful	fine	great

For example, someone describing a vacation says, "I had a good trip." What does *good* mean? Was the vacation relaxing, stimulating, eventful, or exciting? The reader cannot tell from the adjective *good*. Or suppose you say, "My best friend is a good person." What does *good* mean here? Does it mean worthy, moral, admirable, kind, or helpful? Be specific in your descriptions.

EXERCISE 9.10

Replace each adjective in bold type with a more specific synonym. Use the first sentence as an example. You may use a thesaurus (see Chapter 8), but be sure that the synonym fits the sentence.

1. The sunset was **pretty**.   radiant _____

2. My new coworker is **nice**.   _____

3. Last night's home-cooked meal was **fine**.   _____

4. The thunderstorms yesterday were **bad**.   _____

5. All teachers want **good** students.   _____

6. The **beautiful** horse won the prize at the fair.   _____

7. The biology test last week was **okay**.   _____

8. The new student government president has done a **good** job.   _____

9. The new Spanish teacher is **great**.   _____

10. I was feeling **bad** last weekend.   _____

Some adverbs are also overused, especially the adverbs *really*, *pretty*, and *very*. (The word *pretty* can be an adjective or an adverb, depending on how it is used.) For instance, suppose a writer describes a kitchen this way:

The kitchen in our house is pretty big.

What do the words *pretty big* mean? What are the dimensions of the room? The following sentence is more specific:

Measuring 15 feet by 20 feet, the kitchen in our house is **spacious.**

The adjective *spacious* combined with the dimensions of the room makes the sentence specific rather than vague.

Here is another example:

The food at Luigi's Italian Restaurant on the corner of Main and Fifth Street is very good.

What is the difference between *good* and *very good?* Is all the food good, or just some of it? This sentence is better:

The manicotti at Luigi's Italian Restaurant on the corner of Main and Fifth Street is **delicious.**

Here the word *delicious* and the mention of a specific entrée, manicotti, improves the wording of the sentence.

Avoid overusing the adverbs *really, pretty,* and *very,* especially when they are combined with vague adjectives. Remember that your goal is to create a specific image in the mind of the reader.

Replace each boldfaced phrase with a single specific adjective. Use the first sentence as an example.

EXERCISE 9.11

1. The tornado was **very bad.**   devastating

2. The horror movie on television last night was **really good.**   _____

3. My grade on the next history test is **very important.**   _____

4. The race cars are **really fast.**   _____

5. Hugh and Karen are a **pretty good** couple.   _____

6. The championship basketball game was **really great.**   _____

7. The movie was **okay.**   _____

8. He's a **very nice** person.   _____

9. Our committee meeting was **fine.**   _____

10. That last math test was **pretty bad.**   _____

In each blank space, write a replacement for the vague words in parentheses.

EXERCISE 9.12

El Mexicano is a (*really good*) _____ restaurant. The dining room is (*very little*) _____ with just ten tables for its customers. As customers walk into the restaurant, they see a (*very beautiful*) _____ mural on the wall. The mural features a colorful map of Mexico surrounded by flowers. To the right is a mural of a cathedral in Mexico

City. In the center of the room are ten (*very nice*) _____ tables set with bright red tablecloths and decorated with vases of red hibiscus flowers. The service is also (*really good*) _____. The servers welcome the customers with (*very great*) _____ smiles. They patiently explain the menu to those customers who are (*really clueless*) _____. For a (*really fun*) _____ evening, El Mexicano is the place to go.

Using Similes

One way to improve descriptive writing is to use similes. A *simile* is a comparison between two unlike things that uses the word *like* or *as*. The purpose of a simile is to help the reader connect an idea to something familiar.

One writer describing a sprinter at a track meet compares the runner to a jackrabbit:

> She sprinted toward the finish line **like a jackrabbit running across a road.**

The reader may not have had the experience of seeing this sprinter, but through the power of language, the reader can associate the experience with the common sight of a rabbit running across a road.

EXERCISE 9.13

Complete the following sentences to create similes.

1. The crowded gym was as noisy as _____.
2. The waters of the spring were as cold as _____.
3. My friend was as happy as _____.
4. Making a good grade on a test is like _____.
5. The first day of a new job is like _____.
6. The full moon is as bright as _____.
7. Leftover pizza tastes like _____.
8. Winning the race was like _____.
9. The man's snoring was as loud as _____.
10. The bouquet was as lovely as _____.

FOCUS ON EDITING

As you compose a paragraph describing a person or a place, you need to observe two rules about the use of specific names and places:

- Capitalize proper nouns.
- Use commas with appositives.

Capitalizing Proper Nouns

A *proper noun*, as opposed to a general noun, names a specific person, place, or thing. Proper nouns are capitalized.

General Noun	Proper Noun
city	Clayton
county	Rabun County
state	North Carolina
country	Zimbabwe
lake	Lake Michigan
river	Tallulah River
mountain	Pocono Mountains
street	Alpine Drive
uncle	Uncle Eddie
aunt	Aunt Mary
cousin	Cousin Sue
grandmother	Grandmother Stevenson
professor	Dr. Rowell
high school	Brookland High School
university	Duke University
building	Longstreet Theater
museum	Museum of Modern Art
mother	Mother

Note: Capitalize *Mother, Father, Grandmother, Grandfather,* and so on when you are using the title as a name. For example:

When are you going to see Evelyn?

When are you going to see Mother? (Evelyn = Mother)

Do not capitalize *mother, father, grandmother, grandfather,* and similar words preceded by the word *a, an,* or *the;* a possessive pronoun (*my, his, her, its, their*); or an adjective.

my mother	her uncle	older sister
his father	their brother	a grandmother

Capitalize where needed.

EXERCISE 9.14

1. My father is a kind, generous person.

2. My grandmother has a sister, aunt mary, and two deceased brothers, hugh and phil.

3. The two sisters, ruth and elizabeth, were both born in atlanta, georgia.

4. Have you ever been rafting on the nantahala river in the blue ridge mountains?

5. Melissa graduated from a high school in evanston, illinois.

6. One of my cousins is going sailing with me next weekend on lake burton.

7. Our new neighbors used to live across the street from the metropolitan museum of art in new york city.

8. The new math teacher, dr. estes, used to teach high school in indiana.

9. The fox theater shows classics as well as new films.

10. My brother's family, including his wife and two children, lives in east calais, vermont.

Using Commas with Appositives

When you introduce a person or a place for the first time, you often use an appositive. An *appositive* is a noun that renames or identifies the noun immediately preceding it. Many appositives are proper nouns. A comma should appear immediately before and after the appositive.

> Our neighbor, **Ms. Sanderson,** is going on vacation next week.

Ms. Sanderson is an appositive because this proper noun identifies the noun *neighbor* (*Ms. Sanderson = neighbor*).

It is also possible to write this sentence with the proper noun appearing first:

> Ms. Sanderson, **our neighbor,** is going on vacation next week.

In this case, *our neighbor* is an appositive because it renames the noun, *Ms. Sanderson*. In both cases, commas set off the appositive.

> The new school, **Miles Hall Elementary,** is only a mile from my home.

> Miles Hall Elementary, **the new school,** is only a mile from my home.

Again, the appositives are set off by commas.

EXERCISE 9.15

Insert commas around appositives. Capitalize where necessary.

A lovely old log cabin in a remote area of macon county, north carolina, sits surrounded by pines. A rough gravel driveway off wayah road leads to the front porch. A wooden sign hanging over the small porch states the cabin's name hidden cove as well as the names of the owners joe and louise smith. On the porch, four rocking chairs, two to the left and two to the right, welcome visitors. No one is home; the front door is locked. A peek inside the front window reveals a large area the living room and its main attraction a stone fireplace. A pathway leads around the house to a small backyard, perhaps forty by sixty feet. The backyard ends on the banks of a small creek hidden cove creek. The peacefulness of this place is inviting.

PRONOUN AGREEMENT

As you learned earlier in this chapter, writers frequently use personal pronouns to provide transition and unify paragraphs. Remember, pronouns are words that substitute for nouns. The noun that the pronoun substitutes for is called the *antecedent.*

Personal pronouns are either *singular* (representing *one*) or *plural* (representing *more than one.*) (See Table 9.1.)

TABLE 9.1 Personal Pronouns	
Singular	*Plural*
I, me, my, mine, myself	we, us, our, ours, ourselves
you, your, yours, yourself	you, your, yours, yourselves
he, him, his, himself (male)	they, them, their, theirs, themselves
she, her, hers, herself (female)	
it, its, itself (neuter)	

Note: The words *hisself* and *theirselves* are *not* acceptable pronouns.

      antecedent   pronoun

The **airplane** circled because **it** could not land in the fog.

     antecedent   antecedent   pronoun

The **pilot** and **navigator** are looking forwarding to receiving **their** raises.

Pronouns and antecedents must agree.

- A singular pronoun (*it*) requires a singular antecedent (*airplane*).
- A plural pronoun (*they*) requires a plural antecedent (*pilot* and *navigator*).

This principle is known as *pronoun-antecedent agreement.*

Circle each pronoun and draw an arrow back to its antecedent. Use the first sentence as a model.

1. Jorge will be able to pick up his paycheck tomorrow.
2. Students will need their social security numbers for registration.

3. Trudy will make her decision tomorrow.

4. John prepared the meal himself.

5. The college has raised its tuition for the coming academic year.

6. The managers have decided they must hire new workers.

7. My research paper was due today, but it is not yet completed.

8. The Supreme Court held its final session last week.

9. The president must be responsible for her actions.

10. The officers cannot forgive themselves for failing to rescue the victims.

Usually, choosing the correct pronoun is easy, but in some cases, deciding on the correct pronoun can be tricky.

Case 1:   The antecedent of a pronoun never appears in a prepositional phrase.

Prepositional phrases can divide the antecedent (often the subject of the sentence) from the pronoun, as in the following sentence:

The real estate company along with the other businesses in town is working to increase (*its, their*) business.

To choose the correct pronoun, follow these steps:

- **Cross out the prepositional phrases.**

  The real estate company ~~along with the other businesses in town~~ is working to increase (*its, their*) business.

- **Locate the antecedent (ask, "Who?" or "Whose?").**

  Ask, "Whose business is it?" *The real estate company* is not only the subject of the sentence but also the antecedent of the pronoun.

- **Make sure the pronoun and antecedent agree in number.**

  Because *the real estate company* is singular, the correct pronoun is *its*.

EXERCISE 9.17

Use the three-step method to choose the correct pronoun in parentheses, and underline it.

1. One of the girls left (*her, their*) keys in the car.

2. Mark along with his brothers is attending (*his, their*) family reunion this summer.

3. The actors on the stage in front of us speak (*her, their*) lines clearly.

4. Every teacher on the first day of class should hand out (*his or her, their*) syllabus.

5. The architects for the new buildings met to discuss (*his or her, their*) plans.

6. The computer in my parents' office lost (*its, their*) hard drive in the storm last week.

7. The restaurant in the center of town has opened in (*its, their*) new location.

8. The advertisements on the billboards along the highway have lost (*its, their*) appeal.

9. The large boats in the shipping channel are making (*its, their*) way into the harbor.

10. One of the county commissioners will soon announce (*his or her, their*) resignation.

Case 2: Indefinite pronouns are always singular.

any**one**	any**body**	either (of)
every**one**	every**body**	neither (of)
some**one**	some**body**	each (of)
no **one**	no**body**	

These words are called *indefinite pronouns* because it is unclear (indefinite) whether the person being referred to is male or female. Should the writer use *his, her,* or *his or her?* The most generally acceptable pronoun form is *his or her.*

Did **anyone** register for **his or her** classes next semester?

Somebody should register for **his or her** classes next semester.

Either of the students should register for **his or her** classes next semester.

Each of the students should register for **his or her** classes next semester.

The problem with indefinite pronouns is that few speakers or writers observe this rule. Most of us say or write, "Everyone should register for their classes next semester." Because we hear and see pronouns used in this way, we have trouble recognizing the correct usage of indefinite pronouns.

Many writers avoid the problem of indefinite pronouns by using plural antecedents:

All **students** should register for **their** classes next semester.

Most **students** should register for **their** classes next semester.

EXERCISE 9.18

Circle the correct pronoun in parentheses, and draw an arrow to its antecedent. In the blank, rewrite the sentence using a plural antecedent. Use the first sentence as a model.

1. Everyone should be careful about (*his or her*, *their*) diet.

   People should be careful about their diets.

2. Neither of the teachers knows (*his or her*, *their*) teaching schedule for next year.

   _____

3. Everybody should be sure that (*he or she*, *they*) is prepared for the possibility of a hurricane.

   _____

4. Does anybody know (*his or her*, *their*) e-mail address?

   _____

5. Each of the tourists needs (*his or her*, *their*) money exchanged.

   _____

6. No one is sure if (*he or she*, *they*) will be available to work next week.

   _____

7. Each of the crew members made (*his or her*, *their*) preparations for the flight.

   _____

8. Either of the girls will be surprised if (*she*, *they*) wins the lottery.

   _____

9. Neither of the men has decided if (*he*, *they*) will be a Scout leader.

   _____

10. Everyone is thankful for (*his or her*, *their*) blessings.

    _____

Case 3: When the antecedent is a collective noun, the pronoun is singular if it represents a group of people acting as a single unit. It is plural if it represents a group of people acting individually.

The following are common collective nouns:

audience	company	jury
board	crew	squad
class	family	school
committee	group	team

antecedent   pronoun

The **committee** has made **its** final recommendation.

antecedent   pronoun

The **team** won **its** championship game.

antecedent   pronoun

The **team** returned to **their** friends and family after the game.

EXERCISE 9.19

Circle the correct pronoun in parentheses, and draw an arrow to its antecedent. Use the first sentence as an example.

1. The jury returned (*its*, *their*) verdict after three hours of deliberation.
2. The audience was positive in (*its*, *their*) reaction to the play.
3. The family took (*its*, *their*) vacation in August last year.
4. The cheerleading squad won (*its*, *their*) divisional championship.
5. The school met (*its*, *their*) goal of improved test scores.
6. The committee returned to (*its*, *their*) offices after the meeting.
7. The board voted according to (*its*, *their*) individual beliefs.
8. The company finished (*its*, *their*) yearlong project.
9. The class took (*its*, *their*) midterms last week.
10. The police squad entered (*its*, *their*) patrol cars after the group meeting.

Skill Check: Pronoun Agreement

EXERCISE 9.20

Read each sentence carefully. If the pronoun in bold type is correct, write **C** in the blank. If the pronoun is incorrect, write **I** in the blank. Then cross out the incorrect pronoun and write the correct pronoun above it. Use the first sentence as an example.

1. All the rooms in my dream house would have **their** own special features.   **I**

2. However, the master bedroom would have **its** rightful place as the most beautiful room.   _____

3. Anyone seeing the 200-square-foot room would open **his or her** eyes wide in amazement.   _____

4. In the center of the room would be a king-size mahogany bed with a satin bedspread to keep **their** owner warm.   _____

5. If two people shared this splendid room, **they** would find a sitting area on each side of the bed.   _____

6. Each of the sitting areas would have **their** own unique design, including overstuffed chairs, bookcases, and brass reading lamps.   _____

7. Each person would also have **his or her** own walk-in closet.   _____

8. These closets would have **its** own floor-to-ceiling shelving as well as a generous space for hanging clothes.   _____

9. Mirrors would hide each closet so that no outsider could determine **their** exact location.   _____

10. The elegant bedroom would also include large, colorful oil paintings on all four of **their** walls.   _____

11. Unfortunately, many of us cannot afford the bedroom of **their** dreams.   _____

Pronoun Choice

Pronouns can be used as subjects, objects, or possessives.

Subject Pronouns

These words are *subject pronouns:*

I	he	we
you	she	they
	it	

These pronouns function

- **As subjects of sentences**

    She is an excellent student.

    We are looking forward to our next trip.

Be careful when you use a pronoun as a subject following the word *and*. Make sure you use a subject pronoun.

Incorrect: My parents and me have moved to another city.

To check for correct pronoun usage, read the sentence omitting the first subject and the word *and*:

Incorrect: Me have moved to another city.

Correct: **I** have moved to another city.

Then edit the sentence:

Correct: My parents and I have moved to another city.

- **Following linking verbs** (*am, is, are, was, were, will be, shall be,* etc.). (For more on linking verbs, see Chapter 5.)

Suppose you are the president of a major company. Someone calls and asks, "Is that you?" Informally, you might reply, "Yeah, it's me." However, in a formal work situation, your answer should be

Yes, it is **I**.

If the caller asks, "Is this the president of the company?" you should answer

Yes, this is **she**.   *or*   Yes, this is **he**.

- **In some comparisons using *than* or *as***

Writers often use pronouns in comparisons following *than* or *as*.

My brother is taller than **I**.

Joe is the same height as **she**.

The subject pronoun *I* serves as the subject for an understood verb:

My brother is taller than **I** (am).

Joe is the same height as **she** (is).

Note: In both cases, the understood verb follows the pronoun. The use of a subject pronoun in a comparison allows writers and speakers to take a shortcut and omit the verb.

Underline the subject pronoun in parentheses.

1. Kate and (*me, I*) have been friends since sixth grade.
2. Scott is taller than (*I, me*).

3. Children can learn to play the violin faster than (*we, us*).

4. Dana and (*her, she*) will exercise every day.

5. In the play *Hamlet,* when someone questions Hamlet's identity, he responds, "It is (*me, I*), Hamlet the Dane."

6. I am not as committed to studying as (*he, him*).

7. When Tran called me, he asked, "Is that you?" and I answered, "Yes, this is (*him, he*)."

8. They are not as willing to share information as (*we, us*).

9. Maria and (*him, he*) are getting married next weekend.

10. Together (*him, he*) and (*I, me*) will finish the project.

Object Pronouns

The following words are *object pronouns:*

me	him	us
you	her	them
	it	

These pronouns are used

- **Following action verbs**

  Carolyn gave **me** a birthday present.

  The supervisor gave **them** a copy of the company's policies.

- **As objects of the preposition**

As you learned in Chapter 6, a prepositional phrase consists of a preposition followed by a noun or pronoun called an object. Use an object pronoun following a preposition.

Are you going with **her** to the party?

Frank sent **him** a copy of the letter.

Sometimes writers and speakers are confused when the pronoun used as an object is preceded by the phrase *you and.* They think that the words *you and* should always be followed by the pronoun *I.* That is true when the phrase *you and I* functions as the subject of the sentence:

You and I received the highest grades on the test.

However, in the following sentence, the pronoun *me* is correct because the word *to* is a preposition and the words *you and me* form the object of the preposition:

> The scholarship has been awarded to **you and me.**

To check the pronoun, read the sentence and omit the words *you and:*

> The scholarship has been awarded to (you and) **me.**

> What would be the pronoun choice in this sentence?

> The prize was intended for Dan and (*I, me*).

Read the sentence omitting the phrase *Dan and:*

> The prize was intended for **me.**

The pronoun *me* is the correct answer.

This rule also applies to sentences in which the preposition *between* appears:

> Just between **you and me,** I already have plans for Friday night.

- **In some comparisons using *than* or *as.***

In some comparisons, an object pronoun follows *than* or *as:*

> Laughter can help you as much as **me.**
> The mountains are as beautiful to him as **me.**

In these cases, the words that are understood appear before the pronoun:

> Laughter can help you as much as (it can help) **me.**
> The mountains are as beautiful to him as (they are to) **me.**

Underline the correct pronoun in parentheses.

EXERCISE 9.22

1. Please pick up an application for Chris and (*I, me*).
2. The jewelry means more to her than (*I, me*).
3. Just between (*you and I, you and me*), I heard that tuition will increase next year.
4. The tutors will review the math problems with (*you and I, you and me*).
5. The noise from the busy highway disturbs Laura more than (*I, me*).

6. To (*you and I, you and me*), finding a job is not difficult.

7. If (*Beth and I, Beth and me*) have time next week, we'll meet you for lunch.

8. For (*Jennifer and I, Jennifer and me*), studying Spanish is fun.

9. Hugh is a harder worker than (*I, me*).

10. Exercising frequently can help you as much as (*I, me*).

Possessive Pronouns

These words are *possessive pronouns:*

my	his	our
mine	her	ours
your	hers	their
yours	its	theirs

Use these pronouns in the following cases:

- **To show possession**

Note: Possessive pronouns do not have apostrophes. Therefore, the possessive form of *it* is *its*—not *it's* (which means "it is"). The confusion of *its* and *it's* is common. Just remember that *it's* can mean only *it is.*

Correct: The bird built **its** nest in the garage.

Correct: It's time to renew my license. (*It is* time.)

Also, do not confuse the possessive pronoun *theirs* with *there's* (which means "there is").

Correct: The books on the table are **theirs.**

Correct: There's the key we need. (*There is* the key.)

- **Before -*ing* words used as nouns**

His working late cost him valuable study time.

My failing the test does not mean I will fail the course.

EXERCISE 9.23 Underline the correct word in parentheses.

1. (*It's, Its*) important to pay bills on time.

2. (*There's, Theirs*) the car of my dreams.

3. The movie's effect on (*it's, its*) audience was powerful.

4. (*His, Him*) coming late to class every day annoyed the other students in the class.

5. (*Me, My*) being such a good cook should not be such a surprise.

Who and Whom

Who and *whom* are among the most troublesome pronouns. However, a few suggestions can help you use these pronouns correctly.

- ***Who* and *whoever* are subject pronouns that function as subjects for verbs.**

  Who is at the front door? (*Who* is the subject for the verb *is*).

  Margaret is the one **who** will serve as a chaperone. (*Who* is the subject for the verb *will serve*.)

  Whoever applies first will get the job. (*Whoever* is the subject of the verb *applies*.)

  Check your choice of *who* or *whoever* by substituting *he* or *she* for *who*.

  She is at the front door.

  She will serve as a chaperone.

  He applies first.

- ***Whom* and *whomever* are object pronouns, so these pronouns are followed by a subject and a verb.**

  The secretary addressed the letter "To **Whom** It May Concern." (The verb *may concern* does not need a subject; it already has one—the pronoun *it*. Therefore, the object pronoun *whom* is correct.)

  For **whom** is the meal being prepared? (The subject is *meal*; the verb is *is being prepared*. The correct pronoun choice is *whom*.)

  What is the correct choice for this sentence?

  You may attend the reunion with (*whoever, whomever*) you please.

  Notice that the pronoun in parentheses is followed by a subject, *you*, and a verb, *please*. Therefore, the pronoun must be objective.

  You may attend the reunion with **whomever** you please.

  Check your choice of *whom* or *whomever* by creating a sentence beginning with the subject and verb. Then substitute *him* or *her* for *whom* or *whomever* to determine whether your pronoun choice is correct.

  It may concern **him**.

  The meal is being prepared for **him**.

  You please **him**.

EXERCISE 9.24

Underline the correct pronoun in parentheses.

1. With (*who, whom*) are you attending the conference?
2. (*Who, Whom*) will be the next student government president?
3. Phil is the student (*who, whom*) will be representing our class.
4. To (*who, whom*) does this land belong?
5. She is the one to (*who, whom*) Jason is engaged.
6. (*Who, Whom*) is Jason asking to be his best man?
7. (*Who, Whom*) will be her bridesmaids?
8. For (*who, whom*) is the contract being written?
9. (*Who, Whom*) will be the most valuable player of the game?
10. David is the one (*who, whom*) I would select.

EXERCISE 9.25

Skill Check: Pronouns

Underline the correct pronouns in parentheses.

A salesperson and her customer lean intently toward each other as (*he or she, they*) work at a small wooden desk littered with papers. (*He or she, They*) are both looking down at the desk. Each person has (*his or her, their*) arms stretched out over the desk's surface. The salesperson, (*who, whom*) has short, straight, unevenly cut hair with bangs covering her forehead, rearranges the papers like a gambler shuffling a deck of cards. Her brown eyes stare through thick glasses. Only her upper body can be seen above the desk. She is wearing a white shirt that is simple in (*its, their*) appearance. The male customer with (*who, whom*) she is talking is also looking closely at the paperwork. He has extremely short brown hair and blue eyes, and he is wearing a short-sleeved brown shirt and plaid pants. He as well as the salesperson seems serious about (*his, their*) work. Both of (*his or her, their*) faces are expressionless like poker players calling a bluff. Neither the salesperson nor the customer gives any hint of (*his or her, their*) intentions. He is as involved in the work as (*she, her*). The outcome of this meeting is not yet clear.

Troubleshooting Problems with Antecedents

Every pronoun you use should refer to a specific antecedent. Otherwise, your reader will be confused.

Sometimes the antecedent is missing. Two pronouns that often have missing antecedents are *it* and *they*. Consider this sentence:

Writers as Spiders

You can find much descriptive writing about people and places on the World Wide Web.

Web Exercise 1

Use a search engine to locate information about a person you admire. (You might want to visit <http://www.achievement.org/autodoc/pagegen/galleryachieve.html >—see Chapter 7). Find a picture of this person on the web. Then, using this picture, write a paragraph describing the person's physical appearance. Consider this question: What is the relationship between the person's appearance and the qualities you admire in this person?

Web Exercise 2

The World Wide Web has many exciting sites related to travel. Some of these sites feature America's national parks. Using a search engine, locate information about one of these parks. Some possibilities are Yosemite National Park, Grand Canyon National Park, Everglades National Park, and Grand Tetons National Park.

Read some background information about the park. Then locate a photo of the park. Write a description of this photograph. Keep in mind these questions:

1. What makes this national park special?

2. How does this photo demonstrate the special qualities of this national park?

Additional Help

For a complete review of pronoun agreement, including interactive exercises, see

http://ouray.cudenver.edu/~slmckinn/project3/patoc.htm

For exercises on pronoun choice, visit

http://webster.commnet.edu/hp/pages/darling/grammar/pron2_/quiz.htm

Focus on Development by Example

Writers often use examples to develop their paragraphs. The writer makes a point and then supports that point using firsthand experience or observation. Each example the writer uses must support the main idea.

One place to find writing developed by example is the travel section of your local newspaper. Travel writers introduce readers to new places. They give examples of where to stay, where to eat, and where to go. Read this paragraph about a popular vacation spot in Florida:

> The city of St. Petersburg offers family fun in the sun. First, everyone will enjoy a visit to The Pier, a collection of stores and restaurants. Here families can shop for toys, jewelry, clothing, and souvenirs. The Pier even features an aquarium with various marine life exhibits including tropical fish, eels, and sea horses. Second, families that love baseball will delight in the many games played in the area. A trip to a spring training game is fun for all ages. During the regular season, the Devil Rays baseball team thrills the crowds. Third, everyone loves a trip to St. Petersburg Beach. It's clean, safe, and free. Don't forget St. Petersburg for a great family trip on Florida's West Coast.

What are the three examples of family entertainment this paragraph provides?

Example 1: The Pier

Example 2: Baseball games

Example 3: The beach

You can also develop a paragraph with a single example rather than several separate ones. Read this paragraph:

A great teacher encourages students to overcome their fears. My first year in college, I was terrified of writing a paper. Waiting for the words to come, I would stare for hours at a sheet of paper. I finally got up the nerve to tell my English teacher, Ms. Smith. Instead of laughing at me, she told me that I was not the only student scared of writing papers. She advised me to keep a daily journal so I could get used to expressing myself in words. She showed me how to freewrite and brainstorm. She assured me that with practice, my writing would improve. I no longer fear writing papers, thanks to an outstanding teacher, Ms. Smith.

This student uses one extended example to illustrate her topic sentence, "A great teacher encourages students to overcome their fears."

Developing your paragraphs with examples shows your reader that you are knowledgeable about the topic. Also, using examples encourages your reader to think critically about what you have to say. When you use examples, your reader is thinking, "Do I agree with these examples? If so, why? If not, why?"

Development-by-example paragraphs generally begin with a main idea (topic sentence) and then present examples to support it. Supporting examples usually appear in order of importance—from the least important idea to the most important idea. The writer decides on this order, and the order of the ideas lets the reader know which ideas the writer values least and which ideas the writer values most.

When you write a paragraph developed by examples, be sure to

- Select your examples carefully
- Provide a sufficient number of examples
- Arrange your examples logically

CHOOSING A TOPIC

To write your development-by-example paragraph, begin with a general topic of interest to you. The following are just a few topics that you could develop by example:

- Great places to vacation
- Role models in my community

- Today's outstanding recording artists
- Favorite television comedies
- Scary movies

These topics, however, are still general. You could not write a paragraph about *all* of your favorite television comedies without giving generalized, rather than specific, examples. So your first task is to limit the topic.

Suppose you wanted to write about vacation destinations. Here are some possible ways to limit that topic:

Great places to vacation

> San Francisco, California
> New York City
> Boston, Massachusetts

You could then write about one of these cities and develop your paragraph with examples that show your reader what this city has to offer vacationers.

EXERCISE 10.1   List three possible ways to limit each of the following topics.

1.   Great places to vacation

Topic 1: _____

Topic 2: _____

Topic 3: _____

2.   Role models in my community

Topic 1: _____

Topic 2: _____

Topic 3: _____

3.   Today's outstanding recording artists

Topic 1: _____

Topic 2: _____

Topic 3: _____

4.   Favorite television comedies

Topic 1: _____

Topic 2: _____

Topic 3: _____

5. Scary movies

Topic 1: _____

Topic 2: _____

Topic 3: _____

ORGANIZING A DEVELOPMENT-BY-EXAMPLE PARAGRAPH

The keys to a successful development-by-example paragraph are

- Focused topic sentence
- Interesting, organized supporting details
- Effective concluding sentence

The Topic Sentence

After you have chosen a suitable topic, you are ready to write your topic sentence. The topic sentence of a paragraph developed by examples should

- Focus your reader's attention on the limited topic
- State your opinion about the topic

An opinion is, of course, different from a fact. Your reader cannot disagree with a fact. For example, the following statement is a geographical fact:

The city of St. Petersburg is located on Florida's Gulf Coast.

This statement, however, is an opinion:

The city of St. Petersburg offers family fun in the sun.

Your reader does not have to agree with your opinion.

This statement is also a fact:

In 1997, more tourists visited New York City than any other American city.

This statement is an opinion:

New York City is an excellent vacation destination for lovers of art museums.

In sum,

Topic sentence = Limited topic + Writer's opinion about the topic

Read each of the following possible topic sentences. Write the letter **F** in the blank if the sentence is a **fact**. Write **O** in the blank if the sentence expresses an **opinion.**

EXERCISE 10.2

_____ **1.** Last week I saw my former high school principal, Ms. Anthony, speak at a community meeting.

_____ **2.** The scariest movie I have ever seen is *Psycho,* directed by Alfred Hitchcock.

_____ **3.** Wes Craven directed the thriller *Scream.*

_____ **4.** The first television show filmed before a live audience was *I Love Lucy.*

_____ **5.** My former high school principal, Ms. Anthony, is an excellent role model in my community.

_____ **6.** One of Madonna's first hit singles was *Holiday.*

_____ **7.** My favorite television comedy is *Frasier.*

_____ **8.** A multitalented performing artist on today's pop music scene is Sarah McLachlan.

_____ **9.** Sun worshipers should take a summer vacation to Myrtle Beach, South Carolina.

_____ **10.** Disney World in Kissimmee, Florida, attracts more tourists each year than any other theme park in the world.

EXERCISE 10.3

For each of the general topics in Exercise 10.1, write a limited topic and a topic sentence.

1. General topic: Great places to vacation
Limited topic: New York City _____
Topic sentence: New York City is an excellent vacation destination
for lovers of art museums. _____

2. General topic: Role models in my community

Limited topic: _____

Topic sentence: _____

3. General topic: Today's outstanding recording artists

Limited topic: _____

Topic sentence: _____

4. General topic: Favorite television comedies

Limited topic: _____

Topic sentence: _____

5. General topic: Scary movies

Limited topic: _____

Topic sentence: _____

Supporting Details

A key to writing successful development-by-example paragraphs is providing enough details to support the opinion expressed in the topic sentence. If you do not include enough details, the reader may not have confidence that you are knowledgeable about your topic. If you include too many details, you risk overwhelming your reader.

How many supporting details do you need? You generally need three examples to support your topic sentence. Consider the following paragraph:

New York City is an excellent vacation destination for lovers of art museums. Tourists can begin their day at the Guggenheim Museum, located on Fifth Avenue at Eighty-eighth Street. Here art lovers will find special collections, ranging from African masks to motorcycles. The permanent collection includes works of modern artists such as Jackson Pollock and Pablo Picasso. Then they can stroll down Fifth Avenue to the Metropolitan Museum of Art at Fifth and Eighty-second. This museum features a stunning Egyptian collection, including an Egyptian temple that has been reconstructed inside the museum! Furthermore, the ancient Greek collection is vast, with statues of goddesses and nude male athletes. Finally, museum goers can visit the Museum of Modern Art at 11 West Fifty-third Street. This museum features masterpieces by such artists as Vincent Van Gogh, Claude Monet, and Paul Cézanne. Tired feet can rest in the museum's sculpture garden. With these three museums, the Big Apple is an art lover's paradise.

What are the three examples the writer uses to support the topic sentence?

Example 1: _____

Example 2: _____

Example 3: _____

Write three examples to develop each topic sentence you wrote in Exercise 10.3. **Hint:** The examples do not have to be complete sentences. Use the first topic as a model.

EXERCISE 10.4

1. General topic: Great places to vacation

Limited topic: New York City

Topic sentence: New York City is an excellent vacation destination for lovers of art museums.

Example 1:   Guggenheim Museum _____

Example 2:   Metropolitan Museum of Art _____

Example 3:   Museum of Modern Art _____

2.   General topic: Role models in my community

Limited topic: _____

Topic sentence: _____

Example 1: _____

Example 2: _____

Example 3: _____

3.   General topic: Today's outstanding recording artists

Limited topic: _____

Topic sentence: _____

Example 1: _____

Example 2: _____

Example 3: _____

4.   General topic: Favorite television comedies

Limited topic: _____

Topic sentence: _____

Example 1: _____

Example 2: _____

Example 3: _____

5.   General topic: Scary movies

Limited topic: _____

Topic sentence: _____

Example 1: _____

Example 2: _____

Example 3: _____

These examples, however, are not sufficient to develop the paragraph. To satisfy the reader, the writer should add supporting details for each example.

List two examples used to support each major point in the paragraph about art museums.

Example 1:   Guggenheim Museum _____

Supporting detail 1:   Special collections _____

Supporting detail 2:   Permanent collection _____

Example 2: _____

Supporting detail 1: _____

Supporting detail 2: _____

Example 3: _____

Supporting detail 1: _____

Supporting detail 2: _____

The general structure of a development-by-example paragraph appears in Table 10.1.

TABLE 10.1   **Structure of Development-by-Example Paragraph**

Topic sentence
   Example 1
      Supporting details
   Example 2
      Supporting details
   Example 3
      Supporting details
Concluding sentence

In Chapter 4, you learned about outlining. Many writers use outlines during the organizing stage to help them arrange their ideas in logical order. Outlines can be informal (such as your response to Exercise 10.4) or formal. Table 10.2 illustrates formal outline format for a development-by-example paragraph. Table 10.3 outlines the paragraph on New York City's art museums.

TABLE 10.2   **Outline Format for Development-by-Example Paragraph**

  I. Limited topic (or topic sentence) of paragraph
    A. Example 1
      1. Supporting detail 1
      2. Supporting detail 2
    B. Example 2
      1. Supporting detail 1
      2. Supporting detail 2
    C. Example 3
      1. Supporting detail 1
      2. Supporting detail 2

TABLE 10.3	Sample Outline

I. New York City is an excellent vacation destination for lovers of art museums.
   A. Guggenheim Museum
      1. Special collections
      2. Permanent collection
   B. Metropolitan Museum of Art
      1. Egyptian collection
      2. Ancient Greek collection
   C. Museum of Modern Art
      1. Masterpieces
      2. Sculpture garden

Follow these general guidelines when preparing an outline:

- Use key words (rather than complete sentences) for each part of the outline after the topic sentence.
- A Roman numeral identifies the topic (or topic sentence) of a paragraph.
- Follow standard outline form:

   I.
     A.
       1.
       2.
     B.
       1.
       2.
     C.
       1.
       2.

- All levels of the outline (except the topic sentence) must have a minimum of two parts. Every A must be followed by a B, every 1 by a 2.
- Do not outline the concluding sentence.

Your completed outline will help you check the arrangement of your supporting details.

EXERCISE 10.5

Using one of your answers to Exercise 10.4, complete the following outline. Write your topic sentence after the Roman numeral I. List your three examples after the letters A, B, and C. Add two supporting details for each example.

   I. _____
     A. _____
       1. _____
       2. _____

B. _____

   1. _____

   2. _____

C. _____

   1. _____

   2. _____

The Concluding Sentence

Development-by-example paragraphs, like all other paragraphs, need strong ending sentences. The concluding sentence should remind the reader of your main idea and leave the reader focused on what you have to say.

Avoid a general, unfocused concluding sentence such as:

There are many art museums in New York City.

This sentence states a fact—an uninteresting fact. It will not make a good impression on the reader.

This concluding sentence is more effective:

With these three museums, the Big Apple is an art lover's paradise.

It uses New York's well-known nickname (*the Big Apple*) and reinforces the city as a vacation destination (*an art lover's paradise*).

EXERCISE 10.6

Read each sentence. If the sentence would make a good concluding sentence, place a check mark in the blank. If the sentence is too unfocused for a concluding sentence, write the letter **X** in the blank.

_____ **1.** There are so many interesting sites for tourists in this vacation spot.

_____ **2.** Many movies like this one scare audiences each year.

_____ **3.** Every community needs a role model.

_____ **4.** After seeing a thriller like *Scream,* I have nightmares.

_____ **5.** This television comedy is the best.

_____ **6.** For scuba divers, a trip to Cozumel, Mexico, is the ideal vacation.

_____ **7.** The shows on the Nickelodeon channel are all classics.

_____ **8.** Yo-Yo Ma, a cellist, is the most talented recording artist on the classical music scene.

_____ **9.** The hits keep coming for this country singer.

_____ **10.** My role model, Ms. Anthony, is a gift to her community.

EXERCISE 10.7   Write a concluding sentence for each of the topics in Exercise 10.3. Use the first example as a model.

1.   General topic: Great places to vacation

Limited topic: New York City

Topic sentence: New York City is an excellent vacation destination for lovers of art museums.

Concluding sentence: With these three museums, the Big Apple is an art lover's paradise.

2.   General topic: Role models in my community

Limited topic: _____

Topic sentence: _____

Concluding sentence: _____

3.   General topic: Today's outstanding recording artists

Limited topic: _____

Topic sentence: _____

Concluding sentence: _____

4.   General topic: Favorite television comedies

Limited topic: _____

Topic sentence: _____

Concluding sentence: _____

5.   General topic: Scary movies

Limited topic: _____

Topic sentence: _____

Concluding sentence: _____

TRANSITIONS IN DEVELOPMENT-BY-EXAMPLE PARAGRAPHS

You can use transitional words and phrases to help your reader move through your supporting details. In Table 10.4, the letter **T** indicates places where you should consider providing transition.

In Chapter 4, you learned that the following transitional words can be used in a paragraph when you introduce an example:

first	also	in addition	moreover
second	next	additionally	furthermore
third	then		

TABLE 10.4	Transitions in Development-by-Example Paragraphs

Topic sentence
   Example 1
      (T) Supporting details
   (T) Example 2
      (T) Supporting details
   (T) Example 3
      (T) Supporting details
(T) Concluding sentence

These transitional expressions let the reader know that you are providing a supporting detail:

for example	as an illustration	in particular	as a case in point
for instance	to illustrate	in general	

To emphasize a particular example, use

especially	surely	equally important
certainly	above all	most importantly

Underline the transitions in the following paragraph.

EXERCISE 10.8

My favorite television comedy is *The Mary Tyler Moore Show.* The female characters on this show are unforgettable. For instance, Mary, the title character, is a clever, insecure young woman working as assistant producer at a television station in Minneapolis, Minnesota. Her neighbor, Rhoda, is single and sassy, a match for Mary's humor in every way. Also, the male characters are memorable. For example, Ted Baxter, the station's weather reporter, is stiff-backed and dim-witted. Lou Grant, Mary's boss, is loud and rough. Furthermore, the show is full of humor. To illustrate, one of the show's feature characters, Chuckles the Clown, is remembered for these lines: "A little song, a little dance, a little seltzer down your pants." In another episode, Ted Baxter, worried about the IRS, writes this poem to Mary: "Roses are red / So here's a whole bunch / Tell the income tax man / I took you to lunch." Certainly, television comedy fans will always remember Mary, who "can turn the world on with her smile."

FOCUS ON REVISING: SENTENCE COMBINING

Have you ever written a paragraph in which all the sentences sound the same? Maybe every sentence begins with a subject followed by a verb: "I watched . . . ," "He ran . . . ," "She stood . . . ," and so on. Sentences like that can lead to dull writing.

Here is a paragraph with repetitive sentence structure:

A great place to vacation is Disney World in Orlando, Florida. First, the rides are fun at the Magic Kingdom. I can ride the roller coasters, such as Space Mountain and Big Thunder Mountain Railroad. I can enjoy a boat ride through Pirates of the Caribbean. Second, I can visit Epcot. I can view the exhibits on the history of technology in Epcot's geodesic dome. I can see the "countries," such as France, Italy, and Canada. Third, I can tour MGM Studios. I can watch the animators drawing cartoons in their studio. I can then go to the stunt show and ride the Tower of Terror. I am saving my money for my dream vacation.

In this paragraph, every sentence is a *simple sentence*—a sentence with only one subject and verb group. What can you do if you write a paragraph that is full of simple sentences? The following suggestions will help you vary your sentences during the revising stage.

Suggestion 1: Begin sentences with an introductory prepositional phrase.

Original: The rides are fun at the Magic Kingdom.

Revision: At the Magic Kingdom, the rides are fun.

All the writer has done to revise this sentence is move the prepositional phrase from the end of the sentence to the beginning of the sentence. Sometimes you may have to add a prepositional phrase to the beginning of a sentence, like this:

Original: Second, I can visit Epcot.

Revision: After a whirlwind tour of the Magic Kingdom, I can visit Epcot.

EXERCISE 10.9

Rewrite the following sentences so that they begin with one or more prepositional phrases. You can move prepositional phrases already in the sentence or add new ones.

1. Don't forget St. Petersburg for a great family trip on Florida's West Coast.

Revision: _____

2. New York City is an excellent vacation destination for lovers of art.

Revision: _____

3. Tourists can begin their day at the Guggenheim Museum.

Revision: _____

4. The ancient Greek collection is vast, with statues of goddesses and nude male athletes.

Revision: _____

5. Museum goers can visit the Museum of Modern Art at 11 West Fifty-third Street.

Revision: _____

6. Tired feet can rest in the museum's sculpture garden.

Revision: _____

7. Mariah Carey is the best recording artist on today's pop music scene.

Revision: _____

8. *Seinfeld* is my favorite of all television comedies.

Revision: _____

9. I can view the exhibits on the history of technology in Epcot's geodesic dome.

Revision: _____

10. I can watch the animators drawing cartoons in their studio.

Revision: _____

Suggestion 2: Use appositive phrases.

In Chapter 9, you learned about appositive phrases. An *appositive* is a noun that renames or identifies the noun preceding it. Sometimes you can use appositive phrases to combine two simple sentences.

Original: My favorite talk show often features inspirational speakers. The name of this talk show is *Oprah*.

Revision: Oprah, my favorite talk show, often features inspirational speakers. (The appositive, *Oprah*, appears next to the words it renames, *My favorite talk show*.)

Note: You will have to omit words when you revise sentences by using appositive phrases. Remember to use commas on either side of the appositive.

EXERCISE 10.10

Use an appositive phrase to combine each of the following pairs of sentences.

1. A great place for a summer camping vacation is Crater Lake.

Crater Lake is a deep blue lake in southern Oregon.

Revision: _____

2. Thousands of years ago, Crater Lake was formed by a volcano.

This volcano was Mount Mazama.

Revision: _____

3. Summer campers will enjoy the area's wildflowers with their interesting names.

The names of the wildflowers are Lewis monkey flower and glacier lily.

Revision: _____

4. Campers can also see some of the park's wildlife, including the largest animal.

The largest animal in the park is the Roosevelt elk.

Revision: _____

5. Smaller mammals are often seen feeding in the meadows at twilight.

These smaller mammals are mule deer and black-tailed deer.

Revision: _____

6. If they listen carefully, campers can hear a noisy bird.

This bird is called Clark's nutcracker.

Revision: _____

7. Some of the park's birds have funny names.

These birds are hairy woodpeckers and yellow-bellied sapsuckers.

Revision: _____

8. Hikers can also enjoy a view of an island in the middle of the lake.

This island is called Wizard Island.

Revision: _____

9. They will also enjoy seeing the rock island jutting from the water.

This rock island is named Phantom Ship.

Revision: _____

10. A camping trip to Crater Lake is unforgettable.

This lake has been called "the blue gem of the Cascade Mountains."

Revision: _____

In addition to using phrases to combine sentences, you can use coordination.

Suggestion 3:   Join the two simple sentences with a coordinating conjunction.

These are the ways to join independent clauses (see Chapter 7 for a review):

Method 1:   Use a coordinating conjunction.

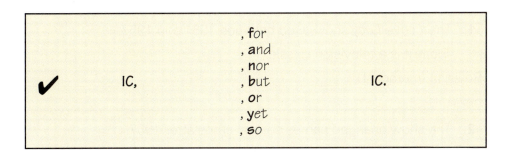

Original: I can ride the roller coasters, such as Space Mountain and Big Thunder Mountain Railroad.
I can enjoy a boat ride through Pirates of the Caribbean.

Revision: I can ride the roller coasters, such as Space Mountain and Big Thunder Mountain Railroad**, and** I can enjoy a boat ride through Pirates of the Caribbean.

Method 2:   Use a semicolon.

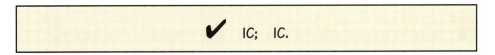

Original: I can ride the roller coasters, such as Space Mountain and Big Thunder Mountain Railroad.
I can enjoy a boat ride through Pirates of the Caribbean.

Revision: I can ride the roller coasters, such as Space Mountain and Big Thunder Mountain Railroad; I can enjoy a boat ride through Pirates of the Caribbean.

Method 3:   Use a conjunctive adverb.

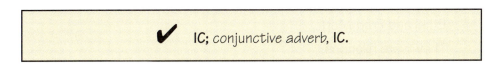

(For a list of conjunctive adverbs, see Table 7.1.)

Original: I can ride the roller coasters, such as Space Mountain and Big Thunder Mountain Railroad.

I can enjoy a boat ride through Pirates of the Caribbean.

Revision: I can ride the roller coasters, such as Space Mountain and Big Thunder Mountain Railroad; **furthermore,** I can enjoy a boat ride through Pirates of the Caribbean.

EXERCISE 10.11

Use the coordination method in parentheses to revise these pairs of sentences.

1. The *I Love Lucy* show aired between 1951 and 1957.

Today it is a television classic.

Revision (method 1): _____

_____

2. The show changed names several times after 1957.

The quality of the show remained high.

Revision (method 3): _____

_____

3. For example, from 1957 to 1958, the show was named *The Lucille Ball–Desi Arnaz Show.*

From 1958 to 1959, the show was called *The Westinghouse Lucille Ball–Desi Arnaz Show.*

Revision (method 1): _____

_____

4. From 1959 to 1960, the show became *Lucy-Desi Comedy Hour.*

This was the show's last season.

Revision (method 2): _____

_____

5. Over the years, 180 half-hour episodes were produced.

Only 13 one-hour episodes appeared.

Revision (method 2): _____

_____

6. The main characters on the show were Lucy and Ricky Ricardo and Ethel and Fred Mertz.

They were hilarious.

Revision (method 1): _____

_____

7. Lucille Ball and Desi Arnaz played Lucy and Ricky Ricardo.

They were married in real life.

Revision (method 2): _____

_____

8. Vivian Vance played Lucy's best friend, Ethel Mertz.

In 1954, she won an Emmy for her work on the show.

Revision (method 1): _____

_____

9. Sadly, the last episode aired on April 1, 1960.

Then Lucille Ball filed for divorce from Desi Arnaz.

Revision (method 3): _____

_____

10. Fans of classic television will always treasure this show.

Today's fans must watch the classic episodes on video.

Revision (method 3): _____

_____

Suggestion 4: Combine sentences using subordination.

When you subordinate, you change one simple sentence to a dependent clause by adding a subordinating conjunction. The dependent clause can come at the beginning of the sentence or at the end.

Method 1: Place the dependent clause at the beginning.

> ✔ *sub. conj.* **DC, IC.**

(For a list of subordinating conjunctions, see Table 7.2.)

Original: The show changed names several times after 1957.
   The quality of the show remained high.

Revision: Even though the show changed names several times after 1957, **the** quality of the show remained high.

Method 2: Place the dependent clause at the end.

> ✔ **IC** *sub. conj.* **DC.**

Original: The show changed names several times after 1957.
The quality of the show remained high.

Revision: The quality of the show remained high **even though** the show changed names times after 1957.

EXERCISE 10.12

Use the subordinating conjunction in parentheses to revise the pairs of sentences below. Use either method 1 or method 2.

1. The Appalachian Trail is a trail of many challenges and incredible beauty.

   It is a dream vacation for mountain hikers.

   Revision (*because*): _____

   _____

2. Many mountain hikers have full-time jobs.

   They can only dream about hiking this wonderful trail.

   Revision (*because*): _____

   _____

3. The 2,100-mile Appalachian Trail extends from Georgia to Maine.

   It crosses two national parks, eight national forests, and fourteen states.

   Revision (*as*): _____

   _____

4. Hikers begin the trail.

   They are on Springer Mountain in Georgia.

   Revision (*when*): _____

   _____

5. Hikers complete the journey.

   They will reach Mount Katahdin in Maine.

   Revision (*if*): _____

   _____

6. Hikers reach the highest point of the trail in the Great Smoky Mountains.

   They are standing 6,642 feet above sea level.

   Revision (*when*): _____

   _____

7. Hikers walk along the Hudson River.

   The elevation is near sea level.

Revision (*when*): _____

_____

8. Most of the trail is on public land.

Some stretches are on private land.

Revision (*although*): _____

_____

9. This year ends.

One hundred hikers will have completed the trail.

Revision (*before*): _____

_____

10. It takes four to six months to complete the trail.

It is the experience of a lifetime.

Revision (*even though*): _____

_____

Rewrite the following paragraph, combining sentences as needed. Use any of the suggestions for varying your sentences.

EXERCISE 10.13

Washington, D.C., is a wonderful vacation spot for families. It is America's capital city. Children will enjoy seeing many famous monuments. They have read about these monuments in school. For example, they can visit the monument to Thomas Jefferson. This monument is called the Jefferson Memorial. They will also enjoy climbing the steps of the most famous of all the monuments. This monument is the Washington Monument. Then they can tour the museums of the Smithsonian Institution. This museum system is the largest in the world. The National Air and Space Museum is part of the Smithsonian Institution. This museum is the most popular in the world. It features a touchable moon rock. The National Museum of Natural History is a favorite with children. Its collection includes many dinosaur skeletons. Children may need several days to visit these museums. There is so much to see. Fortunately, many of these sites are free. This is important to many families on a tight vacation budget. This fascinating city is like a treasure hunt for children of all ages.

Revising Tip: Using a Style Checker

Many word processing programs provide style checkers along with grammar and spell checkers. Style checkers can give you information about the number of words in each sentence and paragraph of your composition, calculate the average length of each sentence and paragraph, and even tell you about the "readability" of your writing.

Readability scales are based on mathematical formulas that use the number of words in a sentence and the number of syllables in a word.

Many style checkers also figure the percentage of your sentences that use the passive voice. The term *passive voice*, however, is unfamiliar to many writers. All action verbs in English grammar have voice—either active or passive. A verb is in the *active voice* if the subject is doing the action expressed in the verb:

> Jenny **performed** the voice solo. (Who performed the voice solo? *Jenny*, and *Jenny* is the subject of the sentence. Therefore, the verb *performed* is in the active voice.)

A verb is in the *passive voice* if the subject is receiving the action of the verb:

> The voice solo **was performed** by Jenny. (Who performed the voice solo? *Jenny*, but *Jenny* is not the subject of the sentence. The subject is *voice solo*. Therefore, the verb *was performed* is in passive voice.)

Generally, you want to use passive voice verbs in only a low percentage of sentences. Most readers prefer sentences that use active voice verbs because these sentences are shorter and more direct.

To look for passive voice verbs in your paper, watch for a past participle verb (with a helping verb) followed by a prepositional phrase that begins with *by*.

The paper **was read** *by* Joe.

To change the verb from passive voice to active voice, follow these steps:

- Locate the verb and remove the helping verb.
- Find the performer of the action, and place this subject at the beginning of the sentence (drop the preposition *by*).

Joe **read** the paper.

Be careful when you use a style checker. Depending on your reader and the purpose of your composition, you may want to have a low number of words in each sentence or drop the reading level. However, if you run the style checker on several papers and are concerned about the results, you might want to discuss the statistics with your teacher.

FOCUS ON EDITING

During the editing stage, read your paper looking for choppy, awkward sentences. One strategy you can use to strengthen your sentences is parallelism (also called parallel structure).

Parallelism

Parallelism is a way to join related ideas while giving your sentences rhythm and balance. When you use parallelism, you repeat a grammatical form (such as a noun, a verb, or a prepositional phrase) for emphasis. Consider these two sentences:

> In the summer, I love to go **swimming, sailing,** and **fishing.**
>
> In the summer, I love to go swimming, sail, and fish.

In the first sentence, the words *swimming, sailing,* and *fishing* are parallel—that is, they are all nouns ending in *-ing* (the same grammatical form). The second sentence, however, lacks parallelism, and the result is a choppy sentence.

You can use parallelism to join

- Words in a series
- Phrases in a series

When you join words in a series using parallelism, the words must be similar grammatically—for example, all nouns, all verbs, all adjectives, or all adverbs.

> **Biking, walking,** and **jogging** are three forms of exercise. (all nouns)
>
> Mark can **walk, drive,** or **bike** to work. (all verbs)
>
> The sunset is blazing with **purple, pink,** and **red** streaks. (all adjectives)
>
> Harriett works **quickly, quietly,** and **effectively.** (all adverbs)

Read each sentence, looking carefully at the words in italics. Circle any word or words not in parallel form. Then rewrite the sentence using parallel form. Use the first sentence as a model.

EXERCISE 10.14

1. Suzanne enjoys *gardening, reading, and* (she likes to cook.)
   Suzanne enjoys gardening, reading, and cooking.

2. When I come home from school, I am *hungry, thirsty, and ready to sleep.*

   _____

3. My chores at home include *vacuuming my room, washing my car, and I must clean the kitchen.*

   _____

4. Good parents are *kind, patient, and they try to help their children.*

   _____

5. The sports car in my neighbor's driveway is *new, attractive, and it is expensive.*

   _____

6. My best friend is *honest, loyal, and I can rely on her.*

   _____

7. An athlete must be *quick, strong, and have a lot of energy.*

   _____

8. The player hit the home run *firmly, gracefully, and with lots of power.*

   _____

9. Spouses should treat each other *respectfully, honestly, and be generous.*

   _____

10. The job training classes teach *independence, cooperation, and how to be a leader.*

    _____

11. Brenda *arrived late, chatted loudly, and she left in a hurry.*

    _____

A series of phrases must also be parallel. These phrases include prepositional phrases and infinitive phrases. (See Chapter 6 for more on these types of phrases.)

In his Gettysburg Address, Abraham Lincoln wrote of a government "of the people, by the people, for the people." These three prepositional phrases are parallel:

of the people

by the people

for the people

If you use the same preposition throughout the series, you can either include the preposition just once or repeat it in each part of the series:

I need to go ***to*** *the store, the laundromat, and the post office.*

I need to go ***to*** *the store,* ***to*** *the laundromat, and* ***to*** *the post office.*

The same is true of infinitive phrases:

I need ***to*** *shop, do my laundry, and buy stamps.*

I need ***to*** *shop,* ***to*** *do my laundry, and* ***to*** *buy stamps.*

Rewrite each sentence below using parallel form. Reword the sentences as necessary.

EXERCISE 10.15

1. This year I plan to attend every class, do homework every day, and I'll raise my grades every semester.

   _____

2. My roommate likes to watch television, to listen to the radio, and do her math homework at the same time.

   _____

3. Michelangelo was the greatest painter of the Renaissance because of his abilities as a painter, as a sculptor, and he was also a famous architect.

   _____

4. To be wealthy, to be healthy, and be wise are my dreams.

   _____

5. I promised to love my husband in sickness and in health, for better or worse.

   _____

6. When I graduate, I plan to find a job, marry my girlfriend, and I want to buy a house.

   _____

7. On spring break, I hope to go to the beach, get a tan, and maybe I'll even meet some new friends.

   _____

8. A business owner must be able to track expenses, supervise employees, and he or she must be able to provide customer service.

   _____

9. When I get home from class today, I need to clean out my book bag, to organize my notes, and I have to finish my English homework.

_____

10. Shane has worked as a bartender, he was a contractor, and he was a mechanic.

_____

EXERCISE 10.16

Skill Check: Parallelism

Using parallel structure, rewrite the italicized words and phrases in the following paragraph.

Visitors to Charleston, South Carolina, my favorite city in the Southeast, never lack something to do. For example, they can tour this historical city *by foot, by carriage, or boat*. Tourists can visit homes built before the Civil War, such as Drayton Hall, Middleton Place, *and they can also tour Boone Hall Plantation*. After touring, they can enjoy *golfing, swimming, or they can fish*. Those who enjoy fishing can fish *from piers, or they can try fishing from boats*. When hunger strikes, tourists can choose from a wide variety of restaurants. Many serve traditional Charleston foods: *shrimp with grits, catfish with hushpuppies, and rice that has blackeyed peas served with it*. When exhaustion sets in, tourists can settle in *inexpensive motels or hotels that cost a lot*. This city has survived *hurricanes, earthquakes, and it has also made it through fires*. Fortunately, this treasure of the South never lost *its charm, its beauty, and it has not lost its grace either*.

> **Editing Tip**
>
> To locate sentences that need rewording, try these techniques:
>
> - **Read your paper aloud to yourself or to someone else.**
>   Read exactly, read expressively, and read slowly. Listen to every word. Bring your voice to a full stop at every period. Listen to the rhythm of your sentences. Does your voice stumble over any sentences? Are words omitted? Can some sentences be combined? Are your structures parallel?
>
> - **Ask someone to read your paper to you.**
>   Tell your reader to read exactly what is on the page. Choose someone who reads expressively so you can listen to the rhythm of your words. Are there any sentences that cause the reader trouble?
>
> - **Read your composition line by line.**
>   Use a cover sheet to expose each line of your composition. Slow down your reading, and examine each word carefully.

FOCUS ON PEER REVIEW

Use these questions to help you prepare your development-by-example paragraph:

1. Underline the topic sentence of the paragraph. What is the limited topic of the paragraph? What is the author's opinion about the topic?

2. What are the major points the writer uses to support the topic sentence?

3. Is each of these major points sufficiently developed with additional supporting details? If not, which points need more support?

4. Are the supporting details interesting? If not, what details could be added to interest the reader?

5. Circle the transitional words and phrases the writer uses.

6. Does the concluding sentence reinforce the opinion expressed in the topic sentence? If not, why?

7. Are all sentences clearly worded? If not, circle the sentences that need rewording.

8. Are there any choppy sentences that could be combined? List these sentences.

9. Are there any fragments? If so, where?

10. Are there any run-ons or comma splices? If so, where?

11. Are there any punctuation errors? Where?

12. Are any words misspelled? List them.

13. The strengths of this paragraph are _____

_____

_____.

14. The weaknesses of this paragraph are _____

_____

_____

_____.

In a small group, read the development-by-example paragraph below. Then discuss the answers to the peer review questions.

EXERCISE 10.17

Student Sample

With its many interesting attractions, Nashville, Tennessee, is a wonderful place to visit. As country music fanatics know, Nashville is the country music capital of the world. Fan Fare Week is an annual event. During Fan Fare, country music lovers can watch their favorite stars perform. Tourists can visit Music Row, where the history of country music is displayed at the Country Music Hall of Fame. Furthermore, the Grand Ole Opry House hosts a multitude of country music shows. In addition, Nashville's accommodations are plentiful. As guests enter the massive seven-story Opryland Hotel, elegance and charm overwhelm them. A water and lights display called Cascades is breathtaking. Pathways meander through luscious greenery in a two-acre atrium, and the sounds of waterfalls and soothing harp music help relax any weary traveler. Anyone can see why Nashville is a lovely place to visit.

—Jane Dietz

WRITING ASSIGNMENT

Write a development-by-example paragraph using the steps of the writing process. You can develop one of the topics from Exercise 10.1, or you can choose from one of these topics:

- Irritating commercials
- Favorite professional sports teams
- Effective study habits
- Special family occasions

Writers as Spiders

Suppose you are a travel agent preparing to lead a group on a city tour. Using a search engine, enter the name of a city you would like your group to visit. Then read through several web sites about this city. Write a paragraph focusing on the selected city as a tourist destination. Give three examples of things tourists can do while visiting this city.

Additional Help

For additional practice combining sentences, see

http://wserver.arc.losrios.cc.ca.us/~jukesb/sentenc1.html

http://wserver.arc.losrios.cc.ca.us/~jukesb/sentenc2.html

If you would like additional exercises on parallelism, visit

http://webster.commnet.edu/hp/pages/darling/grammar/parallelism.htm

CHAPTER 11

Focus on Process

In this chapter, you will learn to write a process paragraph. When you write about a process, you tell how to do something step by step. You already have many examples of how-to writing—for example, the manual to your videocassette recorder, the instructions for your new coffeepot, or even a cookbook. Newspapers and magazines are filled with process writing, with articles on topics from how to make a set of bookends to how to order plans for a log cabin. Here is a process paragraph from a car manual:

> To change a flat tire, follow these directions. Open the trunk and re-move the tool bag and spare tire. To loosen the spare tire bolt, use the end of the jack rod located in the tool bag. Next, remove the jack from the trunk. Position the jack under the jack-up point, fitting the jack head be-tween the notches. Remove the hubcap. Then with the wheel nut wrench, turn each wheel nut counterclockwise. Loosen the nuts, but do not remove them. Turn the jack to raise the vehicle until the tire is off the ground. Then remove the wheel nuts and the tire. Install the new tire. Screw on the wheel nuts and tighten them with your fingers. Using the jack, lower the vehicle until the tire touches the ground. Finish tightening the wheel nuts. Replace the hubcap. Remove the jack and return the jack, the tool bag, and the damaged tire to the trunk. If you follow these steps, you should be able to change the tire efficiently and safely.

This example points out some of the challenges of writing a process para-graph. First, you must keep your audience in mind. What if the reader of this paragraph does not know what a jack rod is? Second, your directions must be complete. Omitting a step from this process of changing a tire could cause a serious accident. Third, you must be sure to list the steps in the proper order, mentioning all the required tools or materials. Otherwise, your reader will be confused.

A process paragraph begins with a clear topic sentence that focuses the reader's attention on the task to be explained. The paragraph's supporting details are then presented in chronological order. For example, the paragraph above begins with removing the tool bag and spare tire from the trunk and ends with returning the tool bag and the damaged tire to the trunk. In between, the steps are given in exact 1-2-3 order.

A process paragraph relies on exact details to

- Keep the reader focused on the task
- Provide the step-by-step instructions necessary to complete the task successfully

An effective process paragraph explains the steps so carefully that your reader can follow your directions and achieve the desired results.

CHOOSING A TOPIC

A process paragraph requires a sharp, focused topic. If the topic is too general, you will not be able to discuss the process completely in a single paragraph. Also, you need to choose a topic that you are knowledgeable about. Otherwise, it is unlikely that you will be able to provide your reader with detailed instructions.

Here are some ideas to help you choose a topic:

- How to cook _____ (Name a particular food.)

- How to make _____ (Choose a simple how-to project.)

- How to _____ (Identify a habit you want to overcome.)

- How to _____ (Focus on something you do at work or at home.)

- How to plan _____ (Name a specific event.)

You can choose your topic by listing some possible topics and then deciding which one is the most suitable for a single paragraph.

How to cook vegetable lasagna

How to cook chile rellenos

How to make a picture frame

How to plan a romantic dinner for two

EXERCISE 11.1   List two possible topics for each process.

1.   How to cook   _____   (Name a particular food.)

Topic 1:   _____

Topic 2:   _____

2.   How to   _____   (Choose a simple how-to project.)

Topic 1:   _____

Topic 2:   _____

3.   How to   _____   (Identify a habit you want to overcome.)

Topic 1:   _____

Topic 2:   _____

4.   How to   _____   (Focus on something you do at work or at home.)

Topic 1:   _____

Topic 2:   _____

5.   How to plan   _____   (Name a specific event.)

Topic 1:   _____

Topic 2:   _____

ORGANIZING A PROCESS PARAGRAPH

A process paragraph has all the basic elements of effective paragraphs:

- Topic sentence
- Supporting details
- Concluding sentence

The Topic Sentence

An effective topic sentence of a process paragraph lets the reader know

- The specific process the writer will explain
- The promised outcome of the process
- What the reader has to do

Look again at the topic sentence of the paragraph from the car manual:

To change a flat tire successfully, follow these directions.

- **What is the specific process the writer will explain?**

  How to change a flat tire

- **What is the promised outcome of the process?**

  The flat tire will be changed, and the driver will be able to drive the car again.

- **What does the reader have to do?**

  Follow these directions.

When you write your topic sentence, be careful not to create a fragment (incomplete sentence). Suppose you are writing a paragraph about how to prepare homemade pizza. Do not write the topic

How to prepare homemade pizza

as your topic sentence. First, these words do not form a sentence. Second, the reader doesn't know what he or she is supposed to do. Instead, begin your topic sentence with the specific process (including the promised outcome) and the directions to the reader:

To prepare a delicious homemade pizza, complete these steps.

Or you can reverse the order:

Complete these steps to prepare a delicious homemade pizza.

- **What is the specific process the writer will explain?**

  How to prepare a homemade pizza

- **What is the promised outcome of the process?**

  A delicious pizza (In this case, the adjective *delicious* states the promise.)

- **What are the directions to the reader?**

  Complete these steps.

For a process paragraph,

> **Topic sentence = Identification of a specific process +**
> **Promised outcome + Directions to the reader**

Place a checkmark in the blank by each effective topic sentence below. Write an **X** in the blank by each sentence that would not be a good topic sentence.

EXERCISE 11.2

_____	**1.**	How to write an effective business letter.
_____	**2.**	To plan an elegant, romantic dinner for two, follow these instructions.
_____	**3.**	To lose ten pounds in six weeks.
_____	**4.**	How to cook chile rellenos with salsa and cheese.

_____   **5.** Complete these steps to create a beautiful picture frame.

_____   **6.** How to prepare an effective résumé.

_____   **7.** To prepare for a successful job interview, follow these steps.

_____   **8.** You can take an excellent photograph if you plan carefully.

_____   **9.** How to stop procrastinating.

_____   **10.** You can plan a beautiful small wedding if you follow these guidelines.

EXERCISE 11.3

In Exercise 11.1, you developed some possible topics for the following processes. Choose one topic for each process, and write a topic sentence.

1. How to cook _____ (Name a particular food.)

Topic sentence: _____

2. How to make _____ (Choose a simple how-to project.)

Topic sentence: _____

3. How to _____ (Identify a habit you want to overcome.)

Topic sentence: _____

4. How to _____ (Focus on something you do at work or at home.)

Topic sentence: _____

5. How to plan _____ (Name a specific event.)

Topic sentence: _____

Supporting Details

To write a successful process paragraph, you must carefully list all the steps of the process using time order. Without clear, specific directions, the reader will not be able to complete the process successfully. You must, therefore, choose a topic you know well. At the same time, be aware that being familiar with the process can lead you to make assumptions about what the reader knows.

How can you avoid confusing your reader? Here are some suggestions.

Ask Questions

Before you begin your draft, ask yourself questions so you can gather the necessary supporting details. These questions will get you started:

1. What materials or ingredients will the reader need to complete the process?

2. What tools or equipment will the reader require?

3. Does the reader need any special knowledge to complete the process?

4. What are the key steps in the process?

5. What parts of the process are the most difficult to accomplish? Why?

6. How long should the process take?

7. What can the reader expect to accomplish at the end of the process?

Suppose you were writing a process paragraph on how to make biscuits. Here are some possible answers to the questions listed above:

1. What materials or ingredients will the reader need to complete the process?

   • Self-rising flour

   • Milk

   • Shortening

2. What tools or equipment will the reader require?

   • Standard oven

   • Baking sheet

   • Large bowl

   • Measuring cups (1 cup and 1/3 cup)

   • Cutting board

   • Large fork and spoon

   • Biscuit cutter (or glass with a diameter of at least two inches)

3. Does the reader need any special knowledge to complete the process?

   No.

4. What are the key steps in the process?

   • Gather ingredients and equipment.

   • Preheat oven.

   • Measure ingredients.

   • Cut biscuits.

   • Mix ingredients.

   • Bake biscuits.

5. What parts of the process are the most difficult to accomplish? Why?

   The hardest part of making biscuits is mixing the biscuits. If there is too little milk, the dough won't hold together. If there is too much milk, the dough will be too sticky to cut.

6. How long should the process take?

   Preparing the biscuits for the oven takes ten to fifteen minutes. Baking them takes ten to twelve minutes.

7. What can the reader expect to accomplish at the end of the process?

   Delicious homemade biscuits!

EXERCISE 11.4

Choose one of your topics from Exercise 11.1 and answer the questions below.

1. What materials or ingredients will the reader need to complete the process?

2. What tools or equipment will the reader require?

3. Does the reader need any special knowledge to complete the process?

4. What are the key steps in the process?

5. What parts of the process are the most difficult to accomplish? Why?

6. How long should the process take?

7. What can the reader expect to accomplish at the end of the process?

Arrange the Steps in Order

After you have answered the questions, you are ready to arrange the steps in chronological order. To make biscuits, the writer has listed these necessary steps:

- Gather ingredients and equipment.
- Preheat oven.
- Measure ingredients.
- Cut biscuits.
- Mix ingredients.
- Bake biscuits.

But are these steps in the correct order? Using a flow chart will help answer this question.

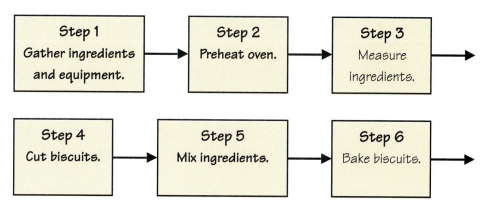

A close look at this flow chart reveals that some of the steps (in bold print) are out of order. The correct order follows:

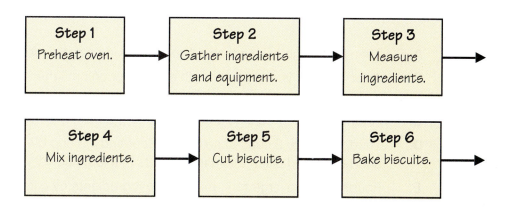

Some steps require further supporting details when they appear in the paragraph. For example, when the writer introduces step 1, "Preheat oven," the temperature must also be included. Step 2, "Gather ingredients and equipment," must include a list of ingredients and a list of equipment. The key is to include enough details so that the reader can complete the process successfully.

Develop a flow chart using the steps you listed in question 4 of Exercise 11.4. As you prepare your flow chart, visualize yourself completing each step. Have you omitted any steps? If so, add these steps to your flow chart. Be sure you arrange the steps in chronological order.

EXERCISE 11.5

The following details support steps 1 and 2 on the second flow chart above. Place each detail in time order by writing the appropriate number in the blank.

EXERCISE 11.6

Topic sentence: Preparing delicious homemade biscuits is an easy task if you follow these directions.

_____ **A.** Second, gather the necessary ingredients and equipment.

_____ **B.** After you have located the ingredients, get a large bowl, measuring cups (1 cup and 1/3 cup), a cutting board, a large fork and spoon, a large bowl, a biscuit cutter (or a glass with a diameter of at least two inches), and a baking sheet.

_____ **C.** The ingredients are self-rising flour, milk, and shortening.

_____ **D.** First, preheat the oven to 450 degrees.

EXERCISE 11.7 The following details support steps 3 and 4 in the second flow chart. Place each detail in time order by writing the appropriate number in the blank.

_____ **A.** Then pour slightly less than a cup of milk and set it aside.

_____ **B.** After the milk is added, stir with a large spoon until the ingredients are mixed. (Dough will be lumpy).

_____ **C.** After the dry ingredients are mixed, add the milk.

_____ **D.** Third, measure 2 cups of self-rising flour and 1/3 cup of shortening and place these ingredients in a large bowl.

_____ **E.** Fourth, using a large fork, mix the dry ingredients by cutting the shortening into the flour.

EXERCISE 11.8 The following details support steps 5 and 6 in the second flow chart. Place each detail in time order by writing the appropriate number in the blank.

_____ **A.** Pour the biscuit dough onto a cutting board covered lightly with flour.

_____ **B.** Then, again with your hands, pat the dough gently until it is spread out about 1/4 to 1/2 inch thick.

_____ **C.** With your hands, roll the dough into a loose ball.

_____ **D.** Bake for ten to twelve minutes.

_____ **E.** After you have prepared the dough, dip the biscuit cutter (or glass) in flour.

_____ **F.** Serve the biscuits piping hot and enjoy!

_____　**G.**　Place the biscuits on a baking sheet and put the sheet in the preheated oven.

_____　**H.**　Cut ten to twelve biscuits.

The Concluding Sentence

Your process paragraph needs a strong concluding sentence. Do not end your paragraph with the last step, this way:

> Serve these biscuits to your guests.

Also avoid generalized concluding sentences such as these:

> All these steps are very important.

> Following these steps is easy.

Instead, remind your readers what they will accomplish if they follow the directions you have provided. For example, the paragraph from the car manual ends this way:

> If you follow these steps, you should be able to change the tire efficiently and safely.

This concluding sentence is effective because it gives the reader confidence that the process will not take too much time and will not end in an accident.

Here is a possible concluding sentence for the paragraph on making biscuits:

> Not only will your dinner guests appreciate these tasty biscuits, but they will also be impressed with your cooking skills.

This concluding sentence reminds the reader that the time it takes to complete the process will be rewarded. All readers want to know that their efforts are recognized.

Place a checkmark in the blank by each good concluding sentence. Write an **X** in the blank by each example that would not be a good concluding sentence.

EXERCISE 11.9

_____　**1.**　This paragraph has told you how to write an effective business letter.

_____　**2.**　When planned well, a romantic dinner for two is unforgettable.

_____　**3.**　Losing ten pounds in six weeks will improve not only your self-esteem but also your health.

_____ **4.** Procrastination is a hard habit to overcome.

_____ **5.** A well-constructed picture frame is a treasure.

_____ **6.** Preparing thoroughly for a job interview improves your chances of landing the job.

_____ **7.** There are many steps to prepare an effective résumé.

_____ **8.** Following these directions, you can take photographs that you will cherish for years to come.

_____ **9.** Remove the chile rellenos from the oven.

_____ **10.** Serve wedding cake to each of your guests.

EXERCISE 11.10

Write a concluding sentence for each of the topics in Exercise 11.3.

1. How to cook _____ (Name a particular food.)

Topic sentence: _____

Concluding sentence: _____

2. How to make _____ (Choose a simple how-to project.)

Topic sentence: _____

Concluding sentence: _____

3. How to _____ (Identify a habit you want to overcome.)

Topic sentence: _____

Concluding sentence: _____

4. How to _____ (Focus on something you do at work or at home.)

Topic sentence: _____

Concluding sentence: _____

5. How to plan _____ (Name a specific event.)

Topic sentence: _____

Concluding sentence: _____

TRANSITIONS IN PROCESS PARAGRAPHS

Transitions are critical in process paragraphs because your reader needs to be able to follow each step of the process in order to achieve the promised result. Transitional words and phrases help your reader to move smoothly from one step to the next.

The transitional words and phrases used in process paragraphs are similar to those used in narrative paragraphs. Both types of paragraphs are organized according to time order. Some transitional expressions often found in process paragraphs are

before	meanwhile	immediately	finally
previously	in the meantime	later	to begin
earlier	at the same time	then	first
after	now	gradually	second
afterward	presently	eventually	third

EXERCISE 11.11

Underline the transitional words and phrases in the following process paragraph.

You can enjoy gardening in a small space if you build a planter box. Before you begin building, locate a flat area in your yard, on your patio, or on a rooftop. This area should be approximately 4 feet by 4 feet and in a sunny location. After you have located a spot, you are ready to build. To begin, buy four 1-by-6-inch boards, each 8 feet long. First, cut each board in half. Second, take four of the boards and nail them together to form a square. Third, take the other four boards and form another square. If you want a portable box, nail a sheet of plywood to one square to form the bottom of the box. Then carry the squares to the desired location and place one on top of the other. Now you are ready to fill the box with soil and plant a vegetable or flower garden. A planter box is not difficult to make, and it makes gardening in a small space a pleasure.

EXERCISE 11.12

Underline the transitional words and phrases in the following process paragraph. **Hint:** Use the paragraph to check your answers to Exercises 11.6 through 11.8.

You can make delicious homemade biscuits by following these directions. First, preheat the oven to 450 degrees. Second, gather the necessary ingredients and equipment. The ingredients are self-rising flour, milk, and shortening. After you have located the ingredients, get a large bowl, measuring cups (1 cup and 1/3 cup), a cutting board, a large fork and spoon, a large bowl, a biscuit cutter (or a glass with a diameter of at least two inches), and a baking sheet. Third, measure 2 cups of self-rising flour and 1/3 cup of shortening and place these ingredients in a large bowl. Then pour slightly less than a cup of milk and set it aside. Fourth, using a large fork, mix the dry ingredients by cutting the shortening into the flour. After the dry ingredients are mixed, add the milk. After the milk is added, stir with a large spoon until the ingredients are mixed. (Dough will be lumpy.) Pour the biscuit dough onto a cutting board covered lightly with flour. With your hands, roll the dough into a loose ball. Then, again with your hands, pat the dough gently until it is spread out about 1/4 to 1/2 inch thick. After you have prepared the dough, dip the biscuit cutter (or glass) in flour. Cut ten to twelve biscuits. Place the biscuits on a baking sheet and put the sheet in the preheated oven. Bake for ten to twelve minutes. Serve the biscuits piping hot and enjoy! Not only will your dinner guests appreciate these tasty biscuits, but they will also be impressed with your cooking skills.

FOCUS ON REVISING

When you write a process paragraph, you need to express each sentence clearly and directly to the reader. During the revising stage, you can work to improve the clarity of your writing by checking for

- Shifts in person
- Gender bias

Shifts in Person

As you learned in Chapter 9, writers use personal pronouns to help unify their paragraphs. Personal pronouns are grouped as follows:

First person	I, me, my, mine, myself, we, us, our, ours, ourselves
Second person	you, your, yours, yourself, yourselves
Third person	he, him, his, himself, she, her, hers, herself, it, its, itself, they, them, their, theirs, themselves

Writers generally use first person and/or third person pronouns when they write. Process paragraphs, however, are often written in second person. In whatever writing you do, however, keep your pronoun use consistent. If you begin in first person, stay in first person; do not shift from first or third person to second person or third person.

Consider this sentence:

If I want to host a surprise birthday party, you should plan several weeks in advance.

This sentence shifts from the second person pronoun *you* to the third person pronoun *we*. Here are several ways to correct this sentence:

> If **you** want to host a surprise birthday party, **you** should plan several weeks in advance. (Both pronouns are in the second person.)

> If **we** want to host a surprise birthday party, **we** should plan several weeks in advance. (Both pronouns are in the third person.)

> If **someone** wants to host a surprise birthday party, **he or she** should plan several weeks in advance. (This sentence is written in third person.)

Correct the shifts in person in these sentences. Cross out the incorrect pronouns and make corrections above the lines.

EXERCISE 11.13

1. If a person wants to write an effective business letter, you should know the name and position of the person receiving the letter.

2. Used car shoppers should be sure you have the car's blue book value.

3. If I want to lose ten pounds in six weeks, you must eat balanced meals with small portions.

4. To select a college, you should evaluate my long-term career goals.

5. To be sure I do my homework every day, you need to keep a daily calendar listing all assignments.

6. To make myself a good cup of coffee, you follow these simple directions.

7. If someone wants to design an exercise plan, you can contact a personal fitness trainer.

8. If someone needs help writing an English paper, you can visit the learning support center.

9. Garage sale shoppers know you can find great deals in someone else's "trash."

10. You can save money at the grocery store if one uses coupons regularly.

Rewrite the following paragraph, changing all first person pronouns to second person. Make your corrections above the lines.

EXERCISE 11.14

If I want to order from this clothing catalog, I must follow these instructions. First, I must complete the mailing label with my name and mailing address. Then I fill out the item number, the color of the item, the size, the price per item, and the total amount. I can pay by credit card or with cash on delivery, but I must indicate the method of payment on the form. If I pay by credit, my credit card will not be charged until my items are shipped. To complete the form, I include shipping and handling charges and the tax to reach the total for my order. Then I sign the form, tear it out of the catalog, and mail it to the company's address. If I follow these orders exactly, my order should arrive within four to six weeks. Ordering from catalogs like this one will save me time and money.

Gender Bias

You also need to review your paragraphs for gender bias. The term *gender* refers to whether a pronoun is masculine, feminine, or neuter (see Chapter 9). Gender applies only in the singular third person:

Masculine	he, him, his, himself
Feminine	she, her, hers, herself
Neuter	it, its, itself

In most cases the gender is clear, and so is the choice of the pronoun. However, in other cases the pronoun is not clear. In such cases, writers traditionally have used masculine pronouns. Consider the following sentences from an employee's handbook:

> Every employee should make sure **he** is on time for work. If **he** is late, then **he** must inform **his** supervisor immediately.

These sentences are examples of gender bias. The writer of the handbook uses the male pronoun exclusively. What about the female employees?
Some writers try to use both masculine and feminine pronouns:

> Every employee should make sure **he or she** is on time for work. If **he or she** is late, then **he or she** must inform **his or her** supervisor.

The problem with using both masculine and feminine pronouns is that the sentences often sound awkward when these pronouns are used repeatedly.
Here are some other ways to avoid gender bias:

Method 1:   Use first person or second person pronouns.

> **I** must make sure **I** am on time for work. If **I** am late, then **I** must inform **my** supervisor immediately.

You should make sure **you** are on time for work. If **you** are late, then **you** must inform **your** supervisor immediately.

Method 2:   Use plural nouns and pronouns.

Employees should make sure **they** are on time for work. If **they** are late, then **they** must inform **their** supervisors immediately.

Notice that the phrase *your supervisor* changes to *their supervisors* when the sentence is revised using plural nouns and pronouns.

Rewrite the following sentences using one of the above methods. **Hint:** You may have to change some singular nouns to plural nouns.

EXERCISE 11.15

1.   Every employee must carry his social security card.

_____

2.   Each teacher is responsible for setting her attendance policy.

_____

3.   The high school graduate often goes to college because of pressure from his parents.

_____

4.   The writer should be sure that all his paragraphs have clear topic sentences.

_____

5.   Each new committee member must provide his home telephone number.

_____

Use method 2 to eliminate gender bias in the following paragraph. Make your corrections above the lines.

EXERCISE 11.16

To gain admission to this college, a student must meet the following requirements. First, he must complete a formal application for admission by the university's application deadline. He must submit his recommendation letters with the application and include a $20 application fee. If he is applying for in-state tuition, he must also show proof of residency. Second, he must have an overall 2.5 grade point average in high school. To verify his GPA, he must send the college an official copy of his high school transcript. Additionally, he must have a minimum score of 950 on the SAT or 20 on the ACT. Third, he must complete an interview with a member of the admissions committee. If the student meets these conditions, he has an excellent chance of being admitted to the university.

Revising Tip: Using Help

Most word processing programs provide a help feature that will display how-to information about your computer. In one of the most popular help programs, you can type in a question, and the help feature will assist you in finding the answer. For example, suppose you want to know how to format a word using bold print. You can ask, "How do I bold a word?" and the help feature will respond with a list of topics that address this question. You can also access the help feature's table of contents for an alphabetical listing of additional help topics. Next time you are frustrated because you cannot figure out how to do something on your computer, look for help.

Focus on Editing

A *modifier* is a word or phrase that provides additional information about another word or group of words in a sentence. This information changes, or *modifies*, the meaning of the word.

Adjectives and adverbs are modifiers:

> This process is **easy.** (*Easy* is an adjective modifying *process* and answering the question "What kind of process?")

> This task is **quite difficult.** (*Quite*, an adverb modifying *difficult*, answers the question "How difficult?" *Difficult*, an adjective modifying the noun *task*, answers the question "What kind of task?")

Phrases can also be modifiers:

> **Watching the sunset,** the couple held hands. (The phrase *Watching the sunset* describes the couple and answers the question "Which couple?")

When you use a phrase as a modifier, you must place the phrase next to the word or words it modifies. Because modifier errors can weaken your sentences and confuse your reader, be sure to place modifiers correctly in your compositions. If you do not place the modifier correctly, two problems can result:

- Dangling modifiers
- Misplaced modifiers

Dangling Modifiers

Sentences sometimes begin with phrase modifiers. When a phrase modifier appears at the beginning of a sentence, the word that is being described (or modified) must follow immediately.

> **Looking ahead,** the driver focused carefully on the road. (Ask, "Who is looking ahead?" The driver is. This sentence is correct.)

> **Tired of sleeping,** I got up to begin my day. (Ask, "Who is tired of sleeping?" I am. This sentence is also correct.)

Problems occur when the noun following the opening phrase is not the subject. Consider these two sentences:

> Before writing a paragraph, a cluster diagram should be completed.

> To make homemade ice cream, a churn is needed.

Both sentences have logic problems. Who is writing the paragraph? A cluster diagram? In the second sentence, who is making the homemade ice cream? A churn?

Correct a dangling modifier by placing the subject immediately after the opening phrase.

> Before writing a paragraph, **a student should complete** a cluster diagram.

> To make homemade ice cream, **you need** a churn.

Another way is to change the dangling modifier to a dependent clause:

> **Before a student writes** a paragraph, **he or she should complete** a cluster diagram.

> **If you want** to make homemade ice cream, **you will need** a churn.

Read each sentence carefully. If the sentence contains a dangling modifier, write a correct sentence in the blank. If the sentence is already correct, write **C** in the blank.

1. Surprised by the loud boom, a jet flew overhead.

_____

2. Scratching the cat's back, it bit me.

_____

3. After being soaked in a sudden rainstorm, I found my umbrella when I got in the car.

_____

4. After walking along the beach, we headed to a seafood restaurant for dinner.

_____

5. To make a crazy quilt, many pieces of cloth are needed.

_____

6. To throw a fastball, a pitcher must be strong.

_____

7. After receiving an award, the actor made a long speech.

_____

8. To take a digital photograph, a digital camera is needed.

_____

9. Tapping to the beat, the dancers entertained the audience.

_____

10. Using the spell checker, the number of spelling mistakes in my papers has decreased.

_____

Misplaced Modifiers

Another problem with modifiers occurs when the modifier is misplaced. A *misplaced modifier* is a phrase that is separated from the word it modifies. Here is an example:

> My mother died at the age of two.

Did the writer's mother really die at the age of two? One way to correct this sentence is to change the opening phrase to a dependent clause:

> **When I was two years old,** my mother died.

Another possibility is to rewrite the sentence using another subject:

> At the age of two, **I lost** my mother.

Consider these confusing sentences:

> The father rushed his child to the emergency room with pneumonia.

> I gave the suit to a friend I don't want any longer.

Does the emergency room have pneumonia? Do you not want this person to be your friend any more? Correct these misplaced modifiers by moving the modifier next to the word it modifies:

> The father rushed his **child with pneumonia** to the emergency room.

> I gave **the suit I don't want any longer** to a friend.

Underline the misplaced modifiers below. Then correct each sentence.

1. Valerie loaned some money to her friends her father gave her.

   _____

2. My father at the age of twelve took me to the state fair.

   _____

3. We found a trunk in the attic that we had been looking for.

   _____

4. Angela visited the house where George Washington slept on her trip to Williamsburg.

   _____

5. The mother took her child to the doctor with the flu.

   _____

6. Jenny bought ice cream sundaes for her friends with whipped cream.

   _____

7. The cat scratched my feet with sharp claws.

   _____

8. The children fought about what television show they should watch in the backyard.

   _____

9. I read about the mayor's wedding sitting on my back porch.

_____

10. John gave the car to his best friend with the red vinyl interior.

_____

EXERCISE 11.19

Skill Check: Modifiers

Rewrite the following paragraph, correcting dangling and misplaced modifiers. Reword faulty sentences as necessary.

Before planning a wedding, several decisions must be made. First, consider planning the wedding yourself. To plan your own wedding, you in your local bookstore can find many magazines and books offering advice on choosing a location, selecting a color scheme, preparing an invitation list, sending out invitations, and many other decisions you must make. Some books even offer suggestions for writing your own wedding vows. Second, you may want to hire a wedding coordinator. Many couples find that a wedding coordinator among family members reduces conflicts. When selecting a wedding coordinator, it is important to ask for references from others who have used this coordinator. Finally, you can use computer software to plan your wedding. This software can help you manage your time. For example, a person might want assistance with poor time management skills setting up a calendar listing key events related to the wedding. Software can also help you manage your money so that you do not exceed your budget. Careful planning is the key to a beautiful wedding.

Editing Tip

If you need help editing your papers, think about visiting your college's tutoring center. Often a tutor can read your paper and discover errors that you have missed. Here are some suggestions to keep in mind when working with a tutor:

- Before you see the tutor, write a list of questions you have about your paper. Not only will you make a favorable impression but also your conference will be productive.

➡

- Allow plenty of time. Do not see the tutor the day your paper is due. You will need time to think through any corrections that you need to make.
- Take notes during the conference. These notes will guide you as you prepare the final draft of your paper.

FOCUS ON PEER REVIEW

Use these questions as you peer review your process paragraph:

1. Does the topic sentence clearly identify the process the writer will explain?

2. Does the writer state the outcome in the topic sentence?

3. Are the directions in the body of the paragraph complete? If not, which steps are omitted?

4. Are the steps of the process presented in logical order? If not, what steps appear out of order?

5. Does the writer make any assumptions about the reader's knowledge of the topic? Are all terms explained clearly?

6. Are all necessary materials (or ingredients) listed in the paragraph?

7. Does the concluding sentence encourage the reader to complete the process?

8. List three transitional words or phrases in the paragraph.

9. Do any shifts in person occur in the paragraph? If so, where?

10. Are there any misplaced or dangling modifiers? Where do they occur?

11. Are there any errors in sentence structure—fragments, comma splices, or run-ons? If so, where do they occur, and how should they be corrected?

12. List any punctuation errors.

13. List any spelling errors.

14. What are the strengths of this paragraph?

15. What are its weaknesses?

In a small group, read this process paragraph. Use the peer review questions to discuss the paragraph.

Student Sample

You can cook delicious Beef Stroganoff by following these easy steps. To begin, collect all the necessary ingredients: a pound of lean ground beef, an onion, chopped garlic, flour, a can of cream of mushroom soup, sour cream, parsley, pepper, and a pound of egg noodles. Next, you will need a saute pan, a large sauce pot, a cutting board, a knife, measuring spoons, and a measuring cup. Immediately, fill the sauce pan with water and place the pot on the stove, turning the temperature to medium-high. After putting on the water, dice the onion. Then, add 1/2 cup onion, beef, and one tablespoon of garlic to the saute pan and brown on medium. After the meat is cooked, drain off the fat, add two tablespoons of flour, and stir. At this point, it is very important to cook the mixture for five minutes and to stir constantly. This step will cook out the flour taste and keep the mixture from sticking. To finish, mix in the can of soup, one cup of sour cream, two tablespoons of parsley, one teaspoon of pepper, and turn the temperature to low. In the meantime, the water should be boiling, so dump the egg noodles into the water and boil for eight minutes. Finally, drain the noodles and serve with a healthy scoop of Stroganoff. Congratulations on making a delicious, easy meal!

—Ken Sparks

WRITING ASSIGNMENT

Use the stages of the writing process to write a process paragraph. Develop one of the topics from Exercise 11.1.

Writers as Spiders

The World Wide Web has many sites with recipes for adventurous cooks. Using a search engine, locate an interesting recipe. Try it out in your kitchen. Then write a process paragraph based on the recipe.

Additional Help

For more information about gender bias, see

http://owl.english.purdue.edu/Files/26.html

You can find a review of dangling modifiers at this address:

http://owl.english.purdue.edu/Files/24.html

This site features an exercise on misplaced and dangling modifiers:

http://www.uottawa.ca/academic/arts/writcent/hypergrammar/rvmismod.html#q3

APPENDIX A

Spelling

Spelling errors are frustrating for both writers and readers, and editing for spelling errors is time-consuming. The following strategies will help good spellers and poor spellers alike decrease the number of misspelled words in their compositions.

SPELLING RULES

Many English words are spelled according to rules. While each of these rules has some exceptions, mastering them will help you improve your spelling.

Rule 1: Use *i* before *e* except immediately following the letter *c*. Use *ei* immediately following the letter *c* or in words where *ei* sounds like *ay*.

believe	receive	neighbor
niece	conceive	weigh
relieve	deceive	eight

Exception: When the letter *c* makes the *sh* sound, the letter *c* is followed by *ie*.

sufficient	efficient	ancient

Some words do not follow the rules above.

weird	their	foreign
height	neither	either
seize	society	

Rule 2: Drop the final *e* when you add an ending that begins with a vowel. Keep the final *e* when you add an ending that begins with a consonant.

280

ride + ing = riding	move + ing = moving
time + er = timer	manage + er = manager
hope + less = hopeless	move + ment = movement
time + less = timeless	manage + ment = management

Rule 3: When you add letters to a word ending in *y*, change the *y* to *i* if the letter before the *y* is a consonant. Do not change the *y* if a vowel appears before the *y*.

dry + ed = dried	deny + ed = denied	rely + ed = relied
enjoy + ment = enjoyment	delay + ed = delayed	buy + er = buyer
cry + er = crier	relay + ed = relayed	angry + ly = angrily

Exception: Always keep the final *y* when you add *-ing*.

drying	denying	relying
enjoying	delaying	buying

Rule 4: When you form plurals, add *-es* to words ending in *ss, x, z, ch, sh,* or *o*. Always add *-es* when you form a plural by changing a final *y* to *i*.

kisses	tomatoes	countries
axes	potatoes	babies
buzzes	churches	flies

Rule 5: In one-syllable words that end in a single vowel between two consonants, double the final consonant when you add an ending.

stopped	stirring	crammed
rotted	stunning	stubbed

Rule 6: In words of more than one syllable ending in a single vowel between two consonants and with a stress on the second syllable, double the final consonant when you add an ending.

committed	occurring	expelled
transmitted	preferring	compelled

COMMONLY CONFUSED WORDS

Some pairs of English words are frequently confused with each other. Unfortunately, if a writer confuses these words, the sentence's meaning changes, and the reader is often puzzled as well. Learn the meanings of these words.

accept: a verb meaning "to receive"

except: a preposition that means "excluding"

> Will you **accept** this gift?
>
> Everyone is going **except** her.

advice: a noun meaning "help"

advise: a verb meaning "to counsel"

> Your **advice** was helpful.
>
> Can you **advise** me further?

affect: a verb that means "to influence"

effect: a noun meaning "result"

> Will your procrastination **affect** your grade?
>
> The **effect** of the drug is unknown.

breath: a noun pronounced "breth" (short *e* sound as in *death*)

breathe: a verb pronounced "breeth" (long *e* sound; rhymes with *seethe*)

> Take a deep **breath** and then dive into the water.
>
> Singers must learn to **breathe** correctly.

choose: verb meaning "select" (rhymes with *fuse*)

chose: past tense of *choose* (rhymes with *hose*)

> I will **choose** a new couch tomorrow.
>
> I **chose** a new couch last week.

conscience: noun meaning "knowledge of good or bad acts"

conscious: adjective meaning "aware and awake"

> He had a guilty **conscience** because of his misdeeds.
>
> The patient is not yet **conscious.**

hear: verb meaning "to listen"

here: adverb indicating a location

> Did you **hear** Denise say that her parents were **here?**

know: a verb meaning "to understand"

no: opposite of *yes*

> I did not **know** there was **no** food in the house.

knew: past tense of *know*

new: opposite of *old*

> I **knew** we would need a **new** car soon.

lead: verb meaning "to guide" (rhymes with *seed*); noun for a metal (rhymes with *head*)

led: past tense and past participle of *lead*

> I will follow if you **lead** the way.

> I need more **lead** for my mechanical pencil.

> The limousine **led** the funeral procession.

lie: a verb meaning "to recline"

lay: a verb meaning "to place" (present tense); also past tense of the verb *lie*

> My cat likes to **lie** in a sunny place.

> Where did you **lay** her keys?

> Yesterday, I **lay** down for a nap about three o'clock in the afternoon.

loose: adjective meaning "untied" or "unwound" (rhymes with *moose*)

lose: verb that means "to misplace" or "to fail to win" (rhymes with *fuse*)

> The necklace was so **loose** that it nearly fell off her neck.

> Did you **lose** your necklace?

passed: past participle and past tense of verb *to pass*

past: noun referring to a time before the present; preposition that means "beyond"

> The car **passed** by very quickly.

> Did you go **past** our house last night?

> So much has happened in my **past.**

quiet: opposite of *noisy*

quite: synonym for *very*

> I was **quite** happy that my house was so **quiet.**

raise: verb meaning "to lift" or "increase"; noun meaning "increase in salary"

rise: verb meaning "to move without assistance"

> Did you receive that **raise** you asked for?
>
> Every morning I get up before the sun **rises.**

sit: verb; opposite of *to stand*

set: verb meaning "to place"

> Are you planning to **sit** on this couch all day?
>
> Will you **set** those dishes on the table?

than: word used in comparisons

then: adverb that means "later"

> She is a better runner **than** her brother.
>
> I will see you **then.**

their: third person plural possessive pronoun

there: adverb indicating location

they're: contraction for *they are*

> Dan, Pat, and Phil left **their** golf clubs at home.
>
> **There** is the golf course.
>
> **They're** not going to play well **there** without **their** golf clubs.

through: a preposition

threw: past tense of verb *to throw*

> Over the river and **through** the woods is grandmother's house.
>
> She **threw** the ball to home plate.

to: a preposition

too: adverb meaning "also" or "more than enough"

two: a number

> George is going **to** a reunion this weekend.
>
> **Two** of his coworkers are going **too.**

were: plural past tense of verb *to be*

where: adverb indicating direction

> **Where were** you last weekend?

weather: a noun meaning "climactic conditions"

whether: a subordinating conjunction used like *if*

    The **weather** today is stunningly beautiful.

    Do you know yet **whether** you can go with me?

whose: possessive form of *who*

who's: contraction for *who is*

    Whose house is that?

    Who's the new student in the class?

your: second person possessive pronoun

you're: contraction for *you are*

    You left *your* jacket at my house last night.

    You're going to have to go to *your* friend's house without me.

USING A SPELL CHECKER

To improve your spelling, consider purchasing a handheld spell checker. If you are unsure how to spell a word, enter your best guess into the spell checker. The spell checker will check the word against its dictionary and suggest a spelling. This tool is good for writers who have difficulty visualizing the spelling of a word unless they see it.

If you are using a computer to write your papers, be sure that you have access to a spell checker as part of your word processing program. When the spell checker is activated, the program will select possible misspelled words and then ask the writer to verify whether each word is spelled correctly. If the writer is unsure, the spell checker will suggest possible spellings. Then the writer can ignore the suggested spelling or request that the spell checker substitute the correct spelling once or at every occurrence of the word.

Many spell checkers offer the writer a chance to modify the dictionary by adding or excluding words. Check the word processing program's help feature to learn about options specific to your software.

Spell checkers do have some limitations. For example, many spell checkers cannot recognize whether proper nouns are misspelled. They also cannot correct homonyms, words that sound alike but are spelled differently (see "Commonly Confused Words" above). Spell checkers do not note omitted word endings such as *-s*, *-ed*, or *-ing* if the base word is spelled correctly. Finally, a spell checker cannot understand the context in which a word appears. For instance, it cannot distinguish between *from* and *form* or between *an* and *and*. If the word used in the text matches a word that appears in its dictionary, the spell checker will not recognize it as a misspelling.

Even with all those limitations, many writers cannot imagine writing without a spell checker.

Manuscript Form

When you are ready to submit your finished draft to your reader, you should prepare your work so that it creates a positive, lasting impression. Make sure that you have fulfilled any special requests your reader may have made. For example, your reader may ask that you submit your finished work in a folder, turn in all your drafts, or staple your drafts together or that you not write on the backs of the manuscript pages. Taking special care to meet your reader's requirements will help assure that the message of your paragraph or essay is well received.

Many college instructors ask that students prepare manuscripts using the Modern Language Association (MLA) format. The MLA format is one of several major format styles used to prepare manuscripts in college class-rooms. You will learn more about the MLA format when you learn to write research papers. This appendix focuses on

- Preparation of a title page
- Page numbering
- Spacing
- Margins
- Titles

PREPARATION OF A TITLE PAGE

Some manuscripts using MLA format include a title page that is separate from the rest of the text. A sample format for a separate title page is shown in Figure B.1.

As an alternative to a separate title page, MLA format allows you to place a heading in the upper left-hand corner of the first page. The heading is immediately followed by the title of the paper and the beginning of the text (see Figure B.2).

PAGE NUMBERING

If you use a separate title page, begin numbering your document on the first page of text. Place the page number 1 in the upper right-hand corner, and repeat the title (see Figure B.3).

286

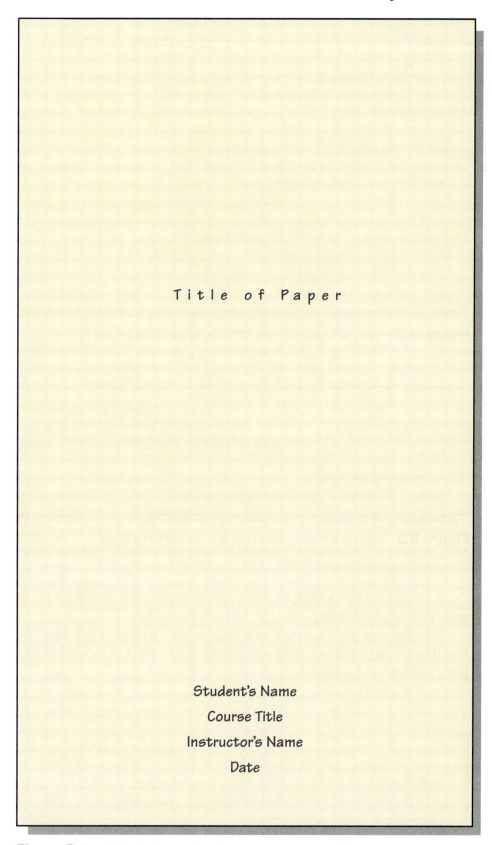

Figure B.1 Sample format for title page—separate page

```
                                                    Student Last Name    1

Student's Full Name

Instructor's Name

Course Title

Date (Day-Month-Year Style)


                              Title of Paper
     Beginning  of  text . . . . . . . . . . . . . . . . . . . . . . . .
. . . . . . . . . . . . . . . . . . . . . . . . . . . . . . . . . . . . .
```

Figure B.2   Sample format for alternative to separate title page

```
                                                    Student Last Name    1
                              Title of Paper
     Beginning  of  text . . . . . . . . . . . . . . . . . . . . . . . .
. . . . . . . . . . . . . . . . . . . . . . . . . . . . . . . . . . . . .
```

Figure B.3   Page numbering when using a separate title page

If you do not use a separate title page, place the page number 1 on the same page as your heading, title, and text (see Figure B.2).

Whether you use a separate title page or not, type your last name followed by the page number in the upper right-hand corner of each subsequent page, as shown in Figure B.4.

```
                                                    Student Last Name    2

     Text . . . . . . . . . . . . . . . . . . . . . . . . . . . . . . .
. . . . . . . . . . . . . . . . . . . . . . . . . . . . . . . . . . . . .
```

Figure B.4   Numbering on subsequent pages

SPACING

If you are word-processing your manuscript, double-space the entire paper. If you are handwriting your manuscript, check with your reader about spacing. Many readers prefer that handwritten manuscripts be double spaced to make them easy to read and edit.

MARGINS

Whether your manuscript is word processed or handwritten, your left and right margins should be defined. For word-processed manuscripts, follow these general guidelines unless your reader has other preferences.

- Set your left margin at 1 to 1.5 inches.
- Set your right margin at 1 inch.
- Set your top margin at 1 inch.
- Set your bottom margin at 1 inch.

TITLES

A title is a phrase (usually three to five words) that appears at the beginning of your composition. Think of your title in the same way you think of a title of a book on a library shelf. Will the title of your composition arouse your reader's interest? Does the title reflect the focus of your composition?

Your title does not have to be catchy to be effective. If you have trouble composing a title for a paragraph, find your topic sentence and write down the key words. Then write a title that includes these words. If you are writing a title for an essay, consider the most important words in your thesis statement.

Follow these guidelines when writing your title:

- Do not place your title in quotation marks (unless, of course, your title is quoting someone else's words).
- Do not underline your title.
- Do not follow your title with a period.
- Capitalize the first and last words.
- Capitalize all other words except conjunctions (*for, and, nor, but, or, yet, so*), articles (*a, an, the*), and prepositions of four letters or less.

Following the guidelines above will help you present a composition pleasing to the eye. Students who prepare their finished drafts carefully are well on their way to achieving success.

Glossary of Key Grammatical Terms

The definitions of key grammatical terms used in this textbook appear below. For further information about each of these terms, consult the pages listed in the index.

Action verb   A word or group of words expressing an action performed by the subject.

Active voice verb   A verb of a sentence in which the subject performs the expressed action.

Adjective   A word modifying (describing) a noun or pronoun by answering the question "What kind of?" "Which one?" or "How many?"

Adverb   A word modifying a verb, adjective, or another adverb by answering "Where?" "When?" or "How?"

Antecedent   A noun that a pronoun is substituting for.

Appositive   A noun renaming or identifying the noun immediately preceding it.

Clause   A group of grammatically related words with a subject and a verb.

Comma splice   Two independent clauses connected by a comma alone (no coordinating conjunction is present).

Complete subject   A noun or pronoun forming the subject (including any descriptive words surrounding it).

Compound subject   A subject consisting of more than one noun and/or pronoun.

Conjunctive adverb   An adverb joining two independent clauses.

Coordinate adjective   Two or more adjectives that can be reversed without changing the meaning of the sentence.

Coordinating conjunction   A word used (with a comma) to join two related independent clauses; FANBOYS (*for, and, nor, but, or, yet, so*).

Coordination   The process of joining two or more related independent clauses.

Dangling modifier   A phrase modifier that appears at the beginning of a sentence but does not modify (describe) the subject of the sentence.

Dependent clause   A group of words with a subject and a verb but without grammatical independence (it does not form a complete thought).

Essential clause   A clause beginning with *who* or *which* and necessary for identification of the noun preceding the clause.

Fragment   Any group of words without grammatical independence (does not form a complete sentence).

Gender   Denotes whether a singular pronoun is male, female, or neuter.

Helping verb   A verb that accompanies (helps) the main action verb of the sentence.

Imperative sentence   A sentence that expresses a command.

Indefinite pronoun   A pronoun that does not refer to a specific person, place, or thing: *anyone, someone, no one, everyone, anybody, somebody, nobody, everybody, each, either, neither, some, all, none, both.*

Independent clause   A group of words with a subject and verb and grammatical independence (forms a complete thought).

Infinitive phrase   A group of words beginning with the word *to* and followed by a verb and sometimes a noun or pronoun (object of the infinitive).

Inverted sentence   A sentence in which the subject does not come before the verb.

Irregular verb   A verb that does not form its past tense by adding *-ed.*

Linking verb   A verb that does not express action but joins the subject to the words that follow the verb and describe or rename the subject.

Misplaced modifier   A modifier that is separated in the sentence from the word it modifies.

Modifier   A word, phrase, or clause that provides additional information about another word or group of words in the sentence.

Nonessential clause   A clause beginning with *who* or *which* and providing additional (but not necessary) information about the noun preceding the clause.

Noun   A word identifying a person, place, or thing.

Number   Denotes whether a noun, pronoun, or verb is singular or plural.

Objective pronoun   A pronoun that is used following an action verb or as an object of the preposition: *me, you, him, her, it, us, you, them.*

Passive voice verb   A verb of a sentence in which the subject receives the expressed action.

Past participle   A verb form used with a helping verb.

Past tense   A verb tense expressing an action or a state of being that has already taken place.

Person   A way of classifying nouns and pronouns: first person, second person, third person.

Personal pronoun   A pronoun referring to a specific person, place, or thing and classified as first person, second person, or third person.

Phrase   A group of grammatically related words without a subject and a verb.

Possessive pronoun   A pronoun that shows possession: *my, mine, your, yours, his, her, hers, its, our, ours, their, theirs*.

Prepositional phrase   A group of words beginning with a preposition and ending with a noun (the object of the preposition).

Present tense   A verb tense expressing action or a state of being that is taking place in the present.

Pronoun   A word that substitutes for a noun.

Pronoun agreement   The grammatical principle which states that a pronoun must agree with its antecedent in number, person, and gender.

Relative pronoun   The pronouns *who, whoever, whom, whomever, whose, which, whichever,* and *that*.

Run-on   Two independent clauses with no punctuation to join them.

Sentence combining   Use of coordination and/or subordination to join sentences.

Shift in person   Unnecessary movement from the use of one type of personal pronoun (e.g., first person) to another type of personal pronoun (e.g., second person).

Simple subject   The main noun or pronoun that forms the subject of a sentence.

Subject   The noun or pronoun that tells who or what is performing the action expressed in the verb or who or what is being discussed in a sentence.

Subject-verb agreement   The grammatical principle which states that a verb must agree with its subject in number and in person.

Subjective pronoun   A pronoun that can be used as the subject of a sentence, following a linking verb, or in most comparisons with *than* or *as: I, you, he, she, it, we, they*.

Subordinate clause   A dependent clause.

Subordinating conjunction   A word or word group that introduces a dependent (subordinate) clause.

Subordination   The process of joining one or more dependent (subordinate) clauses to an independent clause.

Answers to Selected Odd-Numbered Exercises

Exercise 1.3

<u>Editing</u>	Checking for spelling errors
<u>Finishing</u>	Making last-minute corrections
<u>Planning</u>	Gathering your ideas about the topic
<u>Organizing</u>	Arranging your supporting points
<u>Revising</u>	Adding ideas where necessary

Exercise 1.7

G	1.	A restaurant review in a big-city newspaper
S	2.	A review of a ballet in a dance magazine
S	3.	A technical manual for installing a hard drive on a computer
G	4.	A cookbook of easy recipes
S	5.	A repair manual for videocassette recorders
S	6.	A book of quilt patterns for experienced quilt makers
G	7.	A review of a movie for a general newspaper
G	8.	A travel guide for visitors to Chicago
S	9.	An investment guide for stockbrokers
G	10.	A guide to children's health for all parents

Exercise 3.1

1. The advantage of using a spell checker

2. Using a spell checker on a computer can be a great advantage for a writer.

3. Checking spelling; asking the spell checker to suggest a spelling
4. Many writers rely on spell checkers to improve the accuracy of their writing.

Exercise 3.7

1. **B**
2. **D**
3. **B**
4. **D**
5. **C**

Exercise 4.1

1. The writer will list four steps.
2. The writer will give examples of Michael Jordan's skills as a basketball player.
3. The writer will tell what the decision was and how it changed his or her life.
4. The writer will provide examples of effective parents who listen.
5. The writer will describe the jewelry box.

Exercise 4.3

1. Underdeveloped
2. Developed
3. Developed
4. Underdeveloped
5. Underdeveloped

Exercise 4.9

1. **TO**
2. **SO**
3. **TO**
4. **OI**
5. **SO**
6. **TO**
7. **TO**
8. **OI**

9. **TO**

10. **OI**

Exercise 4.11

1. **C**
2. **A**
3. **D**
4. **D**
5. **A**

Exercise 4.13

Other answers are possible.

2. As a case in point
3. For example
4. For instance
5. In particular

Exercise 4.15

One important study skill critical for college success is doing homework completely. Students who are working for academic success know that it is important to follow the directions for each exercise. For example, if the math instructor has asked students to show all their work on a homework assignment, then the students should complete all steps of each problem. Furthermore, serious students review their homework to see if they have followed all the directions. Successful students also attempt to answer all the questions in every homework assignment. If a problem is easy, the student can place a check mark next to it in the margin. If one of the problems is especially difficult, the student can place a question mark next to it as a reminder to ask the instructor for assistance. All in all, students who work hard to complete their homework are well on their way to success in the classroom.

Exercise 5.7

1. My favorite Civil War hero is Confederate General Thomas Jonathan Jackson.

2. General Jackson's (nickname) was "Stonewall."

3. This fierce (warrior) was born in 1824 and died in 1863.

4. (General Jackson) studied at West Point but made poor grades.

5. (He) developed his furious fighting style in the Mexican War.

6. (Prayer) and (fighting) were a man's duties, according to Stonewall Jackson.

7. The (men) under his command respected him and fought by his side.

8. Jackson's strange (habits) led some to call him mad.

9. His own (men) shot him by mistake at the Battle of Chancellorsville in the Civil War.

10. (Jackson) had been riding out amid the fighting during a night attack.

11. His own (soldiers) mistook Jackson for a Union attacker.

12. There were two (officers) with Jackson that night.

13. These two (officers) were killed immediately.

14. The (general) was shot in the right hand and the left arm.

15. The (doctors) in the camp amputated his left arm.

16. (General Jackson) developed pneumonia and asked for his wife.

17. The (doctors) told his wife of her husband's death.

18. Many (mourners) including General Robert E. Lee, cried over Jackson's death.

19. (Jackson) was buried at Virginia Military Institute in Lexington, Virginia.

20. Many (monuments) commemorate Jackson's bravery on the battlefield.

Exercise 5.9

1. Who made that cake?

2. Who will be the next class treasurer?

3. Who sounded the alarm?

4. What will happen next?

5. What is the price?

Exercise 5.11

1. When did the Civil War end?

2. Was President Lincoln assassinated before the end of the war?

3. (You) Name the commanding generals of the Confederate and Union armies at the end of the war.

4. Where was <u>the treaty of surrender</u> signed?
5. <u>Who</u> signed the treaty?
6. What were <u>the terms of the agreement</u>?
7. How <u>many soldiers</u> lost their lives during the Civil War?
8. How did <u>the soldiers</u> get home?
9. Were <u>all the slaves</u> in the South set free?
10. (You) Imagine a world without warfare.

Exercise 5.17

Other answers are possible.

1. will
2. should
3. must
4. had
5. was
6. am
7. had
8. does
9. is
10. has

Exercise 5.19

Other answers are possible.

1. Do
2. will
3. Did
4. will, be
5. is

Exercise 5.21

Other answers are possible.

1. reveal
2. be
3. Look
4. finish
5. close

Exercise 5.23

Other answers are possible.

1. had been
2. has been
3. were
4. tastes
5. will be
6. have, been
7. smell
8. was
9. should be
10. is

Exercise 5.25

Other answers are possible.

1. play, leave
2. laughed, applauded
3. yawn, sleep
4. respect, obey
5. Sit, leave
6. Did, study, remember
7. Will, come, name
8. play, sleep
9. rocked, rolled
10. Bring, prepare

Exercise 5.27

1. General Ulysses S. Grant and his Union officers — were resting
2. A man on a horse — apporached, handed
3. General Lee's offer of surrender — was
4. Only 100,000 men — remained
5. many soldiers — remained
6. Neither General Lee nor his officers — could fight
7. The Union cavalry under General Gordon — had surrounded
8. General Robert E. Lee and General Ulysses S. Grant — met
9. (You) — Imagine

10. (General Lee and his officers)   arrived

11. (General Lee's sword and clean uniform)   were

12. (Neither General Lee nor his officers)   could have predicted

13. (General Grant's boots and pants)   were

14. (The terms of the surrender)   were

15. (The Confederate officers and their soldiers)   could keep

16. (All the soldiers)   could go

17. (Ely Parker, an Iroquois Indian on the staff of General Grant) prepared

18. (General Lee)   left,   returned

19. (A group of tearful soldiers)   met

20. (the soldiers)   went

Exercise 6.7

1. One of the largest rain forests in the world, is in Brazil.,

2. This rain forest is in the Amazon River basin.

3. Tropical rain forests occur in areas along the equator.

4. Rain forests are known for their humid climates.

5. Many rain forests receive more than sixty inches of rain during a year.

6. The abundant rainfall soaks through the trees to the ground.

7. Unfortunately, the large amount of rain in the rain forest drains minerals from the soil.

8. One-third of the world's plants grow within rain forests.

9. Many species of mammals also live in the trees of the rain forest.

10. Without rain forests, the world would lose a valuable natural resource.

Exercise 6.9

1. The rain forest is made (of many layers) (of plant life)

2. The top layer is made (of giant trees)

3. To reach the top, you would have to climb an enormous tree.

4. Monkeys like to jump (from tree) (to tree) (in the highest layer) (of the rain forest)

5. (Below this top layer) is another (of smaller trees)

6. (In this layer) parrots and other tropical birds come <u>to gather food</u> and <u>to make their nests</u>.

7. These two layers combine <u>to form the canopy</u> (of the rain forest.)

8. (Underneath the canopy) is an open space.

9. Monkeys and snakes frequently enter this space <u>to find food</u>.

10. The thick trees allow only a small percentage (of the sunlight) <u>to reach this open space</u>.

11. (Beneath this open space) (of the rain forest) is the floor.

12. Here termites and ants work <u>to feed</u> (on the decomposing leaves) (on the ground.)

13. The tree roots extend (beneath the ground) <u>to form the last layer</u> (of the rain forest.)

14. The plants and animals (of the rain forest) combine <u>to form an important ecosystem</u>.

15. Scientists must continue <u>to study the fascinating rain forest</u>.

Exercise 6.11

Answers will vary.

1. Winning the championship

2. Vacuuming the floors

3. earning a scholarship

4. Taking good notes

5. Cooperating with others

Exercise 6.15

1. **SS**
2. **IC/IC**
3. **IC/IC**
4. **SS**
5. **IC/IC**
6. **IC/IC**
7. **IC/IC**
8. **SS**
9. **IC/IC**
10. **SS**

Exercise 6.19

1. <u>Because the rain forest offers a place for animals to hide</u>, <u>many species call the rain forest home</u>.

2. <u>One of these animals is the jaguar</u>.

3. <u>The jaguar is considered a threatened species</u> <u>because it faces danger from hunters and environmental changes</u>.

4. <u>Although jaguars were once found in the United States</u>, <u>they now live in the rain forests of Central and South America</u>.

5. <u>Adult jaguars are approximately five to seven feet long</u>, and <u>they can weigh up to three hundred pounds</u>.

6. <u>Jaguars roam the undergrowth of the rain forests</u> <u>so that they can capture their prey</u>.

7. <u>Jaguars generally hunt on the ground at night</u> <u>even though they are good swimmers</u>.

8. <u>When the jaguar hunts</u>, <u>its prey includes almost any animal</u>.

9. <u>After the jaguar reaches sexual maturity</u>, <u>it lives with its mate during the mating season</u>.

10. <u>As loggers destroy more rain forests</u>, <u>the jaguar's existence will be constantly threatened</u>.

Exercise 6.21

1. IC/DC
2. IC/IC
3. DC/IC
4. IC/DC
5. DC/IC
6. IC/IC
7. IC/IC
8. DC/IC
9. IC/IC
10. DC/IC
11. IC/IC
12. ID/DC
13. IC/IC
14. DC/IC
15. IC/DC

16. IC/IC
17. DC/IC
18. DC/IC
19. IC/DC
20. IC/IC

Exercise 6.23

When I was in high school, I rarely studied for tests. When I took my first college test, I was in shock. Because I had spent a few minutes looking over the material, I expected to do well on the test. After my instructor returned my test, I knew that my study habits needed to change. After I checked out a book on study skills from the library, I learned that short-term memory differs from long-term memory. When I hear a lecture, the information enters my short-term memory. Unless I do something to send the information into my long-term memory, I will lose the information within a day or so. When I want to move some information into long-term memory, I have to review it, recite it, and repeat it. If I wait too long to review the material, I will have to relearn it. Because I do not often have several hours of uninterrupted time for study, I try to review the class material as soon as possible. Since I have begun these daily reviews, my test grades have improved.

Exercise 6.25

1. My supervisor wants me to work more hours, but I have too much homework.
2. Disciplining children is difficult but necessary.
3. Joe plans to attend college next year, and he is completing his application this week.
4. Christopher has finished college and is working at a computer firm.
5. Joan wants to major in political science, yet she is unsure of her career plans.

Exercise 6.27

1. Leonardo da Vinci, who was a famous Renaissance artist, painted the beautiful mural called *The Last Supper*.
2. Leonardo, moreover, was a child prodigy.

3. *The Last Supper,* which is located in an Italian monastery, was nearly destroyed in a bombing raid in World War II.

4. Leonardo's experimentation with paint, however, was devastating to this famous mural.

5. Today this mural, which is peeling away from the wall, is still a symbol of Renaissance art.

Exercise 6.29

1. Scientists estimate that more than 30 million species of plants and animals live in the rain forest, and most of them live nowhere else.

2. In addition to jaguars and monkeys, other animals such as the giant armadillo, iguana, and bearded pig make the rain forest their home.

3. The giant armadillo, which is covered with bony plates, digs a hole in the forest floor.

4. When an armadillo is hungry, it digs for termites, ants, and snails to eat.

5. Even though many iguanas live in deserts, they also thrive in the trees of rain forests.

6. Iguanas, which can grow up to six feet long, eat flowers, fruits, and tree leaves.

7. The bearded pig is known for its whiskers, narrow body, and bristly hair.

8. The bearded pig eats fruits, but it also feasts on insects and roots.

9. Because these animals are quick to sense danger, they have survived in the rain forests.

10. Their survival in future generations, however, is at risk with as many as 40 million acres of rain forest being destroyed each year.

Exercise 6.31

1. Sarah's car

2. women's clothes

3. employees' time sheets

4. truck's driver

5. director's plans

Exercise 6.33

1. In addition to the many animal species found in the rain forest, millions of plant species thrive there.

2. The rain forest's climate is ideal for many plants.

3. The humidity is generally between 75 and 90 percent, and the temperature is between 75 and 85 degrees Fahrenheit.

4. Over 1,500 types of bromeliads grow in tropical forests.

5. Bromeliads, which are also called air plants, have broad leaves.

6. Air plants grow on other plants such as trees, and they get most of their nutrients from the air.

7. The base of a bromeliad's leaves forms a holding area for water.

8. Frogs, tadpoles, and salamanders can be found in these holding tanks.

9. Other air plants growing in the rain forest include ferns, mosses, and orchids.

10. More than 20,000 species of orchids grow in the wild.

11. Orchids grow on rocks, tree trunks, and tree branches.

12. An orchid plant's size can range from less than 1 inch to more than 80 feet.

13. Although orchids grow in many different regions, they thrive in wet areas.

14. One form of orchid is a wildflower called lady's slipper.

15. It's not widely known that more than one-fourth of the world's medicines come from rain forest plants.

16. Quinine, for instance, comes from the cinchona tree.

17. Many of the world's fruits can be found in rain forests, including bananas, sugar cane, pineapples, and peanuts.

18. Furthermore, chocolate comes from the seeds of the cacao tree, which also grows in the rain forest.

19. It's been estimated that the rain forests' plants might even offer a possible cure for cancer.

20. Shouldn't scientists continue to study the vast resources of the world's rain forests?

Exercise 7.1

1. **X**
2. **N**
3. **X**
4. **N**
5. **N**
6. **X**
7. **N**

8. **X**
9. **X**
10. **N**

Exercise 7.3

1. X
2. ✔
3. X
4. ✔
5. ✔

Exercise 7.7

A. 5
B. 1
C. 8
D. 6
E. 2
F. 4
G. 7
H. 3
I. 9
J. 10
K. 12
L. 11

Exercise 7.11

On a dark, lonely road one summer night, fear turned to laughter. I was on my way home from work and ready to turn into my street when I saw the flashing of police lights in my rearview mirror. <u>Suddenly</u>, I panicked. Why were the police stopping me? Was I speeding? <u>Gradually</u>, I brought my car to a stop. <u>Then</u> I waited for the patrol officer to come to my window. "Can I see your license? he growled. "OK," I responded as I groped for my wallet. "Did you know you were going fifty-five in a forty-mile zone?" he demanded. I said, "See the sign right there. It says fifty-five miles per hour." "I'll be back," he snarled as he returned to his car. I waited impatiently for him to return. <u>Finally</u>, he came back to my window. "Ma'am, I cannot give you a speeding ticket." My heart was pounding rapidly as I heard him speak these words. "The computer in my patrol car is down," he said. <u>Afterward</u>, I pulled into my driveway with a great sigh of relief and a smile on my face.

Exercise 7.13

Other answers are possible.

1. score
2. embarrass
3. envisioned
4. toss
5. sprint
6. tackled
7. executed
8. eluded
9. dashed
10. exclaimed

Exercise 7.17

1. Miguel has to work Saturday night/, so he cannot go with us to the beach.
2. The basketball team won the game/, and they set a new school win-loss record.
3. I need to go buy some new clothes at the mall/, but I have to wait for my sister.
4. You can go to the movies later/, or you can wait until the second showing.
5. We'll stop at Manny's house/, and we'll go to Roxanna's house afterward.

Exercise 7.19

1. Miguel has to work Saturday night/; therefore, he cannot go with us to the beach.
2. The basketball team won the game/; furthermore, they set a new school win-loss record.

3. I need to go buy some new clothes at the mall/; however, I have to wait for my sister.

4. You can go to the movies now/; otherwise, you can wait until the second showing.

5. We'll stop at Manny's house/; then, we'll go to Roxanna's house afterward.

Exercise 7.19

Corrections will vary.

C	1.	Last summer my friend Maria and I set out on a thrilling white-water rafting trip on the San Juan River in Colorado.
RO	2.	That morning we arrived early; soon afterward, we met our guide, Rudy.
RO	3.	Rudy showed us our eight-person raft, and then we met the other rafters.
RO	4.	We couldn't wait to get on the river. We quickly put on our life jackets.
C	5.	As Rudy shouted the safety instructions, we listened to the white water roaring in the river beside us.
C	6.	Maria and I headed to the front of the raft for the best view.
C	7.	Soon we were surrounded by the white-water rapids of the beautiful San Juan.
RO	8.	The landscape flew by quickly as we headed into deep water.
RO	9.	Suddenly, our guide yelled at us to hold on tightly because a difficult rapid was quickly approaching.
C	10.	I grasped Maria's hand and then grabbed the side of the raft.
RO	11.	The front of the raft leaped into the air like a gymnast on a trampoline, and we splashed hard into the river.
RO	12.	I was soaking wet; it was so exciting.
RO	13.	Everyone was safe. No one had tumbled out of the raft.
RO	14.	Fortunately, the next set of rapids was easier to navigate, and our heartbeats returned to normal.
C	15.	After about forty-five minutes of easy rapids, our guide warned us to stay alert.

  RO **16.** The end of our journey was approaching; however, first we had to go over a small waterfall.

  C **17.** We all had to paddle furiously; our raft might capsize in the river.

  C **18.** Suddenly, we were free-falling in foam as our raft dove into the waterfall.

  RO **19.** After our raft regained its position, we all shouted in relief.

  C **20.** For an unforgettably thrilling experience, white water is the greatest!

Exercise 7.23

Corrections to sentences will vary.

  C **1.** Last year on a scorching August afternoon, I witnessed the incredible corn dance at the Santo Domingo pueblo in New Mexico.

  CS **2.** Every August 4, the pueblo celebrates the feast day of St. Dominic. He founded the Dominican order of Catholic friars.

  CS **3.** I was excited because this was my first trip to the Santo Domingo pueblo.

  CS **4.** When I reached the plaza late in the morning, the crowd filled every street of the pueblo.

  CS **5.** I could not believe my eyes; nearly 500 dancers filled the plaza.

  C **6.** The brightly costumed dancers were of all ages, ranging from small children to the elderly.

  CS **7.** The sun's heat did not disturb the dancers' concentration, and they danced in perfect unison.

  CS **8.** The dancers lifted their right legs together; then they pounded the earth.

  CS **9.** Their movements were as quick as lightning, and the noise was like thunder.

  C **10.** Suddenly, the drummers changed the beat; the dancers shifted rhythm.

  C **11.** Then the drumming paused, and the dancers stopped.

CS	12.	Once again, the drummers began their insistent beating as the dancers started to move again.
C	13.	As they moved around the plaza, the dancers formed a snake-like line.
CS	14.	Sometimes the line broke into overlapping lines, but the dancers still moved in unison.
C	15.	Their knees would bend, and their bodies would lean toward the ground.
C	16.	As they danced, the stamping of their feet never stopped.
C	17.	Then they would straighten their bodies, and they would raise their arms to the sky.
CS	18.	The dancing lasted all day; dancers would leave and rejoin the line.
CS	19.	Rain showers arrived at the end of the day, and the rain was a blessing to the dancers and to the crowd.
CS	20.	For the Pueblo Indians, corn represents life, and this dance is a celebration of the joy of life.

Exercise 8.9

My view of Ship Rock on the Navajo Reservation in New Mexico is stunning. <u>At the bottom</u>, rainwater has gathered to form a small stream. <u>Here</u> desert grasses in many shades of green and brown form small clumps in the water. <u>Above</u>, the brown earth stretches out from the stream to the base of Ship Rock. <u>Beyond</u> rises the powerful Ship Rock, a rock formation named for its resemblance to a sailing ship. This "ship" looks gray-black in the morning sun. Ship Rock is so gigantic that it serves as a landmark for desert wanderers. <u>Next to</u> Ship Rock are several rolling hills topped with smaller rock formations. <u>Above</u> is the expansive western sky. Puffy white clouds are mixed with patches of blue. This mixture of rock and water and sky is unforgettable.

Exercise 8.11

1. <u>The</u> <u>abstract</u> painting is <u>colorful</u>.
2. My <u>new</u> truck is <u>bright</u> <u>red</u> with <u>thin</u> <u>blue</u> stripes around <u>the</u> bed.
3. <u>The</u> <u>three-cheese</u> lasagna tastes great.

4. <u>The</u> speakers for <u>my</u> <u>new</u> <u>computer</u> system are <u>large</u>.

5. <u>The</u> <u>fresh</u> bread smells <u>wonderful</u>.

6. <u>The</u> <u>new</u> teacher is <u>nervous</u>.

7. <u>The</u> cover for <u>my</u> <u>English</u> textbook is <u>lively</u>.

8. <u>The</u> <u>grand</u> piano looks <u>small</u> on <u>the</u> <u>huge</u> stage.

9. <u>The</u> <u>political</u> cartoon in <u>the</u> newspaper is <u>funny</u>.

10. <u>The</u> directions on <u>the</u> <u>city</u> map are <u>helpful</u>.

Exercise 8.13

1. <u>Recently</u>, I discovered an old photograph of two children playing <u>happily</u> in the sand.

2. Behind them, the waves <u>gently</u> break against the shoreline.

3. The children are <u>too</u> busy to notice that the waves will reach them <u>soon</u>.

4. The sun must have been shining <u>very brightly</u> on this morning.

5. Light green water <u>completely</u> fills the top of the photograph.

6. The child sitting on the left is <u>nearly</u> six years old.

7. She is turned to the side, and her right arm stretches <u>playfully</u> toward the sand.

8. She is concentrating <u>intently</u> on the sand castle in front of her.

9. <u>There</u> on the right side of the photograph is her four-year-old helper.

10. Her assistant is <u>cautiously</u> pouring water from an orange bucket onto the sand.

11. <u>Slowly</u> the sand castle is taking shape.

12. Four towers have been <u>carefully</u> formed.

13. A <u>newly</u> dug hole forms the center of the castle.

14. The sand castle will disappear <u>soon</u> with the waves <u>quickly</u> coming.

15. The happiness of children is a <u>very</u> great gift.

Exercise 8.19

1. tigers live

2. tigers roam

3. tigers are, tigers reside

4. they are

5. they look, they enter

6. animals lie

7. paws stretch

8. head rests

9. tails curl

10. programs are

Exercise 8.21

1. is

2. are

3. are

4. is

5. provide

6. are

7. plan

8. work

9. are

10. tutor

Exercise 8.23

1. <u>Each</u> <u>is</u>

2. <u>Neither</u> <u>was</u>

3. <u>Either</u> <u>is</u>

4. <u>Each</u> <u>has</u>

5. <u>One</u> <u>works</u>

6. <u>Someone</u> <u>forgets</u>

7. <u>Everybody</u> <u>needs</u>

8. <u>Everyone</u> <u>is</u>

9. <u>Either</u> <u>Works</u>

10. <u>Neither</u> <u>is</u>

Exercise 8.25

1. <u>creatures</u> <u>live</u>

2. <u>one</u> <u>is</u>

3. <u>sharks</u> <u>swim</u>

4. <u>each</u> <u>is</u>

5. <u>reefs</u> and <u>bottom</u> <u>are</u>

6. <u>feature</u> <u>is</u>

7. <u>scientists</u> <u>believe</u>, <u>head</u> <u>acts</u>
8. <u>group</u> <u>provides</u>
9. <u>brain</u> <u>is</u>
10. <u>sharks</u> <u>have</u>
11. <u>eyesight</u> <u>is</u>
12. <u>sharks</u> <u>rely</u>
13. <u>teeth</u> <u>are</u>
14. <u>rows</u> <u>help</u>
15. <u>neither</u> <u>seems</u>
16. <u>tail</u> <u>is</u>
17. <u>slap</u> <u>is</u>
18. <u>tails</u> <u>are</u>
19. <u>sharks</u> <u>swipe</u>
20. <u>everyone</u> <u>seems</u>

Exercise 8.27

1. raced
2. prepared
3. started
4. worked
5. lived
6. crawled
7. crowded
8. listened
9. glistened
10. roared

Exercise 8.29

1. was
2. were
3. had been
4. were
5. have been
6. were
7. has been

8. have been

9. have been

10. has been

Exercise 8.31

1. seen

2. won

3. hid

4. forgiven

5. laid

6. drunk

7. driven

8. became

9. ran

10. eaten

Exercise 9.9

The small city park is deserted on a rainy day. <u>In the center</u> is a large, lonely oak tree. <u>At the bottom</u> of the tree, someone has planted flowers that are drowning in the heavy rain. <u>To the left</u> is an area about ten feet wide and fifteen feet long. <u>Here</u> grass grows in uneven clumps as it stretches toward the city sidewalk. <u>To the right</u> is another grassy area that includes a few brown cement park benches. <u>In front</u> of the tree someone has dumped the remains of a picnic—a bag from a fast-food place and a soda can. <u>Otherwise</u>, the park is clean except for cigarette butts near the benches. <u>Beyond</u>, the tall buildings of the city stretch toward the sky, dwarfing the small park on this dreary morning.

Exercise 9.11

Answers will vary.

2. first-rate

3. crucial

4. speedy

5. exemplary

6. thrilling

7. mediocre
8. pleasant
9. productive
10. difficult

Exercise 9.15

A lovely old log cabin in a remote area of Macon County, North Carolina, sits surrounded by pines. A rough gravel driveway off Wayah Road leads to the front porch. A wooden sign hanging over the small porch states the cabin's name, Hidden Cove, as well as the names of the owners, Joe and Louise Smith. On the porch, four rocking chairs, two to the left and two to the right, welcome visitors. No one is home; the front door is locked. A peek inside the front window reveals a large area, the living room, and its main attraction, a stone fireplace. A pathway leads around the house to a small backyard, perhaps forty by sixty feet. The backyard ends on the banks of a small creek, Hidden Cove Creek. The peacefulness of this place is inviting.

Exercise 9.17

1. her
2. his
3. their
4. his or her
5. their
6. its
7. its
8. their
9. their
10. his or her

Exercise 9.19

2. The audience was positive in (its, their) reaction to the play.
3. The family took (its, their) vacation in August last year.
4. The cheerleading squad won (its, their) divisional championship.
5. The school met (its, their) goal of improved test scores.

6. The committee returned to (its, (their)) offices after the meeting.
7. The board voted according to (its, (their)) individual consciences.
8. The company finished ((its,) their) year-long project.
9. The class took (its, (their)) midterms last week.
10. The police squad entered ((its,) their) patrol cars after the group meeting.

Exercise 9.21

1. I
2. I
3. we
4. she
5. I
6. he
7. he
8. we
9. he
10. He, I

Exercise 9.23

1. It's
2. There's
3. its
4. His
5. My

Exercise 9.25

A salesperson and her customer lean intently toward each other as (he or she, <u>they</u>) work on a small wooden desk littered with papers. (He or she, <u>They</u>) are both looking down at the desk. Each person has (<u>his or her</u>, their) arms stretched out over the desk's surface. The salesperson, (<u>who</u>, whom) has short, straight, unevenly cut hair with bangs covering her forehead, rearranges the papers like a gambler shuffling a deck of cards. Her brown eyes stare through thick glasses. Only her upper body can be seen above the desk. She is wearing a white shirt that is simple in (<u>its</u>, their) appearance. The male customer with (who, <u>whom</u>) she is talking is also looking closely at the paperwork. He has extremely short brown hair, blue eyes, and a short-sleeved brown shirt. He as well as the salesperson seems serious about (<u>his</u>, their) work. Both of (his or her, <u>their</u>) faces are expressionless like poker players calling a bluff. Neither the salesperson nor the customer gives any hint of (<u>his or her</u>, their) intentions. He is as involved in the work as (<u>she</u>, her). The outcome of this meeting is not yet clear.

Exercise 9.27

Answers may vary.

1. Matt wants Tom and Matt's sister to go to the fair.
2. Julie informed Marianna that Julie had made a mistake.
3. My mother and sister visited last weekend, but my mother had to leave early.
4. Christopher helped Miguel move last weekend, and Christopher was exhausted.
5. Danna removed the clothes from the laundry bags and washed the clothes.

Exercise 10.9

1. For a great family trip on Florida's West Coast, don't forget St. Petersburg.
2. For lovers of art, New York City is an excellent vacation destination.
3. At the Guggenheim Museum, tourists can begin their day.
4. With statues of goddesses and nude male athletes, the ancient Greek collection is vast.
5. At 11 West Fifty-third Street, museum goers can visit the Museum of Modern Art.
6. In the museum's sculpture garden, tired feet can rest.
7. On today's pop music scene, Mariah Carey is the best recording artist.
8. Of all television comedies, *Seinfeld* is my favorite.
9. In Epcot's geodesic dome, I can view the exhibits on the history of technology.
10. In their studio, I can watch the animators drawing cartoons.

Exercise 10.11

1. The *I Love Lucy* show aired between 1951 and 1957, and today it is a television classic.

2. The show changed names several times after 1957; however, the quality of the show remained high.

3. For example, from 1957 to 1958, the show was named *The Lucille Ball–Desi Arnaz Show,* and from 1958 to 1959, the show was called *The Westinghouse Lucille Ball–Desi Arnaz Show.*

4. From 1959 to 1960, the show became *Lucy-Desi Comedy Hour;* this was the show's last season.

5. Over the years, 180 half-hour episodes were produced; only 13 one-hour episodes appeared.

6. The main characters were Lucy and Ricky Ricardo and Ethel and Fred Mertz, and they were hilarious.

7. Lucille Ball and Desi Arnaz played Lucy and Ricky Ricardo; they were married in real life.

8. Vivian Vance played Lucy's best friend, Ethel Mertz, and in 1954, she won an Emmy for her work on the show.

9. Sadly, the last episode aired on April 1, 1960; then Lucille Ball filed for divorce from Desi Arnaz.

10. Fans of classic television will always treasure this show; however, today's fans must watch the classic episodes on video.

Exercise 10.15

Other answers are possible.

1. This year I plan to attend every class, do homework every day, and raise my grades every semester.

2. My roommate likes to watch television, to listen to the radio, and to do her math homework at the same time.

3. Michelangelo was the greatest painter of the Renaissance because of his abilities as a painter, as a sculptor, and as an architect.

4. To be wealthy, to be healthy, and to be wise are my dreams.

5. I promised to love my husband in sickness and in health, for better or for worse.

6. When I graduate, I plan to find a job, marry my girlfriend, and buy a house.

7. On spring break, I hope to go to the beach, get a tan, and meet some new friends.

8. A business owner must be able to track expenses, supervise employees, and provide customer service.

9. When I get home from class today, I need to clean out my book bag, to organize my notes, and to finish my English homework.

10. Shane has worked as a bartender, a contractor, and a mechanic.

Exercise 11.7

A. 2

B. 5

C. 4

D. 1

E. 3

Exercise 11.9

1. X

2. ✔

3. ✔

4. X

5. ✔

6. ✔

7. X

8. ✔

9. X

10. X

Exercise 11.11

You can enjoy gardening in a small space if you build a planter box. Before you begin building, locate a flat area in your yard, on your patio, or on a rooftop. This area should be approximately 4 feet by 4 feet and in a sunny location. After you have located a spot, you are ready to build. To begin, buy four 1-by-6-inch boards, each 8 feet long. First, cut each board in half. Second, take four of the boards and nail them together to form a square. Third, take the other four boards and form another square. If you want a portable box, nail a sheet of plywood to one square to form the bottom of the box. Then carry the squares to the desired location and place one on top of the other. <u>Now</u> you are ready to fill the box with soil and plant a vegetable or flower garden. A planter box is not difficult to make, and it makes gardening in a small space a pleasure.

Exercise 11.13

Answers may vary.

1. If you want to write an effective business letter, you should know the name and position of the person receiving the letter.
2. Used car shoppers should be sure they have the car's blue book value.
3. If you want to lose ten pounds in six weeks, you must eat balanced meals with small food portions.
4. To select a college, you should evaluate your long-term career goals.
5. To be sure I do my homework every day, I need to keep a daily calendar listing all assignments.
6. To make myself a good cup of coffee, I follow these simple directions.
7. If you want to design an exercise plan, you can contact a personal fitness trainer.
8. If we need help writing an English paper, we visit the learning support center.
9. Garage sale shoppers know they can find great deals in someone else's "trash."
10. I can save money at the grocery store if I use coupons regularly.

Exercise 11.15

1. All employees must carry their social security cards.
2. Teachers are responsible for setting their attendance policy.
3. High school graduates often go to college because of pressure from their parents.
4. Writers should be sure that all their paragraphs have clear topic sentences.
5. New committee members must provide their home phone numbers.

Exercise 11.17

1. Surprised by the loud boom, I saw a jet fly overhead.
2. As I scratched the cat's back, it bit me.

3. C

4. C

5. To make a crazy quilt, you need many pieces of cloth.

6. C

7. C

8. To take a digital photograph, you need a digital camera.

9. C

10. Using the spell checker, I have decreased the number of spelling mistakes in my papers.

Exercise 11.19

Answers may vary.

Before planning a wedding, you must make several decisions. First, consider planning the wedding yourself. To plan your own wedding, you can find many magazines and books in your local bookstore offering advice on choosing a location, selecting a color scheme, preparing an invitation list, sending out invitations, and many other decisions you must make. Some books even offer suggestions for writing your own wedding vows. Second, you may want to hire a wedding coordinator. Many couples find that a wedding coordinator reduces conflicts among family members. When selecting a wedding coordinator, you should ask for references from others who have used this coordinator. Finally, you can use computer software to plan your wedding. This software can help you manage your time. For example, a person with poor time management skills might want assistance setting up a calendar listing key events related to the wedding. Software can also help you manage your money so that you do not exceed your budget. Careful planning is the key to a beautiful wedding.

Index

A

a, an, the, 68
accept, except, 282
Action verbs, 78–81, 290
Active voice verbs, 248, 290
Adjectives, 169–71, 206–08
   coordinate, 290
   defined, 290
   in description paragraphs, 169–71, 206–08
Adverbs, 144, 171–73, 206–08, 243
   conjunctive, 144, 243, 290
   defined, 290
   in description paragraphs, 171–73, 206–08
advice, advise, 282
affect, effect, 282
Agreement. *See* Pronoun-antecedent agreement; Subject-verb agreement
Antecedents, 211–216. *See also* Pronoun-antecedent agreement
   collective nouns, 215
   defined, 211, 290
   indefinite pronouns, 213–14
   troubleshooting problems, 222–24
any, some, 68
Apostrophes, 97, 121–25
   to form contractions, 121–22
   to show possession, 122–23
   Writers as Spiders, 125
Appositives, 210–11, 241–42, 290
Articles, 68
Audience, 7–8
Auxiliary verbs. *See* Helping verbs

B

Basic verb form, 82
Be, 183
Brainstorming, 16–17
breath, breathe, 282

C

Capitalization, 208–10
Case, pronoun. *See* Pronoun choice
choose, chose, 282

Clauses, 104–114, 243–47. *See also* Dependent clauses; Independent clauses
   coordination of, 142–44, 243–44
   defined, 96, 104–05, 290
   dependent, 105, 108–116, 245–47
   independent, 104–07, 112–16
   nonessential, 119–20
   subordination of, 108–16, 245–47, 292
Clustering, 17–18
Collective nouns, 215
Commands, 75–76
Commas, 97, 117–21, 123–25, 210–11
   with appositives, 210–11
   with coordinating conjunctions, 117–18
   with dates and addresses, 120
   with interrupters, 119–20
   with introductory dependent clauses, 118–19
   with introductory prepositional phrases, 118
   with items in a series, 120
   with nonessential clauses, 119–20
   with numbers, 120
   with transitional expressions, 118
   Writers as Spiders, 125
Comma splices, 148–52, 157, 290
Commonly confused words, 282–85
Complete subjects, 69–70, 290
Compound subjects, 76–77, 290
Compound verbs, 88
Concluding sentences, 29, 54–56
   in description paragraphs, 167–68, 202–04
   in development-by-example paragraphs, 237–38
   in narrative paragraphs, 135–36
   in paragraphs, 28–29
   in process paragraphs, 265–66
Conjunctions. *See* Coordinating conjunctions; Subordinating conjunctions
Conjunctive adverbs, 144, 243
   list, 144
conscience, conscious, 282
Contractions, 121–22
Coordinating conjunctions, 142, 148, 243, 290
Coordination, 142–44, 243–44, 290. *See also* Independent clauses

321

Count nouns, 67–68
Cut and paste, 140

D

Dangling modifiers, 272–74, 279, 290
Dependent clauses,105, 108–116, 245–47,
    290
  beginning with subordinating
      conjunctions, 145–46
  commas with introductory dependent
      clauses, 118–19
  defined, 105, 290
  sentence combining, 245–47
Dependent clause fragments, 105, 108–116
Description paragraphs, 158–227
  choosing a topic, 159–60, 196–97
  concluding sentence, 167–68, 202–04
  describing people, 195, 227
  describing places, 195–96, 227
  diction, 169–73, 205–08
  organizing, 160–69, 197–99
  peer review, 190–91, 225
  professional writing sample, 226
  student sample, 191
  supporting details, 162–67, 199–202
  topic sentence, 160–62
  transitions, 168–69, 204–05
  Writers as Spiders, 192
  writing assignment, 191–226
Determiners, 68
Development-by-example paragraphs,
    228–255
  choosing a topic, 229–231
  concluding sentence, 237–238
  organizing, 231–138
  peer review, 253
  student samples, 253–54
  supporting details, 233–35
  topic sentence, 231–32
  transitions, 238–39
  Writers as Spiders, 255
  writing assignment, 254
Diction. *See also* Adjectives; Adverbs; Editing
    strategies; Gender bias; Shift in
    person; Similes
  in description paragraphs, 169–73,
    205–08
  in narrative paragraphs, 137–39
Drafts:
  edited, 23–24
  experimental, 20–21
  finished, 25–26
  revised, 22–23

E

Edited drafts, 23–24. *See also* Editing
Editing, 3, 23–24, 117, 153, 190, 224, 252,
    276–77, 280–85

commonly confused words, 282–85
  spelling, 280–85
  tips, 117, 153, 190, 224, 252, 276–77
English as a Second Language:
  a, an, the, 68
  any, some, 68
  basic verb form, 81–82
  count nouns, 67–68
  helping verbs, 74, 81–82
  -ing verbs, 79
  interrogative sentences, 74
  inverted sentences, 74
  modals, 82–83
  negatives, 83
  noncount nouns, 67–68
  nouns, 66–69
  past tense, 83
  prepositions, 98–99
  questions 74
  simple present tense, 78–79
  verbs, 74, 78–79, 81–83
  Writers as Spiders, 12–13
  writing style, 21–22
  writing versus speaking, 22
Essential clauses, 291
Example fragments, 93–94
Experimental drafts, 20–21

F

Facts, 231–32
FANBOYS. *See* Coordinating conjunctions
Finished drafts, 25–26
Finishing, 3, 24–26
First person pronouns, 175
Fragments, 90–95
  defined, 90, 291
  dependent clause, 114–17
  example, 93–94
  -ing, 91–92
  missing helping verbs, 92–93
  missing subjects, 90–91
  Writers as Spiders, 95, 156
Freewriting, 15–16
Fused sentences. *See* Run-ons

G

Gender, 194, 291
Gender bias, 270–72, 279
General readers, 8–10
Gerunds, 103–04
Grammar checker, 224
Guide questions. *See* Peer review

H

hear, here, 282
Helping verbs, 74, 81–84, 291

I

Identifying subjects, 66–77
Identifying verbs, 77–90
Imperative sentences, 291
Indefinite pronouns, 213–14, 291
Independent clauses, 104–07, 112–16
   coordination of, 142–44
   defined, 104, 291
   joined by coordinating conjunctions,
      142–43, 148
Infinitive phrases, 101–02, 291
-ing fragments, 91–92
Internet, 11
Inverted sentences, 72, 118–19, 291
Irregular verbs, 186–87, 291

J

Journal writing, 19–20, 27

K

knew, new, 283
know, no, 283

L

lead, led, 283
lie, lay, 283
Linking verbs, 86–88, 291
Loose, lose, 283

M

Main clauses. *See* Independent clauses
Manuscript form, 286–89
Margins, 289
Misplaced modifiers, 272, 274–76, 279, 291
Modals, 83
MLA format, 286–88
   page numbering, 286, 288
   title page, 286–88
Modern Language Association. *See* MLA
   format
Modifiers, 272–76, 279
   dangling, 272–74, 279
   defined, 272, 291
   misplaced, 272, 274–76, 279, 291
   Writers as Spiders, 279

N

Narrative paragraphs, 126–57
   choosing a topic, 128–29

   concluding sentence, 135–36
   diction, 137–39
   organizing, 129–37
   peer review, 153–54
   student sample, 155
   supporting details, 132–34
   topic sentence, 129–32
   transitions, 136–37
   Writers as Spiders, 156
   Writing assignment, 155
Negatives, 83
Noncount nouns, 67–68
Nonessential clauses, 119–20, 291
Nouns:
   collective, 215
   common, 67–69
   count, 67–68
   defined, 66, 291
   noncount, 67–68
   proper, 66, 209–10
Number:
   defined, 291
   of pronouns, 211
   of subjects, 175–76
   of verbs, 175–76

O

Object pronouns, 218–20, 291
Objective observations, 164–67, 201–02
Objects of phrases, 97–98, 101
   infinitive, 101
   prepositional, 97–98
Opinions, 231–32
Order of importance, 48–50
Organizing:
   description paragraphs, 160–69, 197–99
   development-by-example paragraphs,
      231–38
   narrative paragraphs, 129–37
   process paragraphs, 258–68
   stage of writing process, 2, 20–21
Outlining, 50, 235–37

P

Page numbering, 286, 288
Paragraphs, 28–41. *See also* Description
      paragraphs; Development-by-example
      paragraphs; Narrative paragraphs;
      Process paragraphs
   concluding sentence, 28–29
   elements, 29
   topic sentence, 28–41
Parallelism, 249–252, 255
passed, past, 283
Passive voice verb, 248, 291
Past participle, 83, 186–89
   defined, 291

Past tense, 184–89
   defined, 291
   irregular verbs, 186–89
   past participles, 83, 186–89
   regular verbs, 184–86
Peer review:
   for description paragraphs, 190–91, 225
   for development-by-example paragraphs, 253
   for narration paragraphs, 153–54
   for process paragraphs, 277
Person, 291
Personal pronouns, 175, 291
Phrases, 97–104
   defined, 96, 291
   gerunds, 103–04
   infinitive, 101–02, 291
   -ing phrases, 103–04
   modifiers, 272–76, 279
   prepositional, 97–101, 292
   present participle phrases, 102–03
Planning, 2, 14–20
Plural. *See also* Number
   pronouns, 211
   subjects, 176
   verbs, 176
Possessive pronouns, 220–21, 291
Prepositional phrases, 97–101
   defined, 292
   objects in, 97–98
   sentence combining, 240–41
Present tense, 78–79, 175, 292
Process paragraphs, 256–59
   choosing a topic, 257–58
   concluding sentence, 265–66
   organizing, 258–68
   peer review, 277
   student sample, 278
   supporting details, 260–65
   topic sentence, 258–60
   transitions, 266–68
   Writers as Spiders, 279
   writing assignment, 278
Professional writing sample, 226
Pronouns, 211–26, 268–70. *See also*
         Pronoun-antecedent agreement;
         Pronoun choice
   antecedents, 211–16
   defined, 69, 292
   indefinite, 213–14, 291
   number, 291
   personal, 211, 291
   plural, 211
   relative, 292
   shift in person, 268–70
   singular, 211
   used as subjects, 69
Pronoun-antecedent agreement, 211–16
   with collective nouns, 215
   defined, 292
   with indefinite pronouns, 213–14
   with prepositional phrases, 212–13
   Writers as Spiders, 227

Pronoun choice, 216–220, 227
   object pronouns, 218–220, 291
   possessive pronouns, 220–21, 291
   subject pronouns, 216–218, 292
   Writers as Spiders, 227
Proper nouns, 66, 209–10
Punctuation
   apostrophes, 97, 121–25
   commas, 97, 117–121, 123–25, 210–11
Purposes of writing, 3–7
   to entertain, 5
   to express feelings, 3–4
   to inform, 5–6
   to persuade, 6

Q

Questions, 73–75
quiet, quite, 283

R

raise, rise, 284
Readers, 8–10. *See also* Audience
   general, 8–10
   specialized, 8–10
Regular verbs, 184–86
Reporters' questions, 43–44
Revised drafts, 22–23. *See also* Revising
Revising, 3, 21–23, 139–40, 174, 240–47, 268–72
   gender bias, 270–272
   sentence combining, 240–47
   shifts in person, 268–70
   tips, 140, 174, 248, 272
   unrelated details, 139–40
Run-ons, 141–47, 156–57

S

-s ending on verbs, 175
Second person pronouns, 175
Search engines, 26
Semicolons, 148–49, 243
Sensory details, 162–67, 199–202
Sentence combining, 240–47, 255
Sentences:
   commands, 75–76, 85–86
   complete, 64–65
   inverted, 72, 74
   questions, 73–75, 84–85
Shift in person, 268–70
Similes, 208
Simple subjects, 70–71, 292
Singular. *See also* Number
   pronouns, 211
   subjects, 175

verbs, 175
sit, set, 284
Spacing, 289
Spatial order, 52–54
Speaking versus writing, 7–8
Specialized readers, 8–10
Spelling rules, 280–81
  double consonant, 281
  final *-e*, 280–81
  i before *e*, 280
  plurals, 281
  y to *i*, 281
Spell checker, 285
Student samples:
  brainstorming, 16–17
  clustering, 18
  description paragraphs, 191
  development-by-example paragraphs,
    253–54
  edited drafts, 23–24
  experimental drafts, 19–20
  finished drafts, 25
  freewriting, 15
  journal writing, 19
  narrative paragraphs, 155
  process paragraphs, 278
Style checker, 248
Subject pronouns, 216–18, 292
Subjects. *See also* Identifying subjects
  in commands, 75–76
  complete, 69–70, 290
  compound, 76–77, 290
  defined, 64, 292
  in inverted sentences, 72
  nouns as, 66–68
  plural, 176
  pronouns as, 69
  simple, 70–71, 292
  singular, 175
  understood, 75–76
Subjective observations, 201–02, 164–66
Subject-verb agreement, 175–84, 192–93
  defined, 292
  with indefinite pronouns, 181
  with prepositional phrases, 177–79
  with subjects joined by *and*, 179
  with subjects joined by *or, nor, either . . .
    or, neither . . . nor*, 180–81
Subordinate clauses. *See* Dependent clauses
Subordinating conjunctions, 145
  defined, 292
  list, 145
Subordination, 108–116, 245–47, 292. *See
  also* Dependent clauses.
Supporting details, 28–29, 42–63, 132–34,
  162–67, 199–202, 233–35,
  creating, 42–43
  for description paragraphs, 162–67,
    199–202
  for development-by-example paragraphs,
    233–35
  for narrative paragraphs, 132–34
  order of importance, 48–50

organizing, 48–54
for process paragraphs, 260–65
related, 56–59, 139–140
spatial order, 53–54
sufficient, 45–48
time order, 51–52
Writers as Spiders, 63

T

Tense. *See* Verb tense
than, then, 284
their, there, they're, 284
Thesaurus, 157, 173–74
Third person pronouns, 175
Three-step method of finding subjects,
  71–73
through, threw, 284
Time order, 51–52
Title page, 286–88
Titles, 289
to, too, two, 284
Topic, choosing a:
  for description paragraphs, 159–60,
    196–97
  for development-by-example paragraphs,
    229–31
  for narrative paragraphs, 128–29
  for process paragraphs, 257–58
Topic, limiting, 30–31
Topic sentence, 28–41
  defined, 28, 32
  in description paragraphs, 160–62
  in development-by-example paragraphs,
    231–32
  as first sentence, 34–35
  focused, 33–34
  implied, 36
  as last sentence, 35
  in narrative paragraphs, 129–32
  in process paragraphs, 258–60
  in textbooks, 39–40
  unfocused, 33–34
  Writers as Spiders, 41
Topic sentence paragraphs, 24–25
Topics. *See* Topic, choosing a
Transitions:
  defined 59
  in description paragraphs, 204–05
  in development-by-example paragraphs,
    168–69, 204–05
  in narrative paragraphs, 136–37
  in paragraphs, 59–62
  in process paragraphs, 266–68
Transitional words and phrases. *See*
  Transitions

U

Understood subjects, 75–76

V

Verbs. *See also* Action verbs; Compound verbs; Helping verbs; Identifying verbs, Linking verbs; Verb tense
  basic verb form, 82
  in commands, 85–86
  defined, 64
  English as a Second Language,78–79, 81–83
  irregular, 186–89, 193, 291
  linking, 86–88, 291
  modals, 82
  negatives, 83
  plural, 176
  present participle, 82–83
  past participle, 83, 186–89
  in questions, 84–85
  regular, 184–86, 193
  singular, 175
Verb tense:
  defined, 175
  past, 184–89, 291
  simple present tense, 78–79, 175–184, 292

W

weather, whether, 285
were, where, 284
who, whoever, 221–22
whom, whomever, 221–22
whose, who's, 285
World Wide Web, 11–12
Writers as Spiders
  apostrophes, 125
  comma splices, 157
  commas, 125
  dangling modifiers, 279
  description paragraphs, 192, 227

development-by-example paragraphs, 255, 279
  English as a Second Language, 12–13
  fragments, 95, 156
  gender bias, 279
  identifying subjects, 95
  introductory paragraphs, 198
  irregular verbs, 193
  journals, 27
  misplaced modifiers, 279
  narratives, 156
  parallelism, 255
  pronoun agreement, 227
  pronoun choice, 227
  regular verbs, 193
  run-ons, 156–57
  search engines, 26
  sentence combining, 255
  subject-verb agreement, 192–93
  test anxiety, 63
  topic sentences, 41
  verbs, 95
  writing centers, 63
Writer's inventory, 1
Writing assignments, 11, 26, 40, 62, 95, 124, 155, 101, 226, 254, 278
Writing for rewards, 10–11
Writing process, stages of, 2–3, 14–26
  editing, 3, 23–24
  finishing, 3, 24–26
  organizing, 2, 20–21
  planning, 2, 14–20
  revising, 3, 21–23
  Writers as Spiders, 26–27
Writing with a computer:
  editing tips, 224
  revising tips, 140, 248, 272

Y

your, you're, 285